CHAPTER 1: INTRODUCTION TO RACKET AND FUNCTIONAL PROGRAMMING

In this opening chapter, we embark on a comprehensive exploration of Racket, a prominent dialect of Scheme, and delve into the foundational principles of functional programming that underpin its design and usage. Racket stands out within the Lisp family for its remarkable versatility and its ability to cater to a wide range of programming paradigms, although it is particularly esteemed for its functional programming capabilities.

Our journey begins with an examination of the core concepts of functional programming, focusing primarily on immutability and first-class functions. These principles form the bedrock of functional programming and are crucial for mastering Racket.

To understand immutability, it is essential to grasp the concept of data that cannot be altered once created. In Racket, this principle is not merely a convention but a fundamental aspect of the language's design. Immutability in Racket ensures that once a data structure is created, it remains unchanged throughout its lifecycle. This characteristic leads to several benefits, including the elimination of side effects and the facilitation of reasoning about code. For instance, consider a simple Racket expression that creates a list:

```racket
(define my-list (list 1 2 3 4))
```

In this expression, `my-list` is bound to a list containing the elements `1`, `2`, `3`, and `4`. Once defined, this list cannot be modified; any attempt to alter its contents would involve creating a new list rather than changing the existing one. This immutable nature of data structures helps to prevent unexpected modifications and promotes consistency in the code.

In addition to immutability, Racket's functional programming paradigm emphasizes the use of first-class functions. In functional programming, functions are treated as first-class citizens, meaning they can be passed as arguments, returned as values, and assigned to variables. This capability allows for a high degree of abstraction and flexibility in programming. To illustrate this concept, consider the following example where a function is defined to add two numbers:

```racket
(define (add x y)
  (+ x y))
```

Here, `add` is a function that takes two parameters, `x` and `y`, and returns their sum. We can then use this function as an argument to another function, demonstrating its status as a first-class citizen. For instance:

```racket
(define (apply-function func x y)
```

```
    (func x y))
```

In this case, `apply-function` takes a function `func` and two numbers `x` and `y`, and applies the function to these numbers. We can call `apply-function` with the `add` function as follows:

```racket
(apply-function add 3 5) ; This will return 8
```

This ability to treat functions as values enhances modularity and code reusability, allowing for sophisticated programming techniques such as higher-order functions and function composition.

Next, we turn our attention to Racket's approach to defining and manipulating functions, which further exemplifies its functional programming ethos. Functions in Racket are defined using the `define` keyword, and they can be used to construct more complex functions. For example, consider a function that calculates the factorial of a number:

```racket
(define (factorial n)
  (if ( n 0)
      1
      ( n (factorial (- n 1)))))
```

This recursive function showcases Racket's support for functional programming constructs, such as recursion, which is a common technique in functional languages. The `factorial` function calls itself with a decremented value of `n`, demonstrating how functions can be defined in terms of themselves to solve problems.

In Racket, higher-order functions are a natural extension of the first-class function concept. These are functions that take other functions as arguments or return functions as results. For example, the `map` function is a higher-order function that applies a given function to each element of a list:

```racket
(define (square x)
 ( x x))

(map square (list 1 2 3 4)) ; This will return (list 1 4 9 16)
```

Here, `map` takes the `square` function and a list of numbers, applying `square` to each element of the list. This example highlights how higher-order functions can facilitate operations on collections of data in a concise and expressive manner.

As we delve deeper into Racket, we will encounter additional features that support functional programming, such as closures and continuations. Closures, for instance, are functions that capture the environment in which they were created, allowing them to access variables from that environment even after it has exited. This capability is integral to creating functions with persistent state or partial application.

In conclusion, this chapter sets the stage for understanding Racket by introducing the core concepts of functional programming. Immutability and first-class functions are fundamental to Racket's design and provide a foundation for writing clean, maintainable code. As we progress, we will explore more advanced topics and techniques that leverage these principles, enabling us to harness the full power of Racket's functional programming paradigm.

Lucas's confession hung in the air, a palpable tension that made the rehearsal room feel smaller and more confining.

Emily's eyes widened, and her breath caught in her throat as she absorbed his words. The intensity in Lucas's gaze was a mix of vulnerability and determination, a stark contrast to the usual calm and collected demeanor he displayed. For a moment, time seemed to stretch out, the bustling activity of the rehearsal around them fading into the background.

Emily struggled to find her voice, her mind racing through a tumult of emotions. She had always valued Lucas's friendship, his support throughout the audition process, and their growing connection during rehearsals. But Tyler's recent advances had thrown her into a state of confusion, making it difficult to discern her own feelings clearly. Lucas's revelation added another layer of complexity to her internal struggle. She felt a deep sense of guilt for not recognizing her feelings sooner, mixed with a growing clarity that perhaps her emotions for Lucas were more profound than she had allowed herself to acknowledge.

"I—I didn't know," Emily finally managed to stammer, her voice trembling slightly. She took a step back, attempting to collect her thoughts and compose herself. "Lucas, I appreciate your honesty. I really do. But... I'm not sure what to say."

Lucas's expression shifted from hope to a mixture of sadness and resignation. The fear of rejection was evident in the way his shoulders slumped slightly. He had laid his feelings bare, a bold move driven by his frustration with the situation and his desire to be honest with Emily. The air between them crackled with an unspoken tension as he searched her face for any sign of reciprocation.

"I understand," Lucas said softly, trying to mask the hurt in his voice. "I didn't want to pressure you or make things awkward. I just needed you to know how I feel. If you need time to figure things out, I get that."

Emily nodded, her heart aching at the sight of Lucas's

vulnerable state. She had always known him as a steady, reliable friend, and seeing him so open about his emotions was both surprising and deeply moving. She wanted to reassure him, but she was also grappling with her own feelings. The attention from Tyler had stirred something within her, but she couldn't ignore the growing affection she felt for Lucas.

"Thank you for being honest with me," Emily said, her voice gaining a steadiness she hadn't felt moments before. "I really need to think about this. There's a lot going on right now, and I don't want to make any decisions I might regret later."

Lucas gave a small, understanding nod. "Take all the time you need," he replied. "I'm here if you want to talk or if you just need a friend. I just hope you know that you mean a lot to me."

Emily's heart swelled at his words, touched by his consideration and the depth of his feelings. She appreciated his willingness to give her space while still expressing his affection. It was clear to her now that Lucas had been a steadfast support, someone who had always been there for her even when she hadn't fully recognized her own feelings.

The rehearsal room, once filled with the clamor of stage directions and lines being rehearsed, seemed to settle into a quieter, more introspective atmosphere. Emily's thoughts were in disarray as she tried to reconcile her emotions. She knew that Lucas's confession had changed the dynamics between them, but she was also aware that Tyler's persistence was a significant factor in her emotional turbulence.

As the rehearsal continued, Emily found it difficult to focus on her performance. Her mind was preoccupied with thoughts of Lucas and the complex feelings she was sorting through. The lines she had once known by heart now seemed to blur together, her concentration fractured by the emotional whirlwind she was experiencing.

The dynamic between Lucas and Tyler had created a rift that was becoming increasingly difficult to navigate. Emily's interaction with Tyler had started to feel more like a performance rather than genuine connection. She couldn't ignore the fact that his attention, though flattering, felt somewhat intrusive. His attempts to monopolize her time were starting to wear on her, making her question his true intentions.

Lucas's protective nature had always been one of his most endearing qualities, and his willingness to stand up to Tyler for her sake was both comforting and unsettling. It was clear that his feelings ran deeper than mere friendship, and that realization made her reassess her own emotions.

After rehearsal, as the cast began to disperse, Emily found herself alone in the emptying theater, reflecting on the conversation with Lucas. The space was filled with the remnants of their performance—a half-constructed set, scattered scripts, and the echo of laughter now replaced by silence. It was in this quiet solitude that Emily began to understand the weight of her decision.

Her thoughts drifted back to Lucas's confession and the sincerity behind his words. He had been her constant through the trials of rehearsals, and his support had been unwavering. The friendship they had shared was something she valued deeply, and the prospect of losing that over a misunderstanding was something she wanted to avoid.

At the same time, she couldn't ignore the unsettling feeling that Tyler's interest had stirred within her. The attention she received from him was undeniably alluring, but it lacked the depth and genuine connection she felt with Lucas. She knew she needed to approach this situation with clarity and honesty, both for her sake and for Lucas's.

As the final notes of the day's rehearsal echoed in her mind, Emily resolved to take the time she needed to navigate her feelings. She needed to separate the emotional confusion caused by Tyler's advances from the genuine affection she felt for Lucas. The next steps were crucial, and she wanted to ensure that whatever decision she made was based on a true understanding of her own heart.

With a deep breath, Emily prepared herself to face the coming days with a renewed sense of purpose. She knew that the path ahead would require honesty, both with herself and with Lucas. The play, which had initially been a means of creative expression, had now become a backdrop to a more profound personal journey.

The rehearsal room buzzed with the muted clamor of students preparing for the next scene, yet the tension between Emily and Lucas remained palpable, an invisible barrier that separated them from the rest of the group. Emily took a deep breath, trying to quell the rising tide of emotions that threatened to overwhelm her. She had always prided herself on her ability to manage her feelings with a level head, but this situation was different—it was personal, intimate, and deeply disorienting.

"Lucas," Emily began, her voice steadying as she chose her words carefully, "I've been confused about a lot of things lately. Tyler's attention, the play, our growing closeness… it's all been a whirlwind. I didn't mean to give you the impression that I didn't value what we have. I just didn't see it clearly before."

Lucas looked up, his eyes reflecting a mixture of hope and wariness. He seemed to be hanging onto her every word, as if this conversation could determine the course of their friendship and perhaps something more. His shoulders relaxed slightly, though the strain was still evident.

"I know," Lucas said quietly, "and I didn't mean to add more pressure. I just needed you to know how I felt because it's been eating me up inside. I can't keep pretending that I'm okay with how things are when I'm not."

Emily's heart ached at the sincerity in his voice. She took a step closer to him, closing the distance that had seemed to stretch between them. "I care about you a lot, Lucas. More than I realized until now. But I need to sort out my own feelings before I can give you any answers. It wouldn't be fair to you otherwise."

Lucas nodded, his expression softening. "I understand. I don't want to rush you or make you feel pressured. I just want you to know where I stand."

The conversation left Emily with a sense of both relief and unease. While she was grateful for Lucas's honesty and his willingness to give her space, she couldn't ignore the fact that her own emotions were still in flux. The thought of Tyler's persistent attention and the uncertainty of what lay ahead only added to her internal conflict.

As the rehearsal resumed, Emily found it challenging to concentrate. Her interactions with Tyler had become increasingly uncomfortable, a stark contrast to the ease she experienced with Lucas. Tyler's charm had initially drawn her in, but his aggressive pursuit now seemed overwhelming, and his behavior began to feel more intrusive than flattering. The realization that she was using Tyler as a distraction from her true feelings only compounded her confusion.

During breaks and between scenes, Emily observed Lucas from a distance. His usual confidence was tempered with an air of cautious optimism. He had always been a reliable presence in her life, and now his support felt even more significant. Despite her turmoil, there was a clear and reassuring consistency in the way he treated her. It was a stark contrast to the unpredictable nature of her interactions with Tyler.

The days leading up to the play's opening night were a blur of rehearsals, mounting stress, and unresolved emotions. Emily found herself caught between the two poles of her conflicting feelings: the allure of Tyler's attention and the comfort of Lucas's unwavering support. Each day brought its own set of challenges, but none were as difficult as the internal battle she faced.

On the eve of the play's debut, Emily decided to have a heart-to-heart conversation with Tyler. She had realized that continuing to avoid the issue was not fair to either of them. If she were to move forward with any semblance of clarity, she needed to address her feelings honestly. She approached him after rehearsal, feeling the weight of the upcoming conversation as she walked towards him.

"Tyler," Emily began, her voice firm yet gentle, "I need to talk to you about something. Lately, I've felt uncomfortable with the way things have been between us. I value your attention and appreciate that you've been so kind to me, but I need you to understand that I'm not in a place where I can pursue anything further. I hope you can respect that."

Tyler's face fell, his charm momentarily giving way to a look of genuine disappointment. "I see," he said, his tone subdued. "I didn't mean to make you uncomfortable. I thought... I thought we had something."

Emily shook her head, her heart aching at the look of hurt in his eyes. "It's not about what we had or didn't have. It's about me needing to figure out where I stand before I can be fair to anyone, including you."

Tyler nodded, though his expression was tinged with sadness. "Okay. I appreciate your honesty. I'll give you the space you need."

As Tyler walked away, Emily felt a sense of relief mixed with regret. She had faced one of her challenges head-on, but the path forward was still uncertain. The opening night of the play loomed, bringing with it the culmination of the hard work she and Lucas had invested. The resolution of her personal conflicts seemed intertwined with the outcome of their performance.

Back in the rehearsal room, Emily found Lucas waiting for her, his demeanor a comforting anchor amidst the storm of her emotions. She offered him a tentative smile, knowing that despite the unresolved nature of her feelings, there was something undeniably special about the connection they shared.

The play's opening night approached, and with it, the promise of resolution—both on stage and in Emily's own heart.

CHAPTER 2: SETTING UP YOUR RACKET ENVIRONMENT

To begin programming in Racket, it is crucial to establish a proper development environment that will support efficient and effective coding. This involves installing both the Racket programming language and DrRacket, the integrated development environment (IDE) specifically designed to work with Racket. This section provides a comprehensive guide to setting up your environment, ensuring that all necessary components are correctly installed and configured.

First, visit the official Racket website to download the latest version of Racket. The website provides different versions for various operating systems, including Windows, macOS, and Linux. Choose the appropriate version for your operating system and download the installer. Once the download is complete, run the installer. For Windows users, this involves double-clicking the `.exe` file and following the on-screen instructions. On macOS, open the `.dmg` file and drag the Racket icon to your Applications folder. For Linux, you may need to follow additional instructions specific to your distribution, often involving the use of package managers like `apt` or `yum`.

After installing Racket, the next step is to set up DrRacket. DrRacket is the official IDE for Racket and provides an integrated environment for writing and debugging code. It is included in the Racket installation package, so there is no need for a separate download. However, ensure that DrRacket is installed correctly by launching the application from your installed programs or applications folder. The initial launch may take a few moments as DrRacket configures itself for the first use.

Upon opening DrRacket, you will be greeted with a user-friendly interface that includes several key components: the definitions window, the interactions window, and various menu options. The definitions window is where you will write and edit your Racket code. The interactions window allows you to run expressions and see the results immediately, providing a way to test and debug your code interactively.

It is essential to configure DrRacket to suit your development needs. Start by accessing the preferences or settings menu, usually found under the "Edit" menu or accessible via a gear icon, depending on your version of DrRacket. Here, you can customize various aspects of the IDE, such as font size, color schemes, and the layout of the interface. Adjusting these settings can enhance readability and make the coding process more comfortable.

One important configuration step is setting the language level. Racket supports multiple language levels, ranging from beginner to advanced, depending on your familiarity with the language and your specific project requirements. For beginners, the "Beginning Student" language level is recommended, as it provides a simplified set of features and a more manageable learning curve. As you become more comfortable with Racket, you can gradually switch to more advanced language levels.

Another crucial aspect of your Racket environment setup is managing libraries and packages. Racket's extensive library ecosystem provides a wide range of additional functionality that can be incorporated into your projects. To manage these libraries, open the Racket package manager, accessible from within DrRacket or via the command line. From here, you can browse available packages, install new libraries, and keep your existing packages up to date. It is good practice to periodically check for updates to ensure compatibility and access to the latest features.

Additionally, consider setting up version control for your projects. Tools like Git can be integrated into your workflow to keep track of changes to your code and collaborate with others. This involves creating a Git repository for your project and committing changes regularly. If you are new to version control, various online resources and tutorials are available to help you get started.

Once Racket and DrRacket are installed and configured, it is beneficial to familiarize yourself with the basic workflow of the IDE. Start by creating a new file in DrRacket and writing a simple Racket program. This will help you understand how to use the definitions window for code input and the interactions window for executing and testing code. Experiment with different features of the IDE, such as breakpoints and debugging tools, to become more proficient in navigating and utilizing the environment.

In summary, setting up your Racket environment involves downloading and installing Racket and DrRacket, configuring the IDE to your preferences, managing libraries and packages, and integrating version control if needed. By following these steps, you will create a robust and effective development environment that supports your Racket programming endeavors, laying the groundwork for successful coding and project management.

As you configure DrRacket, pay particular attention to the language settings to ensure that the environment is optimized for Racket development. DrRacket supports a variety of Racket dialects, and you should verify that the language you are using matches the requirements of your projects. To do this, navigate to the language selection menu, typically found in the bottom-left corner of the IDE or within the "Language" menu at the top. Here, you can select from a range of Racket languages and variants, including the standard Racket language or specific teachpacks if you are following a particular curriculum or tutorial.

Configuring the environment for optimal performance also involves setting up the appropriate file directories for your projects. DrRacket allows you to specify a default directory for saving and opening files, which can streamline your workflow. To set this up, go to the preferences or settings menu and locate the file management section. Here, you can designate a default project folder, making it easier to organize your code and related files.

Furthermore, familiarize yourself with DrRacket's integrated debugging tools. These tools are essential for troubleshooting and refining your code. In DrRacket, you can use features such as breakpoints and step-through debugging to examine the flow of execution and monitor the state of your program. To set a breakpoint, simply click in the margin next to the line of code where you wish to pause execution. This allows you to inspect variables and understand the program's behavior at specific points in its execution.

DrRacket also supports a powerful REPL (Read-Eval-Print Loop), which is a fundamental component of interactive programming. The REPL is available in the interactions window and allows you to evaluate expressions and see immediate results. This is particularly useful for testing small code snippets and experimenting with Racket's features. You can input expressions directly into the interactions window and receive instant feedback, facilitating an iterative and exploratory approach to coding.

Another critical aspect of setting up your Racket environment is integrating additional libraries and packages. Racket's ecosystem includes a rich collection of libraries that extend its capabilities. To manage and install these packages, you will use the Racket package manager, available through DrRacket. Access the package manager by navigating to the "File" menu and selecting "Package Manager." Here, you can browse available packages, install new ones, and manage your existing libraries. This feature is invaluable for incorporating external functionality into your projects and keeping your development environment up to date with the latest tools and libraries.

Consider also configuring version control within your development setup. Version control systems like Git are essential for managing changes to your codebase, collaborating with others, and tracking the evolution of your projects. DrRacket itself does not include built-in version control, but you can use external tools like Git to manage your source code. Set up a Git repository for your project directory and use commands like `git init`, `git add`, and `git commit` to track changes. Integrating Git with your workflow will provide a robust mechanism for managing code revisions and collaboration.

Lastly, ensure that your development environment includes adequate documentation and resources for learning and troubleshooting. The Racket documentation is extensive and includes reference guides, tutorials, and examples. You can access this documentation through DrRacket's help menu or online at the Racket website. Familiarize yourself with these resources, as they will be invaluable as you advance in your learning and encounter new challenges in your coding journey.

By carefully configuring DrRacket and your Racket environment, you create a solid foundation for effective and productive programming. This setup not only enhances your coding experience but also equips you with the tools and resources necessary to tackle complex problems and develop sophisticated Racket applications. As you progress, remember that a well-organized and well-configured environment can significantly impact your efficiency and success in learning and applying Racket's functional programming principles.

Once you have installed DrRacket and configured the basic settings, it is prudent to delve into more advanced configuration options that can enhance your development experience. One such option is customizing the appearance of DrRacket to reduce eye strain and improve readability. The IDE allows you to choose from various color themes and font settings. Navigate to the preferences menu, find the "Editor" or "Appearance" section, and select a theme that suits your preferences. You might find that dark themes are easier on the eyes during extended coding sessions, or you may prefer a light theme for better contrast.

In addition to appearance settings, consider adjusting the editor preferences to match your coding style. DrRacket supports various code formatting and indentation options. You can configure automatic indentation, bracket matching, and syntax highlighting preferences to ensure that your code is consistently formatted and easy to read. These settings can usually be found under the "Editor" or "Formatting" section in the preferences menu. Proper configuration of these options helps in maintaining a clean codebase, which is crucial for effective debugging and collaboration.

Next, integrate version control into your workflow. Version control systems such as Git are invaluable for managing changes to your code, especially in collaborative environments. While DrRacket does not include built-in version control support, you can use external tools to manage your repositories. Set up a local Git repository in your project directory by using the command line or a Git GUI client. Ensure that you regularly commit your changes and push them to a remote repository if you are working with a team. This practice not only helps in tracking changes but also provides a backup of your work.

To further streamline your development process, you might want to explore integrating DrRacket with other tools and services. For instance, if you are working on a large project, you may find it beneficial to use an external text editor for certain tasks. DrRacket supports integration with external editors, which can be configured in the preferences menu. This allows you to use specialized tools for code editing while still benefiting from DrRacket's debugging and execution features.

Another aspect to consider is setting up a testing framework for your Racket projects. Automated testing is a key practice in software development that helps ensure the reliability and correctness of your code. Racket supports various testing libraries that can be integrated into your projects. You can explore libraries such as `rackunit`, which provides a framework for writing and running unit tests. To include such libraries in your project, use the Racket package manager to install them, and then import them into your code as needed.

Maintaining an organized workspace is crucial for productivity. Create a clear directory structure for your projects, separating source code, documentation, and any other resources. DrRacket allows you to open multiple files and projects simultaneously, but it is helpful to keep related files grouped together in a logical manner. This organization will make it easier to navigate your projects and manage your files effectively.

Finally, familiarize yourself with the documentation

and community resources available for Racket. The Racket documentation is extensive and provides valuable information on the language's features, standard libraries, and best practices. Access the documentation through DrRacket's help menu or visit the Racket website for online resources. Additionally, engaging with the Racket community through forums, mailing lists, and online discussions can provide support and insights that enhance your development experience. The Racket community is an excellent resource for learning from others, sharing knowledge, and staying updated with the latest developments in the language.

By carefully setting up and configuring your Racket environment, you will create a solid foundation for developing Racket applications. Ensuring that your development tools and settings are aligned with your coding practices will help you write clean, efficient, and maintainable code. The effort invested in setting up your environment will pay off in terms of productivity and the quality of your code.

CHAPTER 3: BASIC SYNTAX AND DATA TYPES

To effectively engage with Racket, it is essential to grasp its syntax and basic data types, which are the building blocks of programming in this language. This exploration of Racket's fundamental elements will provide a solid foundation for understanding how the language supports functional programming principles. We begin with an overview of Racket's syntax, followed by a detailed examination of its primary data types, including numbers, strings, lists, and pairs.

Racket's syntax is designed to be both simple and expressive, adhering to the Lisp family of languages, which emphasizes minimalism and uniformity. The core syntax of Racket is built around the concept of expressions, where every construct is an expression that evaluates to a value. This is in line with the functional programming paradigm, where functions and expressions are the primary means of computation. In Racket, an expression is typically enclosed in parentheses, with the operator or function appearing first, followed by its arguments. This prefix notation, or Polish notation, can initially appear unconventional, but it facilitates a consistent and predictable structure for expressions.

For example, a simple arithmetic expression in Racket might

look like this: `(+ 3 5)`. Here, `+` is the operator, and `3` and `5` are the operands. The expression evaluates to `8`, and the result is produced by applying the operator to the operands. This uniform syntax extends to more complex expressions, allowing for nested operations and combinations of different functions. For instance, the expression `(( + 2 3) (- 7 4))` demonstrates nesting, where the result of `(+ 2 3)` is multiplied by the result of `(- 7 4)`.

Variables in Racket are defined using the `define` keyword, which assigns a value to a symbol. The syntax for defining a variable is straightforward: `define` is followed by the variable name and its value. For example, `(define x 10)` creates a variable `x` with a value of `10`. Once defined, the variable `x` can be used in subsequent expressions, and its value can be accessed or modified as needed. Racket also supports local bindings with the `let` keyword, which allows for temporary variables within a specific scope. For example, `(let ([a 5] [b 10]) (+ a b))` defines local variables `a` and `b`, and evaluates their sum.

Understanding Racket's data types is crucial for effective programming. The language supports several basic data types, each with its own role and characteristics. Numbers are one of the simplest and most commonly used data types. Racket handles both integer and floating-point numbers, allowing for precise arithmetic operations. For example, `3`, `-4`, and `2.5` are valid numeric literals in Racket. Racket also includes a variety of numerical operations, such as addition, subtraction, multiplication, and division, which can be performed on these literals.

Strings are another fundamental data type in Racket, used to represent sequences of characters. Strings are enclosed in double quotes and can include any combination of letters, digits, and symbols. For instance, `"Hello, world!"` is a string literal in Racket. Strings support a range of operations, including concatenation, substring extraction, and pattern matching. The `string-append` function, for example, concatenates two or more strings into a single string.

Lists are a core data type in Racket and are particularly important in the context of functional programming. A list in Racket is an ordered collection of elements, enclosed in parentheses and separated by spaces. Lists can contain elements of different types, including other lists. For example, `(list 1 2 3)` creates a list with three integer elements, while `(list 1 "two" (list 3 4))` creates a list containing a mixture of integers, strings, and nested lists. Lists are central to many functional programming tasks, such as recursion and data manipulation.

Pairs, another important data type, are used to construct more complex data structures in Racket. A pair is a two-element structure that can be created using the `cons` function. For instance, `(cons 1 2)` creates a pair with `1` as the first element and `2` as the second. Pairs are commonly used to build lists and other data structures. The `car` function retrieves the first element of a pair, while the `cdr` function retrieves the second element. For example, if you have a pair `(cons 1 2)`, `(car (cons 1 2))` returns `1`, and `(cdr (cons 1 2))` returns `2`.

By understanding these basic syntax elements and data types, you are well-equipped to begin writing and manipulating Racket code. These foundational concepts provide the basis for more advanced programming techniques and enable you to leverage Racket's powerful features effectively. As you continue to explore Racket, you will discover how these elements come together to support a variety of programming tasks and paradigms.

In addition to the core data types, Racket supports more complex and compound data structures, notably lists and pairs, which are fundamental to its functionality and flexibility. Lists in Racket are a versatile and essential data type, allowing for the representation of sequences of elements. Lists are created using parentheses, with elements separated by spaces. For instance, the list `(1 2 3 4)` consists of four numeric elements. Lists can contain any type of data, including other lists, enabling the creation of nested structures.

To access elements within a list, Racket provides several built-in functions. The `car` function retrieves the first element of a list, while `cdr` returns the remainder of the list after the first element. For example, given the list `(1 2 3 4)`, `(car '(1 2 3 4))` evaluates to `1`, and `(cdr '(1 2 3 4))` evaluates to `(2 3 4)`. These functions are fundamental for list manipulation, allowing you to decompose and work with lists effectively.

Lists are not only for storing data but also for expressing computations. Racket's syntax supports functional operations on lists, such as mapping, filtering, and reducing. The `map` function applies a given function to each element of a list, producing a new list with the results. For instance, `(map (lambda (x) ( x 2)) '(1 2 3 4))` returns `(2 4 6 8)`, where each element in the original list has been doubled. Similarly, the `filter` function selects elements from a list that satisfy a given predicate, while `foldl` and `foldr` reduce a list to a single value using a binary function.

Pairs are another fundamental data type in Racket, closely related to lists but more flexible. A pair is a two-element structure, often used to build lists or represent simple data records. Pairs are created using the `cons` function, which takes two arguments and returns a pair. For example, `(cons 1 2)` creates the pair `(1 . 2)`. This notation indicates that `1` is the first element, and `2` is the second element of the pair. Pairs can be used to construct lists by chaining multiple pairs together. For instance, `(cons 1 (cons 2 (cons 3 '())))` creates the list `(1 2 3)`.

Understanding pairs and lists in Racket also involves grasping the concept of recursion, a key feature of functional programming. Recursion is a method of solving problems by defining a function in terms of itself. Lists and pairs are often processed recursively, as many operations on these data structures naturally fit a recursive pattern. For example, a function that sums the elements of a list can be defined recursively by summing the first element and the result of summing the rest of the list.

In addition to these basic data types, Racket supports other types such as symbols, which are used to represent unique identifiers. Symbols are written with a preceding single quote, like `'symbol`. They are often used for labels or keys in associative data structures, and their equality is based on identity rather than value.

Strings are another important data type in Racket, used for representing sequences of characters. Strings are enclosed in double quotes, such as `"Hello, World!"`. Racket provides a variety of functions for manipulating strings, including concatenation with the `string-append` function, extraction of substrings with `substring`, and querying string properties with functions like `string-length`.

As you become more familiar with Racket's syntax and data types, you will notice that the language's design encourages a functional approach to programming. This means that instead of changing data in place, you will often work with immutable data and functions that produce new values based on existing ones. This approach aligns with Racket's emphasis on functional programming principles, promoting code that is more predictable and easier to reason about.

To reinforce your understanding, consider working through various exercises that involve manipulating lists and pairs, defining recursive functions, and utilizing the provided functions for strings and symbols. These exercises will help you solidify your grasp of Racket's syntax and data types, setting a strong foundation for more advanced topics in functional programming.

Pairs, when used in combination with lists, provide a powerful tool for structuring and managing data. While a single pair might represent a simple tuple or coordinate, pairs are typically employed as building blocks for more complex list structures. For example, the list `(1 2 3 4)` can be constructed using pairs as `'(1 (2 (3 (4))))`, which illustrates how pairs are recursively nested to form lists. This recursive nature of pairs and lists in Racket is a fundamental characteristic that supports the language's functional programming paradigm.

The manipulation of pairs and lists extends beyond basic access and construction. Racket provides a suite of functions for working with these data structures, enabling more sophisticated operations. For instance, `append` concatenates two lists into a single list, while `length` returns the number of elements in a list. Functions like `reverse` allow you to reverse the order of elements within a list, and `member` checks for the presence of a particular element in a list. Understanding and utilizing these functions is crucial for effective data handling and algorithm implementation in Racket.

In addition to lists and pairs, Racket supports several other essential data types that facilitate various programming tasks. Strings, for instance, represent sequences of characters and are used for text manipulation. Strings in Racket are enclosed in double quotes, such as `"Hello, World!"`. Racket provides numerous functions for working with strings, including `string-append` for concatenation, `string-length` to obtain the length of a string, and `substring` to extract a portion of a string. These functions enable you to perform a range of operations on text data, from simple concatenations to more

25

complex parsing and formatting tasks.

Another significant data type in Racket is the symbol, which represents an atomic, unique identifier. Symbols are often used in Racket for identifying keys in association lists or for creating unique identifiers in symbolic expressions. Symbols are written with a leading single quote, such as `'example`. Unlike strings, symbols are not mutable and are used primarily for their identity rather than their content.

Racket also supports more advanced data types, such as structs, which are user-defined types that group related data together. Structs are particularly useful for organizing complex data and can be defined using the `define-struct` construct. This allows you to create new types with specified fields, providing a way to model more complex data structures. For example, defining a struct for a point in a 2D space might look like this: `(define-struct point (x y))`. This definition creates a new type `point` with two fields, `x` and `y`, which can be accessed using accessor functions automatically generated by the `define-struct` construct.

Additionally, Racket's type system supports the concept of contracts, which are used to specify and enforce the expected types of function arguments and return values. Contracts provide a form of runtime checking that ensures functions are used with appropriate types, helping to catch errors early in the development process. For instance, a contract might specify that a function expects a list of numbers and returns a number. By using contracts, you can make your code more robust and reliable.

In summary, understanding Racket's basic syntax and data types is fundamental to leveraging its functional programming capabilities effectively. The language's syntax, characterized by its use of prefix notation and uniform expression structure, supports a functional approach to programming where functions and expressions are central. Basic data types such as numbers, strings, lists, and pairs, along with more advanced constructs like structs and contracts, provide a rich set of tools for data manipulation and program construction. Mastery of these elements will enable you to write clear, efficient, and maintainable Racket code, setting a solid foundation for more advanced programming concepts and techniques.

CHAPTER 4: FUNCTIONS AND FUNCTION APPLICATION

Functions are the core of Racket programming, reflecting the language's emphasis on functional programming principles. Understanding how to define and apply functions is crucial for effective Racket programming. This section will delve into the mechanisms of function definition, the application of functions, and the concepts of parameters and return values. We will examine different methods for defining functions, including both named functions and lambda expressions, and explore how these constructs interact with scope and function application.

In Racket, functions can be defined using the `define` keyword, which allows you to create both named and anonymous functions. A named function, also known as a procedure, is defined with a specific name and can be called multiple times throughout your code. The basic syntax for defining a named function is as follows: `(define (function-name parameter1 parameter2 ...) (body))`. Here, `function-name` is the identifier for the function, `parameter1`, `parameter2`, etc., are the parameters that the function accepts, and `body` contains the expressions that are evaluated when the function is called. For example, the function to calculate the square of a number can be defined as `(define (square x) ( x x))`. This function takes one parameter, `x`, and returns the result of `x` multiplied by itself.

Lambda expressions offer a more concise way to define functions without giving them a name. This is particularly useful for functions that are used temporarily or as arguments to higher-order functions. The syntax for a lambda expression is `(lambda (parameter1 parameter2 ...) (body))`. For instance, the lambda expression to compute the square of a number is `(lambda (x) ( x x))`. Lambda expressions are often used in contexts where functions are required as arguments, such as with the `map` function, which applies a given function to each element of a list. For example, `(map (lambda (x) ( x x)) '(1 2 3))` applies the lambda function to each element of the list, resulting in `(1 4 9)`.

Function application in Racket involves invoking a function with arguments, which is a straightforward yet powerful operation. When a function is applied, the arguments provided are substituted for the parameters in the function definition, and the body of the function is executed with these substitutions. For example, applying the `square` function defined earlier with an argument of `5` results in `(square 5)`, which evaluates to `25`. The order of arguments in function application is crucial, as Racket, like many functional languages, adheres to strict left-to-right evaluation.

Scope plays a critical role in function application, determining which variables are accessible within a function. In Racket, variables defined within a function are local to that function, meaning they cannot be accessed outside of it. This principle ensures that functions maintain a clear and predictable behavior by encapsulating their operations and preventing unintended side effects. For instance, in the function `(define (add x y) (+ x y))`, the variables `x` and `y` are local to the `add` function. Any attempts to access these variables outside of the function will result in an error, maintaining the integrity of the function's internal logic.

Higher-order functions further extend the flexibility of function application. These are functions that take other functions as arguments or return functions as results. Higher-order functions enable more abstract and reusable code. For example, the `map` function, which we previously discussed, is a higher-order function because it takes a function as an argument and applies it to each element of a list. Another example is the `compose` function, which creates a new function by combining two functions. If you have two functions `f` and `g`, the composition `compose f g` represents a new function where `g` is applied first, followed by `f`.

Understanding closures is also important when working with functions in Racket. A closure is a function that captures the environment in which it was created, including any variables that were in scope at the time of its creation. This allows the function to maintain access to these variables even after the environment in which it was created has ended. Closures are essential for creating functions with persistent state or behavior, and they are a key concept in functional programming.

The interplay between function definitions, function application, and scope forms the backbone of programming in Racket. By mastering these elements, you will be equipped to write robust and flexible code, harnessing the power of functions to build sophisticated programs. This understanding of functions, coupled with Racket's functional programming capabilities, provides a solid foundation for more advanced programming techniques and concepts.

In Racket, function application involves substituting the arguments provided into the function's parameter list and then evaluating the body of the function with these substitutions. For example, if you have a function defined as `(define (add a b) (+ a b))` and you apply this function with arguments `(add 3 5)`, Racket substitutes `3` for `a` and `5` for `b` in the body of the function, resulting in the evaluation of `(+ 3 5)`, which yields `8`. This straightforward application of arguments to parameters underpins the flexibility and power of function-based programming in Racket.

The concept of scope is integral to understanding how functions work in Racket. Scope refers to the region of the program where a particular variable or function is accessible. In Racket, function parameters are local to the function body; they exist only within the scope of the function. This local scope ensures that variables defined inside a function do not interfere with variables of the same name outside the function. For instance, in the function `(define (multiply x y) ( x y))`, the parameters `x` and `y` are local to the `multiply` function and do not affect any similarly named variables outside of this function. This encapsulation promotes modularity and reduces potential errors due to variable name collisions.

Function definitions in Racket can also include multiple parameters and more complex bodies. The ability to handle a variable number of arguments is facilitated by the `lambda` expression and other advanced features. For example, you can define a function to compute the sum of a variable number of arguments using a lambda expression combined with `apply`, like so: `(define (sum . numbers) (apply + numbers))`. Here, the dot notation `.` in the parameter list allows the function to accept an arbitrary number of arguments, which are collected into a list named `numbers`. The `apply` function then takes this list and applies the `+` operator to its elements, effectively summing them up.

Higher-order functions represent another powerful aspect of functional programming in Racket. These are functions that take other functions as arguments or return functions as results. Higher-order functions leverage Racket's support for first-class functions, allowing for advanced functional composition and abstraction. For example, the `map` function, which we previously mentioned, is a higher-order function. It takes a function and a list as arguments and returns a new list where the function has been applied to each element of the original list. An example usage would be `(map (lambda (x) ( x x)) '(1 2 3))`, which squares each number in the list.

Another notable higher-order function is `filter`, which takes a predicate function and a list, returning a new list containing only the elements that satisfy the predicate. For instance, `(filter (lambda (x) (> x 5)) '(3 4 6 7))` returns `(6 7)`, as these are the elements greater than 5. Similarly, `foldl` and `foldr` are higher-order functions that reduce a list to a single value by applying a binary function across the list's elements, either from the left or the right.

The concept of closures is also crucial in understanding function behavior in Racket. A closure is a function along with its environment, which includes the values of the variables that were in scope when the function was defined. Closures allow functions to capture and remember the environment in which they were created, even after that environment has gone out of scope. This feature is particularly useful for creating functions with persistent state or for implementing function factories. For instance, if you define a function `make-adder` that creates an adder function with a fixed increment, like so: `(define (make-adder increment) (lambda (x) (+ x increment)))`, each instance of the adder created will remember its specific increment value.

Understanding these aspects of functions and their application is vital for leveraging Racket's capabilities effectively. Functions are not just tools for organizing code but are fundamental to the language's approach to computation, promoting clean, modular, and expressive code. Through mastering function definition, application, and higher-order functions, you gain the ability to write more powerful and flexible Racket programs, embodying the principles of functional programming.

Higher-order functions in Racket enable sophisticated programming techniques by allowing functions to operate on other functions. This capability is crucial for abstracting patterns and composing more complex operations from simpler ones. Functions such as `map`, `filter`, and `foldr` are quintessential examples of higher-order functions in Racket.

The `map` function applies a given function to each element of a list, producing a new list containing the results. For instance, if you define a function `(define (square x) ( x x))`, you can use `map` to apply `square` to each element of a list: `(map square '(1 2 3 4))`. This operation yields `(1 4 9 16)`, demonstrating how `map` systematically applies `square` to every item in the list. The `map` function embodies the functional programming principle of treating functions as first-class citizens and using them to transform data structures.

The `filter` function, another higher-order function, is used to extract elements from a list that satisfy a given predicate. For example, if you want to select only the even numbers from a list, you might define a predicate function `(define (even? x) (zero? (modulo x 2)))` and use `filter` as follows: `(filter even? '(1 2 3 4 5 6))`. This results in `(2 4 6)`, where `filter` uses `even?` to determine which elements to include in the output list. The use of `filter` illustrates how higher-order functions can be employed to refine and process data based on criteria.

The `foldr` function (fold right) combines elements of a list into a single value using a binary function. This function processes the list from right to left, applying the binary function cumulatively. For example, to compute the sum of a list, you can use `foldr` with the `+` function: `(foldr + 0 '(1 2 3 4))`. The result is `10`, achieved by applying `+` in a right-associative manner across the list elements. Similarly, `foldl` (fold left) performs this operation from left to right. Higher-order functions like `foldr` and `foldl` are powerful tools for aggregating and accumulating data, essential for various computational tasks.

In addition to their practical uses, higher-order functions highlight Racket's support for functional programming paradigms. They enable concise and expressive coding patterns that emphasize immutability and the use of functions as abstractions for data manipulation. This approach contrasts with imperative programming, where state changes and explicit loops are more common.

Functions in Racket are also subject to scope rules that influence their behavior and interaction with variables. When defining a function, the parameters and local variables are scoped within the function body. This scoping ensures that variables defined inside the function do not affect or get affected by variables outside the function. However, Racket supports lexical scoping, meaning that the function retains access to variables that are in scope at the time of its definition, even if those variables are not directly passed as parameters. This feature allows for closures, where a function captures and retains the environment in which it was created.

Closures are a significant concept in functional programming and Racket. A closure is a function that captures its surrounding environment, including the variables that were in scope when the function was defined. For example, consider the following function definition:

```
(define (make-adder x)
 (lambda (y) (+ x y)))
```

The function `make-adder` returns a lambda expression that adds a given value `y` to `x`. When you create an instance of this function with a specific value, such as `(define add-five (make-adder 5))`, `add-five` becomes a closure that remembers the value `5` even though it was not directly passed to it when called. Thus, `(add-five 10)` evaluates to `15`, illustrating how the closure retains the context of its definition.

Understanding and effectively utilizing functions, including higher-order functions and closures, is crucial for mastering Racket. These concepts not only enable the construction of modular and reusable code but also embody the essence of functional programming, which prioritizes function application and immutability over state and mutable data. As you continue to work with Racket, these principles will become fundamental to your programming practice, enhancing your ability to write expressive and efficient functional code.

CHAPTER 5: CONTROL STRUCTURES AND FLOW OF EXECUTION

In Racket, control structures are essential for directing the flow of execution and managing the logical decisions within your programs. This section explores the primary control structures available in Racket, including conditionals and iteration constructs, which allow you to create dynamic and responsive applications. Understanding these constructs is fundamental to handling different programming scenarios and achieving the desired behavior in your code.

The `if` expression is one of the most fundamental control structures in Racket. It allows you to make decisions based on a condition and execute different code paths depending on whether the condition is true or false. The syntax for `if` is straightforward: `(if condition then-branch else-branch)`. If `condition` evaluates to true, `then-branch` is executed; otherwise, `else-branch` is executed. For example, consider a function that checks if a number is positive and returns an appropriate message: `(define (check-positive x) (if (> x 0) "Positive" "Non-positive"))`. Here, `if` determines which string to return based on whether `x` is greater than 0.

In addition to `if`, Racket provides the `cond` expression,

which is useful for handling multiple conditions. The `cond` expression allows you to test several conditions sequentially and execute the corresponding code for the first condition that evaluates to true. The syntax of `cond` is `(cond [(test1 result1) (test2 result2) ...])`, where each pair consists of a test expression and a corresponding result expression. For instance, you might use `cond` to classify numbers as positive, negative, or zero: `(define (classify-number x) (cond [(> x 0) "Positive"] [(< x 0) "Negative"] [else "Zero"]))`. Here, `cond` evaluates each test in order until it finds one that is true, then executes the associated result.

Iteration constructs are crucial for repeating tasks and managing repetitive processes. Racket offers several ways to handle iteration, including `for` and `while` loops. The `for` loop in Racket is a versatile and powerful construct that supports various iteration patterns. It is commonly used for iterating over sequences or ranges of values. The basic syntax for a `for` loop is `(for ([variable range-or-sequence] ...) body)`, where `variable` takes on each value in `range-or-sequence` during each iteration of the loop. For example, to print numbers from 1 to 5, you could use: `(for ([i (in-range 1 6)]) (displayln i))`. This loop iterates over the range from 1 to 5, printing each number.

Another iteration construct in Racket is the `while` loop, which continues executing a block of code as long as a specified condition holds true. The `while` loop's syntax is `(while condition body)`, where `condition` is a boolean expression and `body` is the code to execute repeatedly. For example, to compute the factorial of a number using a `while` loop, you could write:
```racket
(define (factorial n)
 (let ([result 1]
    [i 1])
```

```
(while (< i n)
 (set! result ( result i))
 (set! i (+ i i)))
result))
```
```

In this function, the `while` loop multiplies `result` by `i` and increments `i` until `i` exceeds `n`, effectively computing the factorial of `n`.

The ability to combine and nest these control structures enhances the complexity of the logic you can express in your programs. For instance, you might use `if` within a `for` loop to handle different conditions based on the values being iterated. This flexibility allows for nuanced control over the execution flow and is vital for implementing complex algorithms and handling diverse scenarios in your applications.

Understanding how to effectively use these control structures enables you to manage the logic and flow of your Racket programs, ensuring they behave as intended and respond appropriately to different inputs and conditions. Through practical examples and exercises, you will become proficient in applying these constructs to a variety of programming challenges, building a solid foundation for more advanced programming techniques.

The `for` loop in Racket is a versatile construct used to iterate over sequences or ranges of values, offering a more declarative approach to looping compared to traditional imperative constructs. The syntax of a basic `for` loop is expressed as `(for ([variable sequence]) body)`, where `variable` is bound to each element of `sequence` in turn, and `body` is the expression executed for each value of `variable`. For instance, if you wish to print each number in a list, you could use a `for` loop like so: `(for ([num '(1 2 3 4 5)]) (displayln num))`. In this example, `num` takes on each value from the list, and
```

`displayln` prints each number to the standard output.

Racket's `for` construct also supports more advanced iteration patterns, including nested loops and iteration with multiple sequences. For example, if you want to generate a list of all pairs from two different lists, you can use a nested `for` loop: `(for/list ([x '(1 2)] [y '(a b)]) (list x y))`. This generates a list of lists containing each combination of elements from `x` and `y`, resulting in `((1 a) (1 b) (2 a) (2 b))`. The `for/list` syntax creates a list of results, demonstrating how nested loops can be combined to produce more complex data structures.

The `while` loop, on the other hand, provides a more traditional form of iteration where the body of the loop is executed as long as a specified condition remains true. The syntax is `(while condition body)`, where `condition` is evaluated before each iteration of the `body`. For example, to sum numbers until a total exceeds a certain threshold, you might write: `(define (sum-until-threshold threshold) (let ([sum 0] [i 1]) (while (< sum threshold) (set! sum (+ sum i)) (set! i (+ i 1))) sum))`. Here, `while` continues to add the current value of `i` to `sum` and increment `i` until `sum` exceeds `threshold`. This demonstrates how `while` can be used for scenarios where the number of iterations is not predetermined but depends on the runtime state of the program.

In addition to basic control structures, Racket supports advanced constructs for more complex control flow. The `begin` expression, for instance, allows you to sequence multiple expressions where only one result is needed. The syntax `(begin expr1 expr2 ...)` ensures that `expr1` is evaluated first, followed by `expr2`, and so on, with the result of the last expression being returned. This can be particularly useful in scenarios where multiple side effects are needed before a final result is produced. For instance, you might use `begin` to print debugging information and then return a final value: `(begin (displayln "Debugging...") (displayln "Done") 42)`. Here, the expressions are executed in order, with `42` being the result.

Racket also features the `case` expression, which is useful for handling multiple potential values of a single variable in a structured manner. The syntax for `case` is `(case key [(test1 result1) (test2 result2) ...] [else default-result])`, where `key` is compared against each `test`, and if a match is found, the corresponding `result` is executed. For instance, to handle different days of the week, you might write: `(define (day-name day) (case day [(1 "Monday") (2 "Tuesday") (3 "Wednesday") (4 "Thursday") (5 "Friday") (6 "Saturday") (7 "Sunday")] [else "Invalid day"]))`. In this example, `case` provides a clean and readable way to match the day number to its name, defaulting to "Invalid day" for out-of-range values.

Understanding these control structures is essential for managing the flow of execution in Racket programs. Whether using `if` and `cond` for conditional branching, `for` and `while` for iteration, or more advanced constructs like `begin` and `case`, you will be equipped to handle a variety of programming scenarios. Each construct provides different capabilities for controlling how and when code is executed, allowing you to create dynamic and responsive applications with precise control over program logic.

When handling control structures in Racket, it's important to understand how they interact with each other and how they influence the flow of execution within a program. The use of conditionals and iteration constructs not only affects the behavior of the code but also impacts performance and readability. Proper application of these constructs is essential for writing efficient and maintainable programs.

One critical aspect of control structures is their interaction with the scope of variables. In Racket, variables can be defined in various scopes, including global, local, and function scopes.

Understanding how control structures operate within these scopes is key to managing side effects and ensuring correct program behavior. For instance, in the context of `for` and `while` loops, variables defined within the loop's body or in its control expression are typically local to that loop. This local scope prevents unintended interference with other parts of the code, which helps in maintaining the integrity of the program's state.

Additionally, the `begin` expression is often used in conjunction with control structures to group multiple expressions into a single block. This is particularly useful when you need to execute multiple statements in contexts where only a single expression is expected, such as within a loop or a conditional branch. The `begin` expression allows you to combine multiple expressions, ensuring they are executed sequentially. For example, within a `for` loop, you might use `(for ([i (range 5)]) (begin (displayln i) (displayln ( i i))))` to print each number followed by its square.

Handling control flow efficiently also involves understanding and managing recursion, a fundamental concept in functional programming. Recursion is often used in place of traditional iteration constructs, such as `for` and `while`, to achieve repetition and iteration. A recursive function calls itself with modified arguments, continuing until a base case is reached. For instance, calculating the factorial of a number can be elegantly done using recursion: `(define (factorial n) (if (zero? n) 1 ( n (factorial (sub1 n)))))`. This recursive approach is a powerful alternative to loops, particularly in functional programming paradigms where immutability and stateless computations are emphasized.

In more advanced scenarios, controlling the flow of execution may involve exception handling. Racket provides mechanisms for managing exceptions and errors through constructs such as `with-handlers`. This allows you to specify how your program should respond to exceptional conditions. For example, you can use `with-handlers` to catch and handle specific exceptions, providing custom error messages or recovery strategies: `(define (safe-divide x y) (with-handlers ([exn:fail:contract? (lambda (e) (displayln "Division by zero!"))]) (/ x y)))`. Here, if a division by zero occurs, the handler displays an error message rather than allowing the program to crash.

In summary, mastering control structures and flow of execution in Racket involves understanding and applying conditionals, iteration constructs, recursion, and exception handling effectively. Each of these elements plays a crucial role in controlling how your programs execute, making decisions, and handling repetitive tasks. By leveraging these control structures properly, you can write robust, dynamic, and responsive Racket programs that handle a wide range of scenarios and requirements. The ability to manage the flow of execution with precision is fundamental to becoming proficient in Racket programming and building complex applications.

CHAPTER 6: WORKING WITH LISTS AND SEQUENCES

Lists in Racket are foundational to many programming tasks, offering a versatile way to handle collections of data. Understanding how to construct, manipulate, and traverse lists is crucial for efficiently managing and processing data within your programs. This section delves into the essentials of list operations and introduces sequences, which provide a more generalized approach to dealing with ordered collections.

A list in Racket is an ordered collection of elements, which can be of any data type. The simplest way to create a list is to use the `list` function, which takes a variable number of arguments and returns a list containing those arguments. For example, `(list 1 2 3 4)` creates a list containing the integers 1 through 4. Lists can also be created using the shorthand notation `(1 2 3 4)`, where elements are separated by spaces and enclosed in parentheses. It is important to note that in Racket, lists are immutable, meaning that once a list is created, it cannot be changed. Instead, operations on lists produce new lists.

To access elements in a list, you use indexing functions such as `first`, `rest`, and `nth`. The `first` function returns the first element of the list, while `rest` returns a list containing all elements except the first. For example, `(first '(1 2 3))` yields `1`, and `(rest '(1 2 3))` yields `(2 3)`. To access an element at a specific index, use the `list-ref` function, which takes a list and an index as arguments. For instance, `(list-ref '(a b c d) 2)` returns `c`.

Manipulating lists involves operations such as adding, removing, and transforming elements. The `cons` function is used to add an element to the front of a list, constructing a new list with the given element as the first element. For example, `(cons 0 '(1 2 3))` produces `(0 1 2 3)`. To append elements to the end of a list, you use the `append` function, which concatenates two lists. For instance, `(append '(1 2) '(3 4))` results in `(1 2 3 4)`.

For removing elements, Racket provides functions like `remove` and `filter`. The `remove` function removes all occurrences of a specified element from a list. For example, `(remove 2 '(1 2 2 3))` yields `(1 3)`. The `filter` function, on the other hand, allows you to retain elements that satisfy a given predicate. For instance, `(filter odd? '(1 2 3 4))` produces `(1 3)`.

Traversing a list is a common operation that involves processing each element in a list sequentially. Racket provides several functions to facilitate list traversal, such as `map` and `for-each`. The `map` function applies a given function to each element of a list and returns a new list with the results. For example, `(map (lambda (x) ( x x)) '(1 2 3))` produces `(1 4 9)`. The `for-each` function performs an action for each element of a list, but unlike `map`, it does not return a new list. For example, `(for-each (lambda (x) (displayln x)) '(1 2 3))` prints each number in the list.

Sequences in Racket provide a more generalized interface for working with ordered collections beyond lists. While lists are a specific type of sequence, the sequence abstraction in Racket allows for more flexible handling of different data structures, such as vectors and strings. Sequences support various operations similar to those available for lists, including iteration, transformation, and access.

The `sequence` function creates a sequence from a list or other collection. For example, `(sequence '(1 2 3))` creates a sequence from the list `(1 2 3)`. Sequences are particularly useful when you need to work with data in a more abstract manner, allowing for operations to be applied across different types of ordered collections. Racket's sequence library includes functions for generating sequences, such as `in-range` for creating a sequence of numbers within a specified range.

One important aspect of working with sequences is the use of `for` loops designed for sequences. For instance, `(for ([x (in-range 5)]) (displayln x))` iterates over a sequence of numbers from 0 to 4, printing each number. This demonstrates how sequences can be utilized in a similar manner to lists, providing a powerful tool for handling ordered data.

Understanding the interplay between lists and sequences equips you with the tools necessary for efficient data manipulation in Racket. By mastering these data structures and their associated operations, you can handle a wide variety of programming tasks and develop robust, efficient solutions to complex problems.

When working with lists in Racket, understanding recursive processing is particularly useful. Since lists are inherently recursive structures, many operations on lists are most naturally expressed through recursion. For example, consider a function to compute the sum of elements in a list. The base case is when the list is empty, in which case the sum is zero. For a non-empty list, you add the first element to the sum of the rest of the list. The recursive definition of this function is:

```racket
(define (sum-list lst)
 (if (null? lst)
    0
    (+ (first lst) (sum-list (rest lst))))))
```

Here, `sum-list` uses `null?` to check if the list is empty. If not, it recursively calls itself with the rest of the list, adding the first element to the result. This pattern—processing the first element and then recursively handling the rest—is common in list operations.

Another important aspect of working with lists is list transformation. Functions like `map`, `filter`, and `foldr` (fold-right) are higher-order functions that operate on lists and are central to functional programming. The `map` function applies a given function to each element of the list and returns a new list with the results. For example, if you want to square each number in a list, you could write:

```racket
(map (lambda (x) ( x x)) '(1 2 3 4))
```

This produces the list `(1 4 9 16)`. The `filter` function, on the other hand, is used to select elements from a list that satisfy a certain condition. For instance, to get only the even numbers from a list, you might use:

```racket
(filter even? '(1 2 3 4 5 6))
```

This yields `(2 4 6)`. The `foldr` function combines elements of a list using a binary function, starting from the right end of the list. For instance, to compute the product of all elements, you could use:

```racket
(foldr 1 '(1 2 3 4))
```

This results in `24`, as it multiplies the elements from right to left.

Sequences in Racket offer a more generalized abstraction for ordered collections, extending beyond simple lists to include other structures like vectors and strings. The sequence library provides functions that work with sequences in a uniform way, which is particularly useful for abstracting over different data types. For example, the `map` function for sequences can operate not only on lists but also on vectors and strings:

```racket
(map (lambda (x) (string-append x "!")) '("Hello" "World"))
```

This transforms each string in the list by appending an exclamation mark. Sequences also support functions like `length`, `take`, and `drop`, which are analogous to their list counterparts but work with any sequence type. For instance, `length` returns the number of elements in a sequence:

```racket
(length "Hello, World!")
```

This yields `13`, the number of characters in the string.

Working with sequences also involves understanding sequence operations such as slicing and concatenation. The `subseq` function allows you to extract a portion of a sequence by specifying a start and end index, which is similar to slicing lists. For example, to get the substring from index 7 to the end of a string, you would use:

```racket
(subseq "Hello, World!" 7)
```

This produces `"World!"`. Concatenating sequences can be achieved with functions like `append`, which merges two or more sequences into a single sequence. For example:

```racket
(append '(1 2 3) '(4 5 6))
```

Results in `(1 2 3 4 5 6)`, demonstrating how different sequences can be combined seamlessly.

To handle more complex data manipulation tasks, combining these operations effectively is essential. For instance, suppose you need to process a list of strings, converting them to uppercase and then filtering out those that start with a specific letter. You can achieve this by composing `map` and `filter` operations:

```racket
(filter (lambda (s) (string-prefix? "A" s))
    (map string-upcase '("apple" "banana" "avocado")))
```

This code first converts each string to uppercase and then filters out the strings that start with the letter "A". The result would be `("APPLE" "AVOCADO")`.

By mastering these list and sequence operations, you gain the tools necessary for effective data manipulation in Racket, enabling you to handle a wide range of programming tasks with clarity and precision.

Understanding sequences in Racket expands our ability to work with ordered collections beyond the capabilities of basic lists. Sequences in Racket are a more generalized concept that encompasses lists but also includes other ordered data structures like vectors and strings. Sequences offer a uniform interface for manipulating and querying these various types of collections, which is especially useful when writing generic functions that need to handle different kinds of ordered data.

To work with sequences, we use a set of functions that are designed to operate on any sequence. The `sequence` module provides several functions that abstract away the specific details of the underlying data structure, allowing you to perform operations like mapping, filtering, and folding in a consistent manner. For example, the `for/list` loop is a versatile construct for generating lists from sequences. It combines the power of iteration with the functional style of list processing. Here is a basic example:

```racket
(for/list ([x (in-range 5)])
  ( x x))
```

This generates the list `(0 1 4 9 16)`, where each element is the square of the numbers from 0 to 4. The `for/list` construct iterates over the sequence provided by `(in-range 5)` and applies the function `( x x)` to each element, collecting the results into a new list.

Another important function in the `sequence` module is `map`, which applies a function to each element of a sequence and returns a new sequence containing the results. This is similar to `map` for lists but works for any sequence type:

```racket
(map (lambda (x) ( x 2)) (in-range 5))
```

This produces a sequence of `(0 2 4 6 8)`. The `map` function here is used with an `in-range` sequence, showcasing its versatility with different types of sequences.

Filtering sequences works similarly to filtering lists. The `filter` function can be used to select elements from a sequence that satisfy a given condition:

```racket
(filter even? (in-range 10))
```

This will yield `(0 2 4 6 8)`, effectively filtering out the odd numbers. The ability to filter sequences in this manner demonstrates how sequences can be processed in a functional style, leveraging the same principles applied to lists.

Sequences also support more complex operations like combining multiple sequences. The `append` function can be used to concatenate sequences:

```racket
(append (in-range 3) (in-range 3 6))
```

This produces a single sequence `(0 1 2 3 4 5)`, combining the elements of two ranges. The `append` function here demonstrates how sequences can be manipulated to form new sequences from existing ones.

For those needing even more flexibility, the `in-order` function provides a way to generate sequences based on specific ordering criteria. For example, you can use it to create a sequence of elements from a collection in a sorted order:

```racket
(in-order (list 3 1 4 1 5 9 2 6 5 3 5))
```

This results in `(1 1 2 3 3 4 5 5 5 6 9)`, a sequence where the elements are sorted. This functionality is particularly useful when dealing with collections where the order of elements is important and needs to be managed explicitly.

The concept of sequences and their associated functions allows for a more abstract and powerful approach to handling ordered data in Racket. By understanding and utilizing these functions, you gain the ability to work with various types of data structures in a consistent and effective manner. This not only simplifies the process of manipulating and querying data but also enhances the flexibility of your code, making it adaptable to different contexts and requirements.

In summary, working with lists and sequences in Racket involves understanding both basic and advanced operations. From constructing and manipulating lists to applying functional programming techniques and leveraging the generalized interface of sequences, mastering these aspects will significantly enhance your ability to handle complex data manipulation tasks. By practicing these concepts and applying them in various scenarios, you will develop a deeper understanding of how to effectively use Racket's data structures and functions to solve real-world problems.

CHAPTER 7: UNDERSTANDING AND USING MODULES

In Racket, modules provide a means to organize and encapsulate code, facilitating both reuse and separation of concerns. By defining and using modules, you can enhance the maintainability of your codebase, promote clearer abstractions, and manage dependencies more effectively. This section will delve into the essentials of modules, including how to define them, import and export their components, and leverage their capabilities for robust application development.

To begin with, a module in Racket is a self-contained unit of code that can include definitions of functions, variables, and other modules. The basic syntax for defining a module is encapsulated within the `module` form. Here is an example of a simple module definition:

```racket
(module my-module racket
  (define (square x)
    (x x))

  (define (cube x)
    (x x x)))
```

```

In this example, `my-module` is a module that depends on the `racket` language. Inside this module, we define two functions: `square` and `cube`. These functions are local to the module and cannot be accessed outside it unless explicitly exported. The key part here is that the `define` statements are scoped within the module, allowing for encapsulation of these functions.

To make the functions available to other modules or code, you need to export them. The `module` form allows you to specify which definitions should be visible externally. This is done using the `provide` clause:

```racket
(module my-module racket
 (define (square x)
  ( x x))

 (define (cube x)
  ( x x x))

 (provide square cube))
```

The `provide` clause specifies that both `square` and `cube` are accessible to other modules that import `my-module`. Conversely, if you want to use functions from another module, you use the `require` form:

```racket
(require my-module)

(square 5) ; Returns 25
(cube 3)   ; Returns 27
```

Here, `require` makes the `square` and `cube` functions available in the current namespace. This mechanism of
```

importing and exporting helps manage dependencies and keeps your code modular.

Modular programming in Racket encourages better organization of code by splitting it into logical units, each with its own namespace. This separation aids in code maintainability and readability. For instance, consider a scenario where you have multiple utility functions spread across different files. Instead of having all functions in a single file, you can organize them into distinct modules, each providing specific functionality. This modular approach also facilitates testing and debugging, as you can isolate and test each module independently.

Racket's module system also supports hierarchical module structures. Modules can be nested within other modules, allowing for a more granular organization of code. For example, you might have a top-level module that requires several submodules:

```racket
(module main racket
 (require "submodule1.rkt"
    "submodule2.rkt")

 (define (compute-result x)
  (let ([result1 (submodule1-function x)]
     [result2 (submodule2-function x)])
   (+ result1 result2)))
```

In this example, `main` is a top-level module that requires two submodules, `submodule1` and `submodule2`. The functions `submodule1-function` and `submodule2-function` are used to compute a result. This hierarchical approach to modules helps in managing complex applications by breaking them into smaller, more manageable pieces.

Moreover, Racket provides a `require` form with a `prefix` keyword to handle naming conflicts and to clarify the source of imported functions. For instance:

```racket
(require (prefix-in sm: "submodule1.rkt"))
(sm:function-name args)
```

Here, `sm:` is a prefix that distinguishes functions imported from `submodule1.rkt`, preventing naming clashes with other functions that might have the same names. This feature is particularly useful in large projects with multiple dependencies.

In summary, understanding and utilizing modules in Racket is fundamental to effective code organization and management. By defining, importing, and exporting modules, you create a well-structured application where code is modular, reusable, and maintainable. The principles of modular programming not only aid in managing code complexity but also enhance collaboration by allowing different team members to work on separate modules independently. As you continue to develop Racket applications, mastering the use of modules will prove invaluable in building robust and scalable software systems.

Building on the fundamental concepts of defining and using modules, it is essential to explore how modules contribute to code organization and manage complexity in larger applications. By leveraging modules, you can structure your Racket code in a way that promotes clarity, reusability, and separation of concerns. This section will delve into more advanced aspects of modules, such as module composition, nested modules, and the impact on application design.

When working with modules, you often need to compose or combine multiple modules to build more complex functionalities. In Racket, this can be achieved through the use of `require` statements within other modules. For instance, consider a scenario where you have a core module that handles mathematical operations and another module dedicated to utility functions. You can create a module that integrates both to provide a cohesive set of features:

```racket
;; core.rkt
(module core racket
  (define (add x y)
    (+ x y))

  (define (subtract x y)
    (- x y))

  (provide add subtract))
```

```racket
;; utils.rkt
(module utils racket
  (define (double x)
    ( 2 x))

  (define (triple x)
    ( 3 x))

  (provide double triple))
```

```racket
;; main.rkt
(module main racket
  (require core)
  (require utils)

  (define (calculate x y)
    (let ([sum (add x y)]
```

    [difference (subtract x y)]
    [doubled (double sum)]
    [tripled (triple difference)])
  (list sum difference doubled tripled)))

(provide calculate))
```

In this setup, `main.rkt` integrates functionalities from both `core.rkt` and `utils.rkt`, providing a unified interface through the `calculate` function. The `require` statements within `main.rkt` bring in definitions from both modules, enabling you to use `add`, `subtract`, `double`, and `triple` within the `calculate` function. This approach exemplifies modular composition, where different modules contribute to the construction of a more complex feature set.

Nested modules offer another layer of modularity by allowing you to define modules within modules. This feature can be particularly useful for organizing code that logically belongs together but requires additional internal structure. For example:

```racket
;; outer-module.rkt
(module outer-module racket
  (define (outer-function x)
    (* x x))

  (module inner-module racket
    (define (inner-function y)
      (+ y y))

    (provide inner-function))

  (provide outer-function (rename outer-function inner-outer-function)))
```
```

In this example, `inner-module` is defined within `outer-module`. The inner module has its own definitions and provides the `inner-function` to be used within `outer-module` or by modules that import `outer-module`. This nested approach helps to encapsulate and organize related functionalities while maintaining the separation of concerns.

Another aspect of modular programming is the use of `define-for-syntax`, which allows you to define syntax-level constructs. This is particularly useful when working with macros and code that manipulates other code. The `define-for-syntax` form is used to define functions and variables that are only visible during the macro-expansion phase, enabling you to create more sophisticated macros and code generation techniques.

```racket
(module syntax-demo racket
  (define-for-syntax (make-adder n)
   (lambda (x) (+ x n)))

  (define-syntax (define-adder stx)
   (syntax-case stx ()
    [(_ n)
     (with-syntax ([adder (make-adder (syntax-e n))])
      (syntax/loc stx
       (define (adder x)
        (adder x))))]))
  (provide (all-from-out 'syntax-demo)))
```

In this code snippet, `make-adder` is defined using `define-for-syntax`, which creates a function for adding a specified number to its argument. The `define-adder` macro then utilizes this function to define an adder function with a given number. This use of `define-for-syntax` illustrates how modules can manage syntax and code generation, expanding the capabilities of modular programming in Racket.

By employing these modular techniques, you can manage complex applications more effectively. Modules provide a structured approach to organizing code, improving readability, and facilitating maintenance. They help in isolating different aspects of an application, allowing for easier testing and debugging. As you continue to build and refine your Racket applications, mastering the use of modules will be crucial in creating scalable and maintainable codebases.

To fully appreciate the power of modular programming in Racket, it's crucial to understand the nuanced aspects of module interactions and how they influence the structure and behavior of your applications. Modules not only facilitate code organization but also enable you to create scalable and maintainable systems by enforcing boundaries and encapsulating functionality. This final discussion will cover advanced module concepts, including module interdependencies, the use of module-level variables, and strategies for effective modular design.

When dealing with interdependencies between modules, it's important to carefully manage how modules interact to avoid circular dependencies and ensure clean integration. Circular dependencies occur when two or more modules depend on each other, creating a situation where the resolution of one module's requirements necessitates the resolution of another's. This can lead to complex interdependencies that are difficult to manage and debug. To illustrate this, consider two modules that each require functionality from the other:

```racket
;; module-a.rkt
(module module-a racket
  (require (submod "module-b.rkt" module-b))
```

```
  (define (use-b-function x)
    (module-b-function x))

  (provide use-b-function))
```

```racket
;; module-b.rkt
(module module-b racket
  (require (submod "module-a.rkt" module-a))

  (define (module-b-function x)
    (module-a-function x))

  (provide module-b-function))
```

In this scenario, `module-a` requires `module-b` and vice versa. This circular dependency is generally discouraged because it can complicate module resolution and lead to initialization issues. To mitigate such problems, consider refactoring your design to eliminate unnecessary dependencies or use intermediate modules to mediate interactions between dependent modules.

Another advanced concept is the use of module-level variables. Racket allows you to define variables at the module level, which are scoped to the module and can be used to maintain state or configuration specific to that module. For example:

```racket
;; config.rkt
(module config racket
  (define default-value 42)

  (define (get-default)
    default-value)
```

```
(provide get-default))
```

In this case, `default-value` is a module-level variable that `config.rkt` uses internally. This value is encapsulated within the module, and only the `get-default` function is exposed to other modules. This encapsulation ensures that the internal state is not directly accessible from outside the module, promoting data integrity and reducing the risk of unintended side effects.

Effective modular design involves organizing your code into cohesive modules that encapsulate specific functionality and interact through well-defined interfaces. When designing modules, consider the following principles:

1. Separation of Concerns: Each module should address a single responsibility or concern. This separation makes your code easier to understand, test, and maintain. For example, a module responsible for data processing should not mix in code related to user interface management.

2. Minimal Interfaces: Expose only the necessary functions and data from a module. By keeping the interface minimal, you reduce the risk of unintended interactions and make the module easier to use and understand.

3. Encapsulation: Hide implementation details within modules and expose only the relevant functionality. This practice shields the internal workings of a module from external changes, allowing you to modify its implementation without affecting other parts of your application.

4. Documentation and Naming: Provide clear documentation and use descriptive names for module functions and variables. Good documentation helps other developers understand the purpose and usage of your modules, while meaningful names improve code readability.

Consider the following example of a well-structured modular system:

```racket
;; user-management.rkt
(module user-management racket
  (define (create-user name email)
    (list name email))

  (define (get-user-name user)
    (first user))

  (define (get-user-email user)
    (second user))

  (provide create-user get-user-name get-user-email))
```

In this module, `user-management.rkt` provides functions for creating and accessing user information. It encapsulates all user-related functionality and exposes a clear interface for interacting with user data. The internal representation of a user is hidden from other modules, which can only interact with user data through the provided functions.

By adhering to these principles and understanding the advanced concepts of modules, you can leverage Racket's modular programming capabilities to build robust, maintainable, and scalable applications. Modules in Racket are a fundamental tool for managing complexity, and mastering their use is essential for effective software development in this language.

CHAPTER 8: INTRODUCTION TO RECURSION

Recursion is a fundamental concept in functional programming, and its significance in Racket cannot be overstated. At its core, recursion involves a function calling itself in order to solve smaller instances of a problem. This technique is invaluable when dealing with problems that exhibit repetitive or hierarchical structures, allowing for elegant and often more intuitive solutions. To appreciate the power of recursion, it is essential to understand how recursive functions work and how they can be applied effectively.

A recursive function is characterized by two main components: the base case and the recursive case. The base case serves as the termination condition for the recursion, specifying when the function should stop calling itself. It provides a straightforward solution for the smallest instances of the problem, ensuring that the recursion does not continue indefinitely. The recursive case, on the other hand, involves the function calling itself with modified arguments, gradually working towards the base case.

Consider the classic example of calculating the factorial of a number, which illustrates the basic principles of recursion. The factorial function, denoted as `n!`, is defined as the product of all positive integers up to `n`. The recursive definition of the factorial function can be expressed as follows:

```racket
(define (factorial n)
 (if ( n 0)
   1
   ( n (factorial (- n 1))))))
```

In this example, `factorial` is the recursive function that calculates the factorial of `n`. The base case is when `n` is equal to `0`, in which case the function returns `1`. For any other value of `n`, the function calls itself with `n-1` and multiplies the result by `n`. This recursive call continues until the base case is reached.

Recursion is particularly useful for traversing data structures, such as lists and trees, where the problem can be broken down into smaller, similar subproblems. For instance, consider a simple list traversal function that computes the sum of all elements in a list:

```racket
(define (sum-list lst)
 (if (null? lst)
   0
   (+ (car lst) (sum-list (cdr lst)))))
```

Here, `sum-list` is a recursive function that computes the sum of elements in a list. The base case checks if the list is empty (`null? lst`), returning `0` if true. For non-empty lists, the function adds the first element of the list (`car lst`) to the sum of the rest of the list (`sum-list (cdr lst)`). This process continues until the entire list is traversed.

Another common application of recursion is in tree data structures. Trees are hierarchical structures with a root node and zero or more child nodes, each of which can also have child nodes. A common problem with trees is to compute the depth or height of the tree. The height of a tree is the length of the longest path from the root to a leaf node. A recursive approach to finding the height of a tree might look like this:

```racket
(define (tree-height tree)
  (if (null? tree)
      0
      (+ 1 (apply max (map tree-height (cdr tree))))))
```

In this function, `tree-height` calculates the height of a tree where `tree` is represented as a list with the root node as the first element and its children as subsequent elements. The base case handles the empty tree by returning `0`. For non-empty trees, the function computes the height of each subtree (i.e., the height of each child) and adds `1` to account for the root node. The `map` function is used to apply `tree-height` to each child, and `apply` along with `max` is used to find the maximum height among the children.

While recursion is a powerful tool, it is important to consider its limitations. One potential issue is the depth of recursion, which can lead to stack overflow errors if the recursion goes too deep. This is particularly relevant for problems with very large input sizes. To address this, one can use techniques such as tail recursion, which optimizes recursive calls to avoid additional stack frames. In tail recursion, the recursive call is the final operation in the function, allowing the language implementation to reuse the current function's stack frame.

Here is an example of tail-recursive factorial calculation:

```racket
(define (tail-recursive-factorial n)
  (define (helper n acc)
```

```
  (if ( n 0)
    acc
    (helper (- n 1) ( n acc))))
(helper n 1))
```

In this implementation, `tail-recursive-factorial` uses a helper function that accumulates the result in an additional parameter `acc`. The recursive call to `helper` is the final operation, making this function tail-recursive and more efficient in terms of stack usage.

Understanding recursion and its applications is crucial for leveraging Racket's functional programming capabilities. By mastering recursive techniques, you will be able to solve a wide range of problems effectively and write elegant, efficient code that harnesses the full power of functional programming.

To deepen our understanding of recursion, it is essential to explore various forms and patterns of recursive algorithms. One crucial aspect of recursion is the difference between direct and indirect recursion. Direct recursion occurs when a function calls itself directly within its definition, as seen in the previous examples of factorial and list summation. Indirect recursion, however, involves a function calling another function, which eventually leads back to the original function. Understanding these concepts helps in recognizing and implementing recursive solutions in diverse scenarios.

Consider a problem where we need to compute the Fibonacci sequence, a series where each number is the sum of the two preceding ones. The Fibonacci sequence is a classic example where recursion is commonly applied. The naive recursive approach to computing the Fibonacci numbers is defined as follows:

```racket
(define (fibonacci n)
```

```
(if (< n 1)
    n
    (+ (fibonacci (- n 1)) (fibonacci (- n 2)))))
```

In this implementation, `fibonacci` calls itself twice to compute the `n-1` and `n-2` values, which are then summed to obtain the Fibonacci number for `n`. While this method clearly illustrates the recursive nature of the problem, it is not efficient due to redundant calculations. Each call to `fibonacci` generates two additional calls, leading to an exponential growth in the number of function calls.

To improve efficiency, we can use a technique known as memoization, which stores previously computed results to avoid redundant calculations. Here's an example of a memoized Fibonacci function:

```racket
(define (fibonacci n)
  (define (fib-memo n table)
    (cond
      [(< n 1) n]
      [(hash-has-key? table n) (hash-ref table n)]
      [else (let ([result (+ (fib-memo (- n 1) table) (fib-memo (- n 2) table))])
              (hash-set! table n result)
              result)]))
  (let ([table (make-hasheq)])
    (fib-memo n table)))
```

In this implementation, `fib-memo` uses a hash table to store the results of previous computations. This approach ensures that each Fibonacci number is computed only once, significantly improving the function's performance.

Another important concept in recursion is tail recursion,

where the recursive call is the final action in the function. Tail recursion is particularly valuable because it allows the Racket compiler to optimize recursive functions by reusing the current function's stack frame, thus preventing stack overflow errors. For a function to be tail-recursive, the result of the recursive call must be directly returned without additional computation.

Consider the tail-recursive version of the factorial function:

```racket
(define (factorial n)
  (define (factorial-tail n acc)
    (if ( n 0)
        acc
        (factorial-tail (- n 1) ( n acc))))
  (factorial-tail n 1))
```

Here, `factorial-tail` is a tail-recursive helper function that accumulates the result in the `acc` parameter. The recursion occurs as the last operation, enabling the compiler to optimize the function effectively.

Recursion is also widely used in algorithms for processing hierarchical data structures, such as trees. A common example is traversing a binary tree, where each node may have up to two children. To perform an in-order traversal of a binary tree, where the nodes are visited in left-root-right order, the recursive algorithm can be defined as follows:

```racket
(define (in-order-traversal tree)
  (if (null? tree)
      '()
      (append (in-order-traversal (left-subtree tree))
              (list (root tree))
              (in-order-traversal (right-subtree tree)))))
```

```
```

In this example, `in-order-traversal` recursively visits the left subtree, processes the root node, and then recursively visits the right subtree. The results from each subtree are combined using `append`, ensuring that the nodes are processed in the correct order.

Understanding recursion also involves recognizing its limitations and potential pitfalls. Recursive functions can lead to stack overflow if the recursion depth is too great or if there are inefficiencies in the function's design. Additionally, recursive algorithms may be more challenging to understand and debug compared to iterative solutions. Therefore, it is crucial to consider the problem's requirements and constraints when choosing between recursion and other techniques.

In summary, recursion is a powerful tool in Racket programming that enables elegant solutions to problems involving repetitive or hierarchical structures. By mastering recursive functions, including their various forms and optimization techniques, you can write more efficient and effective Racket programs. As you continue to explore recursion, you'll gain a deeper appreciation for its role in functional programming and its impact on solving complex computational problems.

To further explore recursion, let us delve into the concept of tail recursion, which is a specialized form of recursion that optimizes performance. Tail recursion occurs when the recursive call is the final operation in the function, allowing the Racket interpreter to optimize the recursive calls to avoid growing the call stack. This optimization is crucial for avoiding stack overflow errors in deep recursion scenarios.

Consider the following example of a tail-recursive function to compute the factorial of a number:

```racket
(define (factorial n)
  (define (factorial-tail n acc)
    (if ( n 0)
        acc
        (factorial-tail (- n 1) ( n acc))))
  (factorial-tail n 1))
```

In this implementation, `factorial-tail` is a tail-recursive helper function. The accumulator parameter `acc` carries the intermediate result of the computation, and the recursive call is the last operation performed. By using tail recursion, Racket can reuse the current function's stack frame for each recursive call, effectively transforming the recursion into a loop.

Another fundamental recursive pattern is the divide-and-conquer approach. This method breaks a problem into smaller subproblems, solves each subproblem recursively, and then combines the solutions. The merge sort algorithm is a classic example of divide-and-conquer recursion. Here is how merge sort can be implemented in Racket:

```racket
(define (merge-sort lst)
  (if (or (null? lst) (null? (cdr lst)))
      lst
      (let ([mid (quotient (length lst) 2)])
        (merge (merge-sort (take lst mid))
               (merge-sort (drop lst mid))))))
```

In the `merge-sort` function, the list `lst` is divided into two halves. Each half is sorted recursively, and then the sorted halves are merged together. The `merge` function, which is not shown here but would be defined separately, is responsible for combining the two sorted lists into a single sorted list.

Recursive algorithms are not limited to numerical computations. They are also invaluable for traversing hierarchical data structures, such as trees. For example, consider a binary tree where each node has a left and a right child. A common recursive task is to compute the height of the binary tree. Here's how you might implement this in Racket:

```racket
(define (tree-height tree)
  (if (null? tree)
      0
      (+ 1 (max (tree-height (left-tree tree)) (tree-height (right-tree tree))))))
```

In this implementation, `tree-height` calculates the height of a binary tree by recursively determining the height of its left and right subtrees and adding one for the current level. This approach works by exploring each subtree until it reaches the leaves, calculating the height as it returns.

Understanding recursion also involves recognizing its limitations and potential pitfalls. For example, infinite recursion occurs when the base case is never reached, leading to a stack overflow. It is crucial to ensure that each recursive function has a well-defined base case to terminate the recursion. Additionally, recursion can be less intuitive for those accustomed to iterative solutions, so it is important to practice and gain familiarity with recursive thinking.

One way to develop recursive problem-solving skills is to use recursive strategies to solve puzzles or problems with well-defined recursive structures, such as the Towers of Hanoi or the n-queens problem. These problems often have elegant recursive solutions that help illustrate the power and flexibility of recursion.

In summary, recursion is a powerful and versatile tool in functional programming, allowing for elegant solutions to problems involving repetition and hierarchy. By mastering recursive functions, understanding tail recursion, and applying divide-and-conquer strategies, you will be well-equipped to tackle complex programming challenges efficiently and effectively. Through practice and exploration, recursion will become a fundamental aspect of your programming toolkit, enabling you to write concise and effective solutions in Racket.

CHAPTER 9: ADVANCED FUNCTIONS AND CLOSURES

When exploring advanced features in Racket, understanding closures and higher-order functions becomes pivotal. Both concepts play significant roles in writing concise, expressive, and modular code. Let us first examine closures, which are fundamental to grasping how Racket and similar functional programming languages manage scope and state.

A closure is a function that retains access to its lexical environment even after the function has finished executing. In simpler terms, a closure captures and "remembers" the bindings of the variables in its surrounding context when it is defined. This behavior allows functions to maintain state between calls in a way that is both powerful and flexible.

Consider the following example to illustrate a closure:

```racket
(define (make-counter)
  (let ([count 0])
    (lambda ()
      (set! count (+ count 1))
      count)))
```

In this example, `make-counter` is a function that creates and returns a new function—a closure. The returned function has access to the local variable `count` defined in `make-counter`. Each time the closure is invoked, it updates and returns the current value of `count`, demonstrating how it retains state between function calls. To use this:

```racket
(define counter1 (make-counter))
(counter1) ; Returns 1
(counter1) ; Returns 2
```

Here, `counter1` is a closure that increments its internal state every time it is called, proving that it "remembers" the environment in which it was created.

Closures are not only useful for maintaining state but also for creating function factories, which generate functions with specific behaviors. For example, a function that generates other functions for multiplying by a given factor can be defined as follows:

```racket
(define (make-multiplier factor)
  (lambda (x)
    ( x factor)))
```

The function `make-multiplier` creates a multiplier function that remembers the `factor` it was given. For instance:

```racket
(define double (make-multiplier 2))
(double 5) ; Returns 10
```

Here, `double` is a closure that multiplies its argument by 2, demonstrating the practical utility of closures in creating specialized functions.

Next, we explore higher-order functions, which are functions that either take other functions as arguments or return functions as results. Higher-order functions enable a high level of abstraction and reuse in programming. A common example is the `map` function, which applies a given function to each element of a list:

```racket
(define (square x) ( x x))
(map square '(1 2 3 4)) ; Returns (1 4 9 16)
```

In this example, `map` is a higher-order function that takes `square` as an argument and applies it to every element of the list `'(1 2 3 4)`. This allows for a concise and expressive way to transform data.

Another useful higher-order function is `foldl`, which reduces a list to a single value by applying a function cumulatively:

```racket
(define (sum a b) (+ a b))
(foldl sum 0 '(1 2 3 4)) ; Returns 10
```

Here, `foldl` uses the `sum` function to accumulate the sum of the list elements, starting from an initial value of 0.

Higher-order functions are particularly powerful for creating abstract and reusable code. For example, consider the `filter` function, which selects elements from a list based on a predicate function:

```racket
```

```
(define (is-even? x) ( (modulo x 2) 0))
(filter is-even? '(1 2 3 4 5 6)) ; Returns (2 4 6)
```

`filter` takes the predicate function `is-even?` and applies it to each element of the list, returning only those elements for which the predicate returns true.

Closures and higher-order functions are integral to functional programming, enabling the creation of flexible and modular code. By leveraging these concepts, you can write programs that are not only more concise but also more expressive and easier to maintain. This advanced understanding of functions enriches your programming capabilities in Racket, allowing you to tackle complex problems with elegant and efficient solutions.

Higher-order functions are a fundamental aspect of functional programming and provide a way to create more abstract, flexible, and reusable code. In Racket, a higher-order function is defined as any function that either takes one or more functions as arguments or returns a function as its result. This capability allows us to abstract and manipulate behavior in powerful ways.

Consider the concept of map, a common higher-order function. The map function applies a given function to each element of a list, returning a new list with the results. This operation is particularly useful for processing lists in a concise and expressive manner. For example:

```racket
(define (square x) ( x x))
(map square '(1 2 3 4 5)) ; Returns '(1 4 9 16 25)
```

Here, `map` is used to apply the `square` function to each element of the list. This operation demonstrates how higher-order functions can streamline repetitive tasks by abstracting the processing logic into reusable components.

Another powerful higher-order function is `filter`, which allows for selective processing based on a predicate function. The `filter` function takes a predicate and a list and returns a new list containing only the elements that satisfy the predicate. For instance:

```racket
(define (is-even? x) (zero? (modulo x 2)))
(filter is-even? '(1 2 3 4 5 6)) ; Returns '(2 4 6)
```

In this example, `filter` uses the `is-even?` predicate to extract only the even numbers from the list. This showcases how higher-order functions can be used to encapsulate complex selection criteria in a reusable manner.

In addition to `map` and `filter`, Racket provides other higher-order functions, such as `foldl` (fold-left) and `foldr` (fold-right), which are used to aggregate elements of a list into a single value. These functions demonstrate the power of functional abstraction, as they generalize operations that would otherwise require explicit iteration and accumulation. For instance:

```racket
(foldl + 0 '(1 2 3 4 5)) ; Returns 15
```

Here, `foldl` is used to compute the sum of the list elements, with `+` as the function to combine elements and `0` as the initial value. Similarly, `foldr` works in a similar fashion but processes the list from right to left.

To further illustrate the versatility of higher-order functions, consider how they can be used to create more abstract operations. For example, we can define a higher-order function `compose` that takes two functions and returns their composition:

```racket
(define (compose f g)
  (lambda (x) (f (g x))))
```

This `compose` function allows us to create new functions by combining existing ones. For instance:

```racket
(define add1 (lambda (x) (+ x 1)))
(define square (lambda (x) (x x)))
(define square-then-add1 (compose add1 square))
(square-then-add1 4) ; Returns 17
```

In this example, `square-then-add1` first squares its input and then adds 1 to the result. This demonstrates how higher-order functions can facilitate complex function compositions and transformations.

Closures and higher-order functions, when used together, can lead to highly modular and expressive code. For instance, closures can capture specific behaviors or states that are then manipulated by higher-order functions. This combination of features supports writing code that is not only more abstract and reusable but also cleaner and easier to maintain.

For example, consider the following implementation of a memoized function using closures and higher-order functions. Memoization is an optimization technique that stores previously computed results to avoid redundant calculations:

```racket
(define (make-memoized-function f)
  (let ([cache (make-hasheq)])
```

```
  (lambda (x)
    (or (hash-ref cache x f)
      (let ([result (f x)])
        (hash-set! cache x result)
        result)))))

(define slow-fib
  (lambda (n)
    (if (< n 2)
      n
      (+ (slow-fib (- n 1)) (slow-fib (- n 2))))))

(define memoized-fib (make-memoized-function slow-fib))
```

In this implementation, `make-memoized-function` creates a closure that maintains a cache for storing results of the `slow-fib` function. This technique illustrates how closures and higher-order functions can be combined to enhance performance and code efficiency.

Understanding and applying these advanced function concepts—closures and higher-order functions—enables more sophisticated and elegant solutions to programming problems. By leveraging these features, you can create highly abstracted, reusable, and maintainable code in Racket, enhancing both your programming skills and your ability to tackle complex problems effectively.

In discussing advanced functions and closures in Racket, it is essential to understand the concept of closures more deeply. Closures are not just about encapsulating functions but also about preserving the environment in which these functions are created. This preservation of the environment allows closures to access variables that were in scope when they were created, even after the original scope has ended.

Consider a scenario where we have a function that generates

another function with a specific behavior. This is where closures excel. For instance, suppose we want to create a function that generates incrementing functions. We can use closures to capture the current state of the increment value:

```racket
(define (make-incrementer step)
 (lambda (x) (+ x step)))


(define inc-by-3 (make-incrementer 3))
(define inc-by-5 (make-incrementer 5))

(inc-by-3 10) ; Returns 13
(inc-by-5 10) ; Returns 15
```

In this example, `make-incrementer` returns a lambda function that increments its argument by the captured `step` value. Each `inc-by-` function retains its own `step` value, demonstrating how closures can capture and maintain specific environments. This capability is particularly useful for creating customized functions without having to repeatedly pass parameters.

Closures also play a crucial role in managing state and creating more sophisticated abstractions. For example, closures can be used to create data structures such as counters or accumulators where the internal state is hidden and protected from external modification. Consider the following implementation of a counter:

```racket
(define (make-counter)
 (let ([count 0])
  (lambda ()
   (set! count (+ count 1))
   count)))
```

```
(define my-counter (make-counter))
(my-counter) ; Returns 1
(my-counter) ; Returns 2
```

In this code snippet, `make-counter` creates a closure that includes a private `count` variable. Each call to `my-counter` increments this internal state and returns the updated count, while keeping `count` hidden from the outside world. This demonstrates how closures can encapsulate state effectively, which is a cornerstone of functional programming.

To further enhance your understanding of higher-order functions and closures, let's explore an example that involves more complex function composition. Function composition allows us to build new functions by combining existing ones. In Racket, this can be achieved with higher-order functions that return other functions. For example, let's define a function that composes two functions:

```racket
(define (compose f g)
  (lambda (x) (f (g x))))

(define add1 (lambda (x) (+ x 1)))
(define square (lambda (x) ( x x)))

(define add1-then-square (compose square add1))
(add1-then-square 3) ; Returns 16
```

Here, `compose` takes two functions `f` and `g` and returns a new function that first applies `g` to its input and then applies `f` to the result. This allows us to build complex functions in a modular and reusable way, further showcasing the power of higher-order functions.

Combining higher-order functions with closures can also

lead to elegant solutions for various programming problems. For instance, consider a scenario where we want to create a function that counts how many times a particular value appears in a list. We can use closures to encapsulate the counting logic:

```racket
(define (make-counter target)
  (let ([count 0])
    (lambda (lst)
      (for ([x lst])
        (when (equal? x target)
          (set! count (+ count 1))))
      count)))

(define count-3 (make-counter 3))
(count-3 '(1 3 2 3 4 3 5)) ; Returns 3
```

In this example, `make-counter` creates a closure that captures the `target` value and maintains a count of occurrences within a list. Each invocation of the resulting function processes a new list, illustrating how closures can be used to create more flexible and reusable abstractions.

Understanding and effectively using closures and higher-order functions will significantly enhance your ability to write expressive and modular Racket programs. By leveraging these advanced features, you can create abstractions that simplify complex logic, manage state effectively, and build reusable components that improve code quality and maintainability.

CHAPTER 10: ERROR HANDLING AND DEBUGGING

In Racket, error handling and debugging are crucial aspects that ensure your programs run smoothly and are free from unexpected issues. Effective error handling allows you to manage and respond to errors in a controlled manner, while debugging techniques help you identify and resolve problems in your code. This exploration begins with understanding the mechanisms Racket provides for error handling and progresses into practical debugging strategies.

To handle errors in Racket, the `error` function is a primary tool. This function allows you to generate custom error messages when something goes wrong. The `error` function is used to raise an exception and terminate the current operation, providing an error message that can help diagnose the issue. For example, consider a simple function that divides two numbers:

```racket
(define (safe-divide x y)
  (if (zero? y)
      (error "Division by zero is not allowed")
      (/ x y)))
```

In this `safe-divide` function, we check if the denominator

`y` is zero before performing the division. If it is zero, we raise an error with a descriptive message. This approach helps prevent runtime errors and provides informative feedback when an invalid operation is attempted.

Racket also supports contracts, which are a way to specify and enforce expectations about function inputs and outputs. Contracts can be particularly useful for catching errors related to incorrect function usage. For instance, if you want to ensure that a function argument is always a positive number, you can use contracts as follows:

```racket
(define/contract (positive-square x)
 (-> (and/c positive?) number?)
 ( x x))
```

Here, `define/contract` is used to define `positive-square`, which specifies that `x` must be a positive number. If `x` does not meet this requirement, Racket will raise an error. Contracts provide a way to enforce constraints and ensure that functions are used correctly, thus enhancing the robustness of your code.

Moving beyond error handling, debugging is an integral part of the development process. In Racket, DrRacket offers several debugging tools that facilitate the process of finding and fixing issues in your code. One of the most valuable tools is the stepper, which allows you to execute your code one step at a time. This incremental execution helps you observe how variables and expressions change, making it easier to trace the flow of execution and identify problematic areas.

To use the stepper, you first need to set breakpoints in your code. Breakpoints are markers that indicate where you want the execution to pause. You can set breakpoints by clicking in the left margin of the DrRacket editor. Once breakpoints are set, you can run your program in the stepper mode. As the code executes, you can step through each line, inspect variable values, and observe how the program state evolves.

In addition to stepping through code, DrRacket provides a built-in debugger that offers a more comprehensive view of your program's execution. The debugger displays the current call stack, local variables, and the environment in which your code is running. This information is invaluable for understanding the context of errors and diagnosing complex issues.

Another important aspect of debugging is writing test cases. Test cases help verify that your code behaves as expected under various conditions. In Racket, you can use the `rackunit` library to write and run unit tests. Unit tests are automated checks that compare the output of your functions against expected results. For example:

```racket
(require rackunit)

(define (add x y)
  (+ x y))

(check-equal? (add 2 3) 5)
(check-equal? (add -1 1) 0)
```

In this example, `check-equal?` is used to assert that the `add` function produces the correct results. Running these tests can quickly reveal if your functions are not behaving as intended, helping you catch errors early.

Combining effective error handling with robust debugging techniques equips you with the tools needed to manage and resolve issues in your Racket programs. By employing error messages, contracts, the stepper, and unit tests, you can ensure that your applications are both resilient and reliable. This holistic approach to error handling and debugging not only improves the quality of your code but also enhances your overall programming skills.

In addition to the `error` function and contracts, Racket provides several other mechanisms for handling errors. For instance, the `guard` function is a powerful tool for handling exceptions in a controlled manner. The `guard` function allows you to catch and manage errors without terminating the entire program. It takes a handler function and an expression, executing the handler if an error occurs during the evaluation of the expression.

Here is an example that demonstrates how `guard` can be used to handle exceptions:

```racket
(define (safe-sqrt x)
 (guard ([(exn:fail:contract? e) (error-message e)])
  (if (negative? x)
       (error "Cannot compute the square root of a negative number")
    (sqrt x))))
```

In this example, `guard` catches any errors that might be raised during the execution of `sqrt x`. If an exception is thrown, the handler function (in this case, `error-message e`) processes it, allowing you to provide a custom response or log the error. This approach enhances error handling by providing a way to recover from errors gracefully and continue program execution.

Another important aspect of error handling is understanding the different types of errors that can occur. Racket categorizes errors into various types, such as `exn:fail:contract`, `exn:fail:syntax`, and `exn:fail:operation`, among others. Each type of exception corresponds to different kinds of issues, such as contract violations, syntax errors, or runtime errors. Recognizing these types can help you implement more precise error handling strategies and debug issues more effectively.

When it comes to debugging, DrRacket offers several features to aid in the process. In addition to the stepper, which allows you to execute code line by line, DrRacket provides an interactive debugging environment with a variety of tools. The interactive debugger includes features such as breakpoints, which enable you to pause execution at specific points in your code. This allows you to inspect the state of variables, evaluate expressions, and understand the flow of execution.

To set a breakpoint in DrRacket, simply click on the left margin of the code editor next to the line where you want to pause execution. When you run your program, it will halt at the breakpoint, giving you the opportunity to examine the current state of your program. You can then use the debugger's controls to step through the code, resume execution, or inspect variable values. This interactive approach makes it easier to diagnose and resolve issues by providing real-time feedback on the program's behavior.

Additionally, DrRacket's debugging tools include a console for evaluating expressions and inspecting results. The REPL (Read-Eval-Print Loop) provides a dynamic environment where you can interact with your code, test individual expressions, and verify the correctness of your functions. The REPL is an invaluable tool for iterative development and troubleshooting, as it allows you to quickly test hypotheses and explore different scenarios.

Another useful feature in DrRacket is the `check-expect` framework, which supports automated testing of functions. By writing test cases and specifying the expected outputs, you can systematically verify that your functions produce correct results. This approach to testing helps identify issues early in the development process and ensures that your code behaves as expected.

For example, consider the following test cases for a function that computes the factorial of a number:

```racket
(check-expect (factorial 0) 1)
(check-expect (factorial 1) 1)
(check-expect (factorial 5) 120)
```

By running these test cases, you can verify that the `factorial` function produces the correct results for various inputs. Automated testing is a key practice in software development, as it provides confidence in the correctness of your code and helps prevent regressions.

Effective debugging also involves understanding common programming pitfalls and learning how to avoid them. For example, issues such as off-by-one errors, incorrect variable scoping, and logical errors can often be resolved by carefully analyzing your code and using debugging tools to track down the source of the problem. Developing a systematic approach to debugging and employing best practices, such as writing clear and maintainable code, can greatly enhance your ability to diagnose and fix issues.

By combining robust error handling techniques with powerful debugging tools, you can create more reliable and maintainable Racket programs. Understanding how to manage exceptions, enforce contracts, and use debugging features will help you address issues effectively and ensure that your applications function correctly.

While DrRacket's debugger and stepper are invaluable for tracking down issues in your code, it is also important to use various strategies to enhance the debugging process. One such strategy is incorporating logging into your programs. By adding logging statements, you can trace the flow of execution and capture the state of variables at various points in your program. This information can be critical for understanding what went wrong and why.

In Racket, you can use the `printf` function to log information. For example:

```racket
(define (divide a b)
  (printf "Dividing ~a by ~a\n" a b)
  (if (zero? b)
      (error "Cannot divide by zero")
      (/ a b)))
```

In this function, `printf` outputs the values of `a` and `b` before performing the division. This kind of logging can help you see the actual values being processed and identify any unexpected behavior.

Another important aspect of error handling is the design of your functions. Ensuring that functions are robust and fail gracefully is crucial. This involves validating inputs to ensure they meet the expected criteria before proceeding with computation. For instance, if you are writing a function that processes lists, you should check that the input is indeed a list and handle cases where it is not.

```racket
(define (process-list lst)
  (unless (list? lst)
    (error "Expected a list, but got ~a" lst))
  ; Rest of the function
)
```

In this example, `unless` is used to verify that `lst` is a list. If it is not, an error is raised with a descriptive message. This preemptive validation helps to avoid errors later in the function when operations are performed on the list.

Additionally, understanding and handling the scope of errors is key to effective error management. Errors that occur in a specific scope might need different handling strategies compared to errors that occur globally. For example, an error within a loop might be handled differently from an error that occurs during a function call. By using Racket's facilities for local and global error handling, you can tailor your responses to different error contexts.

Error handling in Racket also extends to dealing with assertions. The `check-expected` function can be used to test whether a value meets an expected condition, and it raises an error if the condition is not met. This is particularly useful for validating that the outcomes of your functions are as expected.

```racket
(define (factorial n)
  (check-expected (> n 0) "Factorial requires a non-negative integer")
  (if (zero? n)
    1
    ( n (factorial (- n 1))))))
```

In this function, `check-expected` ensures that `n` is a non-negative integer before computing the factorial. If `n` does not meet the condition, an error is raised with a specific message.

When dealing with complex applications, especially those involving multiple modules or external libraries, you may encounter errors related to module imports or interactions. Racket's module system can help manage these scenarios by isolating code into separate modules, but it also requires careful attention to ensure that modules are correctly loaded and that dependencies are met. Ensuring that your modules are properly documented and that their interfaces are well-defined can help mitigate issues related to integration and usage.

Finally, always ensure that your error handling and debugging practices are part of your development process from the start. Implementing robust error handling and debugging strategies early in the development lifecycle can save time and effort later on. Building a habit of writing defensive code, using logging for tracing execution, and systematically testing your functions can greatly enhance the reliability of your programs.

In summary, effective error handling and debugging in Racket involve a combination of using built-in error management functions, leveraging debugging tools, incorporating logging, validating inputs, and understanding the scope of errors. By applying these techniques, you can develop more resilient programs and troubleshoot issues more efficiently.

CHAPTER 11: FILE I/O AND DATA PERSISTENCE

The ability to handle file input and output (I/O) is essential for developing applications that need to interact with external data. In Racket, file I/O operations allow programs to read from and write to files, facilitating data persistence and interaction with the outside world. Understanding these operations is critical for tasks ranging from simple data storage to more complex data management.

To begin with, Racket provides several functions to handle files. The basic operations include opening, reading, writing, and closing files. Opening a file in Racket involves using the `open-input-file` and `open-output-file` functions. These functions establish connections to files, allowing for subsequent read and write operations.

```racket
(define input-port (open-input-file "data.txt"))
(define output-port (open-output-file "output.txt"))
```

The `open-input-file` function creates an input port for reading from the file named "data.txt", whereas `open-output-file` creates an output port for writing to "output.txt". These ports act as conduits through which data flows into or out of the program.

Reading from a file is typically done using functions like `read`, `read-line`, or `file->string`. The `read` function reads the next datum from an input port, while `read-line` reads the next line of text as a string. The `file->string` function reads the entire file content into a single string, which is useful for processing file contents in bulk.

```racket
(define content (file->string "data.txt"))
```

In this example, `file->string` reads the entire content of "data.txt" into the variable `content`, which can then be manipulated or analyzed as needed. For more controlled reading, you might use `read-line` to process the file line by line, which is useful when dealing with large files or when each line needs to be processed independently.

Writing to a file involves similar functions: `write`, `display`, and `fprintf`. The `write` function outputs data to an output port, while `display` writes textual data, and `fprintf` provides formatted output. Using these functions, you can write various types of data to a file, from simple strings to complex data structures.

```racket
(display "Hello, World!" output-port)
```

Here, `display` writes the string "Hello, World!" to the file associated with `output-port`. If you need to write formatted output, `fprintf` can be particularly useful:

```racket
(fprintf output-port "The value is: ~a\n" 42)
```

This line writes the formatted string "The value is: 42" to the file, demonstrating how `fprintf` can include variable values in the output.

Closing files is crucial to ensure that resources are properly released. Racket provides the `close-input-port` and `close-output-port` functions to close input and output ports, respectively. Failing to close files can lead to resource leaks and other issues, so it's important to always close ports when you are done with them.

```racket
(close-input-port input-port)
(close-output-port output-port)
```

Handling different data formats is another important aspect of file I/O. Racket supports various formats, including plain text, binary, and structured data formats like JSON and XML. When dealing with non-text data, you might need to use specific functions or libraries to handle encoding and decoding.

For example, to read and write JSON data, you would use the `json` library in Racket. This library provides functions to parse JSON strings and convert Racket data structures to JSON format. Similarly, for XML, you might use the `xml` library to parse and generate XML data.

```racket
(require json)
(define data (string->jsexpr "{\"name\": \"Alice\", \"age\": 30}"))
```

In this snippet, `string->jsexpr` parses a JSON string into a Racket data structure. Conversely, you can convert Racket data structures to JSON using `jsexpr->string`.

Managing file-based interactions involves more than just reading and writing. Consideration must be given to error handling and data validation. When working with files, errors can occur due to various reasons, such as missing files, permission issues, or malformed data. Handling these errors gracefully is crucial to maintaining robust and user-friendly applications.

To handle file-related errors, you can use Racket's condition system. For instance, you can use `with-handlers` to catch and handle exceptions that occur during file operations:

```racket
(with-handlers ([exn:fail:filesystem? (lambda (exn) (displayln "File error occurred!"))])
  (define input-port (open-input-file "data.txt"))
  (define content (file->string "data.txt"))
  (close-input-port input-port))
```

In this example, `with-handlers` is used to catch filesystem errors and handle them appropriately. This ensures that your program can recover from or provide feedback about file-related issues without crashing.

By mastering file I/O and data persistence, you gain the ability to create applications that not only interact with users but also persist information between sessions. This capability is fundamental to building effective and reliable software, allowing your applications to handle a wide range of data management tasks.

Handling file operations in Racket extends beyond merely opening, reading, writing, and closing files. It is crucial to understand how to manage different file formats and handle errors effectively to ensure robust data processing. Let us delve deeper into the specifics of reading and writing various data formats, as well as the nuances of error handling during file operations.

When dealing with files in Racket, data formats play a significant role. Files can store data in plain text, CSV (comma-separated values), or even binary formats. Handling different formats requires a nuanced approach. For instance, reading and writing CSV files necessitates parsing and formatting strings, whereas binary files involve working with raw data.

For text files, the process is straightforward: you can read the file line by line or in its entirety using functions like `read`, `read-line`, or `file->string`. Once you have the data, you may need to parse it into a more usable form. For example, if you are reading a file where each line represents a record with fields separated by commas, you would use string operations to split each line into its constituent fields.

```racket
(define (parse-csv-line line)
  (string-split line ","))
```

In this example, `parse-csv-line` takes a line of CSV data and splits it into a list of fields. This function can be used in conjunction with `for/list` or similar constructs to process an entire file.

```racket
(define (read-csv file-name)
  (define input-port (open-input-file file-name))
  (define records
    (for/list ([line (in-lines input-port)])
      (parse-csv-line line)))
  (close-input-port input-port)
  records)
```

Here, `read-csv` reads a CSV file and converts each line into a list of fields using `parse-csv-line`. The `for/list` construct iterates over each line in the file, applying `parse-csv-line` to each line and collecting the results into a list. After processing, it is essential to close the input port to free system resources.

Binary file operations in Racket are somewhat more involved. You must use functions designed for handling raw data, such as `open-input-bytes` and `open-output-bytes`, and work with byte streams. Binary files require careful management of data types and sizes. For instance, reading binary data might involve interpreting byte sequences as integers, floats, or other data types.

```racket
(define (write-binary-data file-name data)
    (define output-port (open-output-file file-name :mode 'binary))
  (write-bytes (bytes data) output-port)
  (close-output-port output-port))
```

In the above code snippet, `write-binary-data` opens a file for binary output, writes a sequence of bytes, and then closes the file. Handling binary data requires a precise understanding of the format and encoding of the data you are working with.

Error handling during file operations is another critical aspect. In Racket, file operations can fail for various reasons, such as non-existent files, permission issues, or file corruption. To manage these errors, you can use conditionals to check for potential issues and `with-handlers` to catch and handle exceptions gracefully.

```racket
(define (safe-read-file file-name)
 (with-handlers ([exn:fail:read? (lambda (e)
            (format "Error reading file: ~a" e))])
  (let ([content (file->string file-name)])
    content)))
```

```

In the `safe-read-file` function, `with-handlers` is used to catch exceptions related to file reading. If an exception occurs, an error message is formatted and returned. This approach ensures that your program does not crash unexpectedly and provides meaningful feedback when an error occurs.

Similarly, when writing to files, it is crucial to handle exceptions that may arise. This includes ensuring that files are properly closed even if an error occurs during writing. Using constructs like `with-output-to-file` ensures that files are correctly handled and closed.

```racket
(define (safe-write-file file-name data)
 (with-output-to-file file-name
  (lambda ()
   (display data))))
```

Here, `with-output-to-file` opens a file, writes data to it, and automatically closes the file when done, ensuring that resources are properly released even if errors occur during the writing process.

Effective error handling and careful management of file I/O operations are essential for developing robust Racket applications. By understanding how to handle different data formats and manage exceptions, you will be well-equipped to create applications that interact with files efficiently and reliably.

When dealing with file operations, error handling is paramount to ensure that your program behaves predictably even when things go wrong. In Racket, you can leverage several mechanisms to handle errors gracefully.

One approach is to use the `with-input-from-file` and `with-
```

output-to-file` constructs. These provide a safe way to open a file, perform operations, and automatically close the file when done, even if an error occurs. This reduces the risk of leaving files open inadvertently and handles resources more efficiently.

```racket
(define (safe-read-file file-name)
  (with-input-from-file file-name
    (lambda ()
      (let ([content (file->string file-name)])
        (string-trim content)))))
```

In this example, `safe-read-file` uses `with-input-from-file` to ensure that the file is properly closed after reading its contents. If an error occurs while processing the file, Racket will handle it by closing the file and cleaning up resources.

To handle more complex scenarios, such as when you need to deal with exceptions explicitly, Racket offers the `condition` system. This system allows you to define custom error conditions and handle them in a structured manner. For instance, you might want to catch specific types of exceptions and take corrective actions, such as logging an error message or attempting a retry.

```racket
(define (read-file-with-error-handling file-name)
    (with-handlers ([exn:fail? (lambda (exn) (displayln "File operation failed!") 'failure)])
    (with-input-from-file file-name
      (lambda ()
        (file->string file-name)))))
```

Here, `read-file-with-error-handling` uses `with-handlers` to catch exceptions that are thrown during file operations. If an exception of type `exn:fail?` is encountered, it displays an error message and returns a failure indicator. This approach helps in isolating error-handling logic and ensures that the rest of the program can continue running smoothly.

When working with data persistence, it's often necessary to ensure data integrity and consistency. For instance, when writing to a file, you may need to check if the file already exists, whether it is writable, and ensure that the data is correctly formatted before writing.

```racket
(define (write-data-to-file file-name data)
  (unless (file-exists? file-name)
    (with-output-to-file file-name
      (lambda ()
        (for-each (lambda (line) (displayln line))
           data))))
  (displayln "Data written successfully."))
```

In this example, `write-data-to-file` checks if the file exists before writing. If it does not exist, it creates the file and writes the data to it. This method ensures that you do not unintentionally overwrite existing files unless explicitly intended.

Data validation is also crucial for maintaining data integrity. Before writing data to a file, it is important to validate that the data conforms to expected formats and constraints. For instance, you might need to ensure that numeric data falls within a specific range or that textual data does not contain forbidden characters.

```racket
(define (validate-data data)
  (for-each (lambda (datum)
       (when (not (string? datum))
```

```
      (error "Invalid data format.")))
    data))
```

Here, `validate-data` checks each item in the `data` list to ensure it is a string. If any item fails this check, it raises an error. This type of validation ensures that only data meeting predefined criteria is written to the file, thereby avoiding potential issues later.

Lastly, managing large files or data streams requires special attention. For large files, reading and writing in chunks can improve performance and reduce memory usage. Racket provides functions such as `read-bytes` and `write-bytes` for handling binary data in chunks, which can be particularly useful for processing large datasets or files.

```racket
(define (process-large-file file-name)
  (define chunk-size 1024)
  (define input-port (open-input-file file-name))
  (let loop ()
    (let ([chunk (read-bytes chunk-size)])
      (unless (eof-object? chunk)
        (process-chunk chunk)
        (loop))))
  (close-input-port input-port))
```

In this function, `process-large-file` reads a file in chunks of 1024 bytes. The `process-chunk` function represents a placeholder where you can define how each chunk should be processed. By handling data in chunks, you can efficiently manage large files without overwhelming system memory.

Mastering file I/O and data persistence in Racket equips you with the skills necessary to create applications that interact effectively with external data sources. By understanding and applying these techniques, you ensure that your programs can read, write, and manage data in a reliable and efficient manner.

CHAPTER 12: INTRODUCTION TO MACROS

Macros are a cornerstone of Racket, offering a robust mechanism for extending and customizing the language. They differ fundamentally from functions in that they operate at the syntactic level, transforming code before it is executed. This ability to manipulate code structures before runtime provides a level of abstraction and flexibility that is not achievable with functions alone.

To understand macros, it's essential first to grasp the distinction between functions and macros. Functions in Racket, as in many programming languages, operate on values and are executed at runtime. When you call a function, you pass it arguments, and it returns a result based on these inputs. In contrast, macros operate on the code itself before it is executed. They take code as input and produce transformed code as output, which is then compiled and executed.

This distinction is crucial because it allows macros to perform tasks that would be cumbersome or impossible with functions. For instance, macros can generate new syntactic forms or embed domain-specific languages within Racket, leading to more expressive and concise code.

Let's start with a basic example of a macro. Suppose we want to create a macro that defines a new control structure, such as a `when` construct, which executes a block of code only if a given condition is true. In Racket, we can define this using the `define-syntax` and `syntax-rules` constructs. Here's how we can implement it:

```racket
(define-syntax when
  (syntax-rules ()
    [(when test expr ...)
     (if test (begin expr ...))]))
```

In this example, the `when` macro is defined using `define-syntax` and `syntax-rules`. The `syntax-rules` pattern-matching system is used to match the `when` form and transform it into an `if` expression. This macro will expand the `when` expression into an `if` statement with the provided expressions executed if the condition evaluates to true.

To see how this macro works in practice, consider the following usage:

```racket
(when (> x 10)
  (display "x is greater than 10")
  (newline))
```

Here, `when` will expand into an `if` statement that checks if `x` is greater than 10. If true, it will execute the `display` and `newline` expressions.

Macros are especially useful for creating domain-specific languages (DSLs) or embedding new syntactic constructs that make the code more expressive. For example, consider a macro that provides a DSL for defining simple data structures:

```racket
```

```
(define-syntax defstruct
 (syntax-rules ()
  [(defstruct name (field1 field2 ...))
   (begin
    (define-struct name (field1 field2 ...))
    (define (make-<name> . args)
     (apply make-struct name args))])))
```

In this macro, `defstruct` is used to define a new structure with specified fields. The macro generates both the `define-struct` form and a `make-<name>` function to create instances of the structure. This example demonstrates how macros can encapsulate boilerplate code and simplify the definition of data structures.

Another powerful aspect of macros is their ability to create hygiene and ensure that variable names do not clash unintentionally. Racket's macro system uses hygienic macros, which preserve lexical scoping and avoid variable capture issues. This is accomplished through mechanisms that manage the binding of identifiers within macros, ensuring that the transformation maintains the correct scope and context.

For instance, when defining a macro that introduces new variables, it's crucial to avoid accidentally capturing variables from the surrounding code. Racket's hygienic macros handle this by generating unique variable names internally, thereby preventing unintended interactions between macro-generated code and user code.

Consider the following example of a macro that introduces a new variable binding:

```racket
(define-syntax let-new
 (syntax-rules ()
```

```
  [(let-new ([var val]) body ...)
   (let ([var val])
     body ...)]))
```

Here, `let-new` is a macro that expands into a `let` expression. The variable `var` is bound to the value `val`, and the `body` expressions are executed with this new binding. By using the macro, you can encapsulate variable binding logic and simplify code, while the hygienic system ensures that variable names remain unique and do not clash with those in the surrounding environment.

Macros offer a powerful way to extend Racket's syntax and create abstractions that fit specific needs. By leveraging macros, you can write more expressive and maintainable code, encapsulate repetitive patterns, and define new control structures that enhance the clarity and functionality of your programs. Understanding how to create and use macros effectively will enable you to harness the full potential of Racket's syntactic capabilities, leading to more sophisticated and elegant solutions to programming problems.

The power of macros in Racket lies in their ability to perform syntactic transformations, which opens up numerous possibilities for customizing and extending the language. Unlike functions, which operate on values and execute at runtime, macros transform code at compile time. This transformation capability allows macros to introduce new syntactic constructs or modify existing ones, making them a versatile tool for code abstraction and reuse.

To illustrate the versatility of macros, let's explore the concept of a macro that creates a new syntactic form—one that is more complex than our initial `when` example. Consider the implementation of a `with-resource` macro that manages resources such as file handles or database connections. This macro ensures that resources are properly initialized before use and cleaned up afterward.

Here's how the `with-resource` macro could be defined:

```racket
(define-syntax with-resource
 (syntax-rules ()
  [(with-resource ([resource init] [cleanup]) body ...)
   (let ([resource init])
    (dynamic-wind
     (lambda () resource) ; Initialization
     (lambda () body ...) ; Body
     (lambda () cleanup))) ; Cleanup
   ]))
```

In this macro definition, `with-resource` takes two arguments: a list specifying the resource and its initialization, and a cleanup function. The `dynamic-wind` construct is used to manage the resource's lifecycle. The first lambda initializes the resource, the second lambda executes the body of the macro, and the third lambda performs the cleanup.

The `with-resource` macro can be employed as follows:

```racket
(with-resource ([file (open-output-file "example.txt")]
        (close-output-port file))
 (display "Writing to file")
 (newline))
```

In this code snippet, `with-resource` ensures that the file is opened before the body executes and closed afterward, regardless of whether the body completes successfully or raises an error. This usage exemplifies how macros can encapsulate common patterns and automate resource management tasks.

Beyond creating new syntactic constructs, macros can also be employed to enforce coding patterns and constraints. For example, we might want to define a macro that ensures certain naming conventions or programming patterns are followed within a module. Consider a macro that enforces function names to start with a specific prefix:

```racket
(define-syntax check-function-name
  (syntax-rules ()
    [(check-function-name (name ...) body ...)
     (begin
       (define (name ...) body ...)
       (when (not (string-prefix? "prefix-" (symbol->string 'name)))
         (error "Function name must start with 'prefix-'")))]))
```

This macro `check-function-name` not only defines a function but also performs a compile-time check to ensure that the function name starts with the prefix `"prefix-"`. This kind of macro can be useful for enforcing naming conventions or other code standards within a codebase.

Another advanced feature of macros is the ability to generate code programmatically. This can be particularly powerful when dealing with repetitive code patterns. Suppose you need to generate a set of accessor functions for a data structure. Instead of manually writing each accessor, you can use a macro to generate them automatically:

```racket
(define-syntax define-accessors
  (syntax-rules ()
    [(define-accessors (struct field1 field2 ...) (data-type))
     (begin
       (define (get-field1 data) (struct-field data 0))
```

```
    (define (get-field2 data) (struct-field data 1))
    ...)]))
```

In this macro definition, `define-accessors` takes a list of fields and a data type and generates corresponding accessor functions. This reduces boilerplate code and ensures consistency across different accessors.

The use of macros in Racket extends beyond simple code generation and validation. Macros can also interact with other parts of the language, such as modules and contracts, to provide advanced features like domain-specific languages (DSLs) or customized control structures. By leveraging macros, you can tailor Racket to fit specific needs or domains, enhancing both the expressiveness and maintainability of your code.

In conclusion, the macro system in Racket provides a robust framework for extending the language's capabilities. Macros offer the ability to transform code at compile time, define new syntactic constructs, enforce coding patterns, and automate repetitive tasks. Mastering macros allows you to write more abstract, reusable, and expressive Racket code, making them an indispensable tool in advanced Racket programming.

Building upon the previous discussions on macros, let us now delve into more advanced usage and the intricacies involved in defining and employing them effectively. Understanding the nuances of macro development will provide a deeper grasp of how macros can be harnessed to create elegant and maintainable code.

A crucial aspect of working with macros is understanding macro hygiene, which refers to the mechanism that prevents name clashes between variables in the macro's expansion and those in the surrounding code. This is achieved through the introduction of fresh identifiers that avoid conflicts. Racket's macro system, through its `syntax-rules` and `syntax-case` constructs, automatically ensures macro hygiene by renaming identifiers in a way that prevents unintended interactions.

To explore this concept, consider a scenario where we create a macro that introduces a new variable scope within a function. For instance, suppose we want to define a macro `with-local` that binds a local variable and ensures that it is used within a specific block of code:

```racket
(define-syntax with-local
  (syntax-rules ()
    [(with-local ([var init]) body ...)
     (let ([var init])
       body ...)]))
```

In this macro, `with-local` introduces a new local variable `var` with the value `init`, and the variable is only accessible within the `body`. This approach leverages the lexical scope of `let` to encapsulate the variable, preventing it from interfering with variables outside the macro. The result is that `var` is confined to the scope of the `let`, adhering to the principles of macro hygiene.

However, if we need more control over macro hygiene or wish to manipulate the syntax tree directly, Racket provides the `syntax-case` system. This system allows for more sophisticated macro definitions where patterns and template expressions can be used to generate code. For instance, let us consider a macro `define-invariant` that enforces an invariant condition on function parameters:

```racket
(define-syntax (define-invariant stx)
  (syntax-case stx ()
    [(_ (name x) invariant body ...)
```

```
(with-syntax ([new-x (generate-temporary)])
  '(define (name x)
     (let ([new-x x])
       (if (not (invariant new-x))
           (error "Invariant violation")
           (begin body ...)))))]))
```

In this macro, `define-invariant` introduces a new variable `new-x` to avoid name clashes and checks if the parameter `x` satisfies the `invariant` condition. If the condition fails, an error is raised. This macro showcases how `syntax-case` can be used to manipulate and validate code during the macro expansion phase, adding a layer of robustness and error-checking to the code.

Another sophisticated example of macro usage involves generating repetitive code patterns. Suppose we need to define a set of functions that follow a specific naming convention and implementation pattern. Rather than writing each function manually, we can use a macro to automate this process:

```racket
(define-syntax (define-math-functions stx)
  (syntax-case stx ()
    [(_ (add sub mul div))
     (with-syntax ([add-fn (syntax (λ (x y) (+ x y)))])
       (with-syntax ([sub-fn (syntax (λ (x y) (- x y)))])
         (with-syntax ([mul-fn (syntax (λ (x y) ( x y)))])
           (with-syntax ([div-fn (syntax (λ (x y) (/ x y)))])
             '(begin
                (define add add-fn)
                (define sub sub-fn)
                (define mul mul-fn)
                (define div div-fn))))))]))
```

In this example, the `define-math-functions` macro generates definitions for `add`, `sub`, `mul`, and `div`, each implementing basic arithmetic operations. By employing macros in this way, you can significantly reduce redundancy and maintain consistency across your codebase.

Furthermore, understanding the interplay between macros and Racket's module system can enhance modularity and reusability. Macros can be defined in one module and used across others, enabling the creation of domain-specific languages or APIs tailored to specific needs. For instance, if you have a set of utility macros for handling file operations, you could define them in a module and then import that module wherever those utilities are needed.

The integration of macros with Racket's module system facilitates the development of well-structured and extensible applications. It allows for the encapsulation of macro definitions in libraries that can be shared and reused, fostering better organization and code management practices.

In summary, mastering Racket's macro system involves not only understanding how to define and use macros but also appreciating the underlying principles of macro hygiene, code generation, and integration with the module system. By harnessing the power of macros, you can extend the Racket language to meet your specific programming needs, making your code more expressive, maintainable, and adaptable.

CHAPTER 13: OBJECT-ORIENTED PROGRAMMING IN RACKET

In exploring object-oriented programming (OOP) within Racket, we uncover a paradigm that complements Racket's functional nature by introducing classes and objects as a means of structuring code. Understanding how to define and utilize classes, methods, and other OOP constructs in Racket can enhance your ability to create modular, reusable components, thereby expanding the versatility of your programming approach.

To start, we must understand the fundamental components of OOP: classes and objects. In Racket, classes are defined using the `define-class` construct, which provides a blueprint for creating objects. An object is an instance of a class and encapsulates both state (attributes) and behavior (methods). For instance, let us define a simple class `Person` with attributes `name` and `age`, and methods to access these attributes:

```racket
(define-class Person
 ([name string?]
  [age integer?])
```

```
(define/public (get-name) name)
(define/public (get-age) age))
```

In this example, `define-class` is used to create the `Person` class. The `[name string?]` and `[age integer?]` are attributes of the class, where `string?` and `integer?` are predicates that ensure the attributes adhere to their respective types. The `define/public` constructs define methods that can be called on instances of the `Person` class. `get-name` and `get-age` are accessor methods that return the values of `name` and `age`, respectively.

With this `Person` class defined, creating instances of it is straightforward. For example:

```racket
(define person1 (new Person [name "Alice"] [age 30]))
```

Here, `new Person` creates a new instance of the `Person` class with the provided attribute values. The `person1` object now has methods `get-name` and `get-age` that can be invoked:

```racket
(send person1 get-name) ; Returns "Alice"
(send person1 get-age)  ; Returns 30
```

Encapsulation is a core principle of OOP, wherein the internal state of an object is hidden from outside manipulation. Racket's class system supports encapsulation by allowing access to data only through defined methods. For instance, while we can define methods to get the name and age of a `Person`, we do not expose the internal representation of these attributes directly. This encapsulation promotes a clean interface and prevents unintended interference with the object's state.

Inheritance allows one class to inherit the properties and methods of another, fostering code reuse and hierarchy. In Racket, inheritance is achieved by defining a class that extends another class. Consider an example where we define a `Student` class that inherits from the `Person` class:

```racket
(define-class Student (Person)
  ([student-id string?])
  (define/public (get-student-id) student-id))
```

In this example, `Student` inherits all the attributes and methods from `Person` while adding a new attribute `student-id` and a corresponding method `get-student-id`. Instances of `Student` will have all the methods available in `Person` as well as those specific to `Student`:

```racket
(define student1 (new Student [name "Bob"] [age 22] [student-id "S12345"]))
(send student1 get-name)       ; Returns "Bob"
(send student1 get-age)        ; Returns 22
(send student1 get-student-id) ; Returns "S12345"
```

Polymorphism, the ability for different classes to be treated as instances of the same class through a common interface, is another key principle of OOP. In Racket, polymorphism is facilitated by the class system through method overriding. When a subclass defines a method with the same name as one in its superclass, it overrides the superclass method, providing a specialized implementation. This allows objects of different subclasses to be used interchangeably if they share a common superclass interface.

For example, if we have another subclass `Teacher` that also extends `Person` but includes additional methods:

```racket
(define-class Teacher (Person)
 ([subject string?])
 (define/public (get-subject) subject))
```

Instances of `Teacher` will have access to `get-name` and `get-age` from `Person`, as well as `get-subject` specific to `Teacher`:

```racket
(define teacher1 (new Teacher [name "Dr. Smith"] [age 45] [subject "Mathematics"]))
(send teacher1 get-name)     ; Returns "Dr. Smith"
(send teacher1 get-age)      ; Returns 45
(send teacher1 get-subject)  ; Returns "Mathematics"
```

Here, `Teacher` and `Student` can both be treated as `Person` objects, showcasing the power of polymorphism. This principle allows for more flexible and extensible code, where new classes can be introduced without altering existing code that relies on the common superclass interface.

In summary, Racket's object-oriented features provide a robust framework for creating modular and reusable code through the use of classes and objects. Understanding the concepts of encapsulation, inheritance, and polymorphism allows for effective application of OOP principles, enhancing the design and functionality of Racket programs. As we continue to explore advanced topics in Racket, these OOP fundamentals will serve as a foundation for more complex programming constructs and applications.

To fully grasp the power of object-oriented programming in

Racket, we must delve deeper into the principles that underpin the paradigm. In addition to encapsulation, which we explored previously, inheritance and polymorphism are essential OOP concepts that facilitate code reuse and flexibility.

Inheritance allows a class to inherit attributes and methods from another class, creating a hierarchical relationship between classes. This principle promotes code reuse and helps in building complex systems by extending existing functionality. In Racket, inheritance is implemented using the `inherit` keyword within the `define-class` construct.

For example, consider extending the `Person` class to create a `Student` class, which adds a new attribute, `student-id`, and inherits the attributes and methods from `Person`:

```racket
(define-class Student (inherit Person)
  ([student-id string?])
  (define/public (get-student-id) student-id))
```

In this definition, the `Student` class inherits all attributes and methods from `Person` and adds an additional attribute `student-id`. The `get-student-id` method provides access to this new attribute. When creating an instance of `Student`, you can use the inherited methods from `Person`:

```racket
(define student1 (new Student [name "Bob"] [age 22] [student-id "S12345"]))
(send student1 get-name)       ; Returns "Bob"
(send student1 get-age)        ; Returns 22
(send student1 get-student-id) ; Returns "S12345"
```

This example illustrates how inheritance enables the `Student` class to leverage the existing functionality of the

`Person` class while adding new features specific to students.

Polymorphism is another cornerstone of OOP that allows different classes to be treated through a common interface. In Racket, polymorphism is often realized through method overriding. When a subclass provides a specific implementation of a method that is already defined in its superclass, the subclass's method overrides the superclass's method.

Let's extend the `Person` and `Student` example by introducing a `Teacher` class, which also inherits from `Person` but overrides the `get-name` method to include a title:

```racket
(define-class Teacher (inherit Person)
  ([title string?])
  (define/public (get-name)
    (string-append title " " (send this get-name))))
```

In the `Teacher` class, the `get-name` method overrides the one inherited from `Person`, modifying its behavior to prepend a title to the name. For example:

```racket
(define teacher1 (new Teacher [name "Dr. Smith"] [age 45] [title "Professor"]))
(send teacher1 get-name) ; Returns "Professor Dr. Smith"
```

This ability to override methods allows for flexible and adaptable code that can handle various types of objects through a unified interface. By leveraging polymorphism, you can write code that operates on objects of different classes but treats them in a consistent manner.

Furthermore, Racket's object system supports the creation

of abstract classes, which define a common interface for a group of related classes but do not provide a complete implementation. Abstract classes are useful for setting up a common structure that concrete subclasses must follow. For instance:

```racket
(define-class Animal
  ([name string?])
  (define/public (make-sound) (error "make-sound must be implemented in subclass")))

(define-class Dog (inherit Animal)
  (define/public (make-sound) "Woof"))
```

In this example, the `Animal` class defines a method `make-sound` that is meant to be overridden in subclasses. The `Dog` class provides a concrete implementation of `make-sound`, while `Animal` serves as a base for other animal types that must implement the method.

To conclude, the object-oriented programming features in Racket—encapsulation, inheritance, and polymorphism—offer powerful tools for designing and organizing complex software systems. By understanding and applying these principles, you can create modular, reusable, and adaptable code that aligns with the object-oriented paradigm, enhancing both the clarity and efficiency of your Racket programs.

In addition to inheritance and polymorphism, encapsulation is a foundational concept in object-oriented programming that ensures the internal state of an object is protected from unintended interference and misuse. Encapsulation is achieved in Racket by defining methods with specific access levels, which control how and when the object's data can be accessed or modified.

In Racket, encapsulation is implemented through the use of public and private methods. Public methods are accessible from outside the class and provide the primary interface for interacting with an object, while private methods are only accessible within the class. This separation ensures that the internal workings of a class remain hidden, allowing for a clear and controlled interface.

For instance, let's enhance our `Person` class to use encapsulation. We will make the `age` attribute private and provide public methods to access and modify it. This will prevent direct manipulation of `age` from outside the class, enforcing better control over how this data is managed.

Here is how you might define such a class in Racket:

```racket
(define-class Person
  ([name string?]
   [age (make-parameter 0)])
  (define/public (get-name) name)
  (define/public (set-name new-name) (set! name new-name))
  (define/public (get-age) (age))
  (define/public (set-age new-age)
    (when (and (number? new-age) (> new-age 0))
      (age new-age))))
```

In this definition, `age` is encapsulated using `make-parameter`, which provides a getter and setter while ensuring that the age cannot be set to a negative value. The `get-age` and `set-age` methods offer controlled access to the `age` parameter, enforcing validation and maintaining the integrity of the object's state.

When dealing with more complex scenarios, encapsulation can also be achieved using Racket's `define/private` feature, which explicitly marks methods and attributes as private, inaccessible from outside the class definition. This explicit control over access is crucial for creating robust and maintainable object-oriented designs.

As we progress with Racket's object-oriented capabilities, it is important to consider the practical applications of these principles. For instance, using encapsulation and inheritance, you can create a hierarchical system of classes where base classes encapsulate shared functionality, and derived classes extend or modify this functionality as needed. This design pattern is particularly useful in scenarios where you have a common set of behaviors and attributes shared among different types of objects, but with some variations specific to each type.

Polymorphism allows objects of different classes to be treated through a common interface, which is especially beneficial in scenarios where you need to write code that can operate on objects of multiple types. By defining common methods in a base class and overriding them in derived classes, you can ensure that your code remains flexible and extensible, able to handle new types of objects without modification.

Consider a scenario where you are developing a graphics application. You might define a base class `Shape` with methods for drawing and resizing shapes, and then create subclasses like `Circle`, `Rectangle`, and `Triangle`, each with its own specific implementation of these methods. Polymorphism allows you to write generic code that can operate on any `Shape`, regardless of its specific type, thus simplifying the management of various shape objects within your application.

In practice, effective use of object-oriented principles in Racket involves carefully designing your class hierarchies to promote code reuse, maintainability, and clarity. By leveraging encapsulation to protect object state, inheritance to extend functionality, and polymorphism to handle diverse object types through common interfaces, you can create sophisticated and well-organized Racket programs.

Overall, understanding and applying these object-oriented principles in Racket will enhance your ability to build modular, reusable, and maintainable software systems. By integrating OOP concepts into your programming practices, you will be well-equipped to tackle a wide range of programming challenges and develop robust applications that effectively manage complexity and promote code reuse.

CHAPTER 14: FUNCTIONAL PROGRAMMING PATTERNS

In functional programming, patterns and techniques are crucial for writing clean, efficient, and expressive code. This segment delves into several key functional programming patterns, each of which plays a significant role in leveraging the power of functions as first-class citizens. Understanding these patterns will deepen your grasp of functional programming and enhance your ability to tackle complex problems with elegance and efficiency.

To begin with, higher-order functions are a cornerstone of functional programming. These functions operate on other functions, either by taking them as arguments or returning them as results. This concept allows for the creation of more abstract and reusable code. Higher-order functions enable us to manipulate functions in ways that can simplify complex operations. For example, consider the `map` function, which applies a given function to each item in a list, producing a new list with the results. This can be demonstrated in Racket as follows:

```racket
(define (square x) ( x x))
```

```
(define numbers '(1 2 3 4 5))
(map square numbers) ; > (1 4 9 16 25)
```

In this example, `map` is a higher-order function because it takes `square` as an argument and applies it to each element of the list `numbers`. By leveraging higher-order functions, you can write code that is more modular and easier to understand.

Function composition is another powerful pattern in functional programming. This technique involves combining multiple functions to create a new function. In Racket, function composition can be achieved using the `compose` function, which takes several functions as arguments and returns a new function that applies them in sequence. Here's an example illustrating function composition:

```racket
(define (add1 x) (+ x 1))
(define (multiply2 x) ( x 2))

(define add1-then-multiply2 (compose multiply2 add1))

(add1-then-multiply2 3) ; > 8
```

In this case, `add1-then-multiply2` is a composed function that first adds 1 to its input and then multiplies the result by 2. Function composition allows for the construction of complex behaviors from simpler functions, facilitating code reuse and modular design.

Next, let us explore functional data structures, which are immutable and provide a different approach to handling and manipulating data compared to imperative programming. In functional programming, data structures such as lists, trees, and maps are immutable, meaning once created, they cannot be changed. Instead of modifying a data structure in place, you create new versions with the desired changes.

For instance, consider a simple list in Racket:

```racket
(define original-list '(1 2 3))
```

To add an element to this list, you would create a new list rather than modifying the existing one:

```racket
(define new-list (cons 0 original-list))
```

In this example, `new-list` is a new list created by adding an element to the front of `original-list`. The original list remains unchanged, demonstrating the immutability of functional data structures.

Another important functional data structure is the binary tree, which can be used for efficient searching and sorting. An immutable binary tree in Racket might be defined as follows:

```racket
(define-struct tree (left value right))
```

Here, `tree` is a structure with three components: `left`, `value`, and `right`. Each node in the tree is immutable, and operations on the tree involve creating new nodes rather than altering existing ones.

By understanding and applying these functional programming patterns—higher-order functions, function composition, and immutable data structures—you will enhance your ability to write functional code that is both expressive and maintainable. These patterns not only help in solving complex problems but also promote a functional programming style that emphasizes immutability, abstraction, and the use of functions as core building blocks.

Exploring functional data structures reveals how they can complement the principles of functional programming. Unlike imperative data structures, which often involve mutable state, functional data structures are immutable. This immutability ensures that data structures do not change once they are created, which simplifies reasoning about code and prevents unintended side effects.

One common functional data structure is the immutable list. In Racket, lists are inherently immutable, meaning that operations on a list create new lists rather than modifying the original. This immutability is particularly advantageous when applying functional programming techniques, as it allows for easier manipulation and transformation of data. Consider the following example, where we prepend an element to a list:

```racket
(define original-list '(2 3 4))

(define new-list (cons 1 original-list))
```

Here, `original-list` remains unchanged, while `new-list` is a new list with `1` added at the front. This approach to data handling aligns well with functional programming principles, as it emphasizes the creation of new data structures rather than altering existing ones.

Another important functional data structure is the persistent binary tree. Persistent data structures, such as immutable binary trees, allow for efficient and safe updates by preserving previous versions of the data. In Racket, you can define a simple binary tree structure as follows:

```racket
(define-struct node (value left right))
```

```
(define tree (make-node 1 (make-node 2 '() '()) (make-node 3 '()
'())))
```

In this example, `tree` is a binary tree where each node contains a value and references to its left and right children. When performing operations on a persistent binary tree, such as inserting a new value, the tree is updated in a way that preserves the old structure, ensuring that previous versions remain intact and accessible.

To illustrate the concept further, consider an insertion operation in a binary tree. When inserting a new value, we create a new tree where only the affected nodes are modified, while the rest of the tree remains unchanged. This method is efficient and maintains the immutability of the original data structure:

```racket
(define (insert tree value)
  (cond
    [(empty? tree) (make-node value '() '())]
    [(< value (node-value tree))
     (make-node (node-value tree) (insert (node-left tree) value) (node-right tree))]
    [else
     (make-node (node-value tree) (node-left tree) (insert (node-right tree) value))]))
```

Here, the `insert` function recursively traverses the tree to find the correct position for the new value, creating a new tree with the insertion applied while keeping the original tree unmodified.

Functional programming patterns also leverage recursion for data processing, often used in place of traditional looping constructs. Recursion is particularly well-suited for working with recursive data structures like lists and trees. For example, processing a list using recursion might involve traversing each element and applying a transformation, such as:

```racket
(define (sum-list lst)
 (cond
   [(empty? lst) 0]
   [else (+ (first lst) (sum-list (rest lst)))]))
```

In this function, `sum-list` recursively computes the sum of all elements in a list by breaking down the problem into smaller instances of the same problem. This pattern showcases how recursion can effectively replace iterative approaches, emphasizing the declarative nature of functional programming.

Overall, functional programming patterns, including higher-order functions, function composition, and immutable data structures, provide powerful tools for writing expressive and maintainable code. By embracing these patterns, you can take full advantage of functional programming principles to create elegant solutions to complex problems.

As we delve further into functional programming patterns, another crucial concept is lazy evaluation. Lazy evaluation, or delayed evaluation, is a strategy where expressions are not evaluated until their values are actually needed. This can lead to significant performance improvements, especially when dealing with potentially infinite data structures or when computations are expensive.

In Racket, lazy evaluation can be managed through constructs such as `delay` and `force`. The `delay` function creates a promise, which is an expression that will be evaluated later. The `force` function is used to evaluate a delayed expression.

For instance, consider the following example:

```racket
(define my-promise (delay (+ 1 2)))
(force my-promise) ; This will evaluate to 3
```

Here, `my-promise` is a promise that encapsulates the expression `(+ 1 2)`. The `force` function triggers the evaluation of this expression, returning the result. This approach is particularly useful when dealing with computations that might be expensive or when working with large datasets where not all parts need to be computed immediately.

Lazy evaluation also facilitates the creation of infinite data structures. For example, you can define an infinite sequence of natural numbers using lazy evaluation:

```racket
(define (infinite-naturals n)
  (delay (cons n (force (infinite-naturals (+ n 1))))))
```

In this definition, `infinite-naturals` is a recursive function that generates an infinite list of natural numbers. Each call to `infinite-naturals` creates a new promise that will eventually be evaluated to provide the next element in the sequence. By using `force`, you can access elements of the sequence as needed without computing the entire sequence at once.

Functional programming patterns also encompass the concept of memoization. Memoization is a technique where the results of expensive function calls are cached so that subsequent calls with the same arguments can be answered more quickly. This can be particularly useful in recursive functions or functions with repeated calculations. In Racket, memoization can be implemented using hash tables or specific libraries designed for caching results.

Consider a simple example of memoization for a recursive Fibonacci function:

```racket
(define fib-memo
  (let ([cache (make-hasheq)])
    (lambda (n)
      (cond
        [(hash-has-key? cache n) (hash-ref cache n)]
        [(zero? n) (begin (hash-set! cache n 0) 0)]
        [(= n 1) (begin (hash-set! cache n 1) 1)]
        [else (let ([result (+ (fib-memo (- n 1)) (fib-memo (- n 2)))])
                (hash-set! cache n result)
                result)]))))

(fib-memo 10) ; This will compute the 10th Fibonacci number efficiently
```

In this implementation, `fib-memo` uses a hash table `cache` to store previously computed values. Each call to `fib-memo` checks if the result is already in the cache. If it is, the cached result is returned. Otherwise, the function computes the result, stores it in the cache, and then returns it. This approach significantly improves performance for functions with overlapping subproblems.

Lastly, functional programming patterns often leverage function composition. Function composition involves combining two or more functions to form a new function. In Racket, function composition is typically achieved using the `compose` function, which takes two or more functions as arguments and returns a new function that applies them in sequence.

For instance, suppose we have two functions, `square` and

`add-one`, and we want to create a new function that first adds one to a number and then squares the result:

```racket
(define (square x) ( x x))
(define (add-one x) (+ x 1))

(define square-after-add-one (compose square add-one))

(square-after-add-one 4) ; This will compute (4 + 1) ^ 2 25
```

In this example, `compose` takes `square` and `add-one` and creates a new function `square-after-add-one` that applies `add-one` first and then `square`. Function composition allows for the creation of complex functions by combining simpler ones, enhancing modularity and readability of the code.

Through the exploration of higher-order functions, functional data structures, lazy evaluation, memoization, and function composition, you gain a deeper understanding of functional programming patterns. These techniques provide powerful tools for writing expressive, efficient, and maintainable Racket code, empowering you to tackle a wide range of programming challenges with a functional approach.

CHAPTER 15: WORKING WITH IMMUTABLE DATA

Immutability, a cornerstone of functional programming, ensures that once a data structure is created, it cannot be modified. This characteristic fundamentally impacts how data is handled, offering several advantages including reliability, predictability, and safety. In Racket, understanding and working with immutable data structures such as vectors, sets, and hash tables are crucial for developing robust functional programs.

To begin, let us consider vectors in Racket. Vectors are fixed-size, indexed collections that, in their immutable form, provide a means to store and access a sequence of elements efficiently. While mutable vectors can be modified, immutable vectors cannot be altered after their creation. This immutability ensures that once a vector is established, its contents are consistent throughout its lifecycle. This can prevent unintended side effects and simplify reasoning about the program's state.

For example, creating an immutable vector in Racket is straightforward:

```racket
(define my-vector (vector 1 2 3 4))
```

In this case, `my-vector` is an immutable vector containing the integers 1 through 4. Operations that appear to modify the vector, such as `vector-set!`, do not exist for immutable vectors. Instead, if you need a modified version of the vector, you must create a new one. Here's how you might add an element to an existing vector:

```racket
(define (add-to-vector vec elem)
  (vector-append vec (vector elem)))

(define new-vector (add-to-vector my-vector 5))
```

Here, `add-to-vector` returns a new vector that appends the element `5` to `my-vector`, leaving the original vector unaltered. This approach embodies the principle of immutability, where each modification results in a new data structure rather than altering the existing one.

Similarly, Racket's sets and hash tables can also be used immutably. Sets in Racket, particularly through the `set` and `set-struct` constructs, can be manipulated immutably. For instance, the `set` library provides functions to work with immutable sets, ensuring that any operation on a set produces a new set rather than changing the existing one.

To illustrate, consider creating an immutable set and performing operations:

```racket
(require racket/set)

(define my-set (set 1 2 3))
(define new-set (set-add my-set 4))
```

In this example, `my-set` remains unchanged after adding the element `4`. Instead, `new-set` contains the updated elements. Such immutability prevents bugs that arise from unintended modifications of shared data.

Immutable hash tables, provided through the `racket/hash` library, follow a similar principle. Hash tables in Racket can be created as immutable, and operations such as adding or removing key-value pairs result in new hash tables. This ensures that the original hash table remains consistent and avoids side effects from concurrent operations.

Consider an example of working with immutable hash tables:

```racket
(require racket/hash)

(define my-hash (hash 'a 1 'b 2))
(define updated-hash (hash-set my-hash 'c 3))
```

Here, `my-hash` retains its original key-value pairs, while `updated-hash` includes the new key-value pair. This immutability is particularly advantageous in concurrent programming contexts where data consistency is crucial.

The benefits of immutability are manifold. Firstly, it ensures code reliability by preventing unintended modifications to data. Since immutable structures cannot be changed once created, there is no risk of accidental side effects, leading to fewer bugs and more predictable behavior. This immutability also simplifies reasoning about code, as you do not need to track changes to data structures over time.

Additionally, immutability facilitates functional programming techniques such as recursion and functional composition. Since functions that work with immutable data do not have side effects, they can be more easily composed and reasoned about. This aligns with the functional programming paradigm, where functions are first-class citizens and are expected to produce consistent results based on their inputs.

Furthermore, immutable data structures are inherently thread-safe. In a multi-threaded environment, immutability guarantees that data shared between threads remains unchanged, thus eliminating issues related to concurrent modifications. This allows for safer parallel programming and can lead to performance improvements in concurrent applications.

In summary, working with immutable data structures in Racket—whether vectors, sets, or hash tables—embraces the principles of functional programming by ensuring consistency and safety. The creation of new data structures rather than modifying existing ones prevents unintended side effects and simplifies code management. As you continue to explore functional programming, leveraging immutable data structures will enhance the reliability and robustness of your Racket programs.

Exploring the use of immutable data structures in Racket extends beyond vectors to include sets and hash tables, both of which are crucial for a variety of computational tasks. Immutable sets, like immutable vectors, provide a consistent state throughout their use. Unlike mutable sets, which allow direct modification, immutable sets ensure that each transformation results in a new set. This immutability guarantees that no changes occur to existing sets, preserving the integrity of data.

In Racket, you can work with immutable sets using the `racket/set` library, which provides functionalities for creating and manipulating sets. For instance, consider creating an immutable set and performing operations on it:

```
```racket
lang racket
(require racket/set)
```
```

```
(define my-set (set 1 2 3 4))
(define new-set (set-union my-set (set 5 6)))
```

Here, `my-set` is an immutable set containing the integers 1 through 4. The function `set-union` combines `my-set` with another set containing 5 and 6, producing a new set that includes all elements. Importantly, `my-set` remains unchanged, reinforcing the immutability principle. Such operations return a new set rather than modifying the original one, which aids in maintaining a predictable program state.

Hash tables, which store key-value pairs, can also be immutable in Racket. The `racket/dict` library offers functionality for immutable hash tables. To create and manipulate immutable hash tables, you can use the `hash` function to initialize a table and `hash-set` to add key-value pairs:

```racket
lang racket
(require racket/dict)
```

```
(define my-hash (hash 'a 1 'b 2))
(define new-hash (hash-set my-hash 'c 3))
```

In this example, `my-hash` is an immutable hash table with two key-value pairs. The `hash-set` function creates a new hash table with an additional key-value pair (`'c` mapped to `3`). Once again, `my-hash` remains unchanged, reflecting the benefits of immutability by ensuring that the original data structure is preserved while allowing for new data to be incorporated into a new structure.

To work effectively with immutable data structures, it is essential to understand how functional programming principles—such as avoiding side effects and ensuring referential transparency—are facilitated. Immutability inherently supports these principles by eliminating state changes and ensuring that functions operate consistently on their inputs without unintended modifications. This approach is particularly advantageous in concurrent and parallel programming scenarios, where shared mutable state can lead to complex synchronization issues.

An important consideration when dealing with immutable data is performance. Immutable structures often involve creating new instances for each modification, which can impact efficiency. However, Racket's implementation of immutable data structures is optimized to mitigate performance overhead. Techniques such as structural sharing allow for efficient updates by reusing parts of existing structures, thus minimizing the cost associated with creating new data.

In practical applications, leveraging immutable data structures can lead to cleaner and more maintainable code. For instance, when designing functions that operate on immutable vectors, sets, or hash tables, the assurance that the data will not be modified helps in reasoning about the code's behavior and debugging issues. Immutable data structures also enable functional programming patterns, such as map, filter, and reduce, which are fundamental for expressing transformations and aggregations in a clear and concise manner.

Consider the following example, where we use immutable vectors and functional programming patterns to perform operations on a list of numbers:

```racket
lang racket

(define (double-elements vec)
  (vector-map (lambda (x) ( x 2)) vec))
```

```
(define my-vector (vector 1 2 3 4))
(define doubled-vector (double-elements my-vector))
```

In this code, `double-elements` is a function that takes an immutable vector and returns a new vector with each element doubled. The `vector-map` function applies a given procedure to each element of the vector, producing a new vector with the transformed elements. This example illustrates how immutability simplifies the application of functional patterns, allowing for clear and predictable transformations without altering the original data.

Through these examples and practices, we see that working with immutable data structures in Racket not only adheres to the principles of functional programming but also enhances code reliability and safety. Understanding and applying immutability effectively can lead to more robust and maintainable software, leveraging the strengths of functional programming to manage data and state in a controlled manner.

The concept of immutability extends to more complex data structures in Racket, such as immutable lists and trees. Immutable lists, represented by the `list` data type, are foundational in functional programming. They provide a way to handle sequences of elements without modifying the original list. Operations on lists, such as appending or removing elements, produce new lists rather than altering the existing one.

To illustrate working with immutable lists, consider the following example:

```racket
lang racket

(define my-list (list 1 2 3 4))
```

(define new-list (cons 0 my-list))
```

Here, `my-list` is an immutable list containing the integers 1 through 4. The `cons` function creates a new list, `new-list`, by adding `0` to the front of `my-list`. The original list, `my-list`, remains unchanged, preserving its initial state. This immutability is beneficial as it prevents inadvertent side effects and ensures that lists can be safely shared across different parts of a program without risk of modification.

Similarly, immutable trees are crucial for more complex data structures. Trees, often used in algorithms and data processing, benefit from immutability by ensuring that operations such as insertion or deletion do not alter the existing tree but rather produce new versions. In Racket, immutable trees can be implemented using structures that encapsulate nodes and subtrees, ensuring that the original structure is maintained throughout transformations.

Consider an example of an immutable binary tree:

```racket
lang racket

(struct tree (value left right) :transparent)

(define tree1 (tree 1 (tree 2 empty empty) (tree 3 empty empty)))
(define tree2 (tree 1 (tree 2 empty empty) (tree 4 empty empty)))
```

In this example, `tree1` is an immutable binary tree with nodes containing the values 1, 2, and 3. `tree2` is a new tree derived from `tree1`, where the right child of the root node has been replaced with a new subtree containing the value 4. This new tree, `tree2`, is created without modifying `tree1`, preserving its immutability and ensuring that both trees exist
```

as separate entities.

Working with immutable data structures provides several key benefits. Immutability guarantees that data remains consistent and reliable, as no unexpected modifications can occur. This immutability simplifies reasoning about code, as the state of data structures remains unchanged throughout operations. Consequently, debugging becomes easier, and the potential for subtle bugs related to unintended data modification is significantly reduced.

Another advantage of immutability is its facilitation of functional programming patterns such as persistent data structures. In functional programming, persistence refers to the ability to retain previous versions of data structures while allowing for modifications that produce new versions. Immutable data structures inherently support this by design, as each modification results in a new structure rather than altering the existing one. This approach enables efficient version control and snapshotting, which are valuable in applications requiring history tracking or undo functionality.

Moreover, immutability aids in concurrent and parallel programming by eliminating issues related to shared mutable state. Since immutable data structures cannot be altered after their creation, concurrent processes can safely access and manipulate these structures without concerns about race conditions or data corruption. This characteristic enhances the robustness and scalability of programs, particularly in environments where multiple threads or processes operate simultaneously.

In summary, mastering the use of immutable data structures in Racket is essential for effective functional programming. Whether working with vectors, sets, hash tables, lists, or trees, the principles of immutability provide a solid foundation for writing reliable, maintainable, and scalable code. By understanding and applying these concepts, you can leverage the full power of functional programming to build robust applications that manage data with consistency and integrity.

CHAPTER 16: ADVANCED DATA STRUCTURES

In addressing more sophisticated programming challenges, an understanding of advanced data structures becomes crucial. Racket, being a versatile language, provides a rich set of data structures beyond the basic lists and vectors, including trees and graphs. Each of these structures offers unique capabilities and optimizations, allowing for efficient data representation and manipulation. This exploration into advanced data structures aims to equip you with the knowledge to implement and leverage these structures effectively within Racket.

Trees are fundamental structures in computer science, providing a hierarchical organization of data. In Racket, trees are often implemented using structures, allowing for the creation of nodes with associated values and child nodes. A common type of tree is the binary tree, where each node has at most two children. To implement a binary tree in Racket, you can define a structure as follows:

```racket
lang racket

(struct tree (value left right) :transparent)
```

In this structure, `value` represents the data contained in the node, while `left` and `right` represent the left and right children of the node, respectively. To create a binary tree, you instantiate this structure with specific values and children. For example:

```racket
(define my-tree
  (tree 10
    (tree 5 empty empty)
    (tree 15 empty empty)))
```

Here, `my-tree` represents a binary tree with a root value of 10, a left child with value 5, and a right child with value 15. This tree structure is immutable, meaning that operations such as inserting or deleting nodes will result in a new tree rather than modifying the existing one. Immutable trees are particularly useful in functional programming for ensuring data consistency and avoiding side effects.

More advanced tree structures include AVL trees and red-black trees, which are self-balancing binary search trees. These trees maintain sorted order while ensuring that operations such as insertion, deletion, and search remain efficient. Implementing such trees in Racket involves maintaining additional properties to ensure balance after modifications, which can be more complex but provides significant performance benefits for large datasets.

Graphs, another advanced data structure, represent relationships between entities. Unlike trees, graphs do not have a hierarchical structure and can contain cycles. In Racket, graphs can be implemented using adjacency lists or adjacency matrices. An adjacency list represents a graph using a list of vertices, where each vertex points to a list of its adjacent vertices. This representation is particularly efficient for sparse graphs. An example implementation is:

```racket
lang racket

(struct graph (adjacency-list) :transparent)

(define my-graph
  (graph '((1 (2 3))
           (2 (1 4))
           (3 (1 4))
           (4 (2 3)))))
```

In `my-graph`, the adjacency list represents a graph with vertices 1 through 4. For each vertex, the list contains the vertices it is connected to. For instance, vertex 1 is connected to vertices 2 and 3. This representation allows for efficient traversal and querying of connections within the graph.

Alternatively, an adjacency matrix can be used to represent a graph with a two-dimensional array, where each entry `(i, j)` indicates whether there is an edge between vertex `i` and vertex `j`. This representation is advantageous for dense graphs where edge lookups need to be constant time. Implementing an adjacency matrix in Racket might look like:

```racket
lang racket

(struct graph (adjacency-matrix) :transparent)

(define my-graph
  (graph 2a([[0 1 1 0]
             [1 0 0 1]
             [1 0 0 1]
             [0 1 1 0]])))
```

In this matrix, `my-graph` represents the same graph as

the previous adjacency list example, with `1` indicating the presence of an edge and `0` indicating no edge.

Advanced data structures also include heaps, which are specialized trees used for priority queue operations. Heaps are often implemented as binary heaps where each parent node is greater than or equal to its children in a max-heap, or less than or equal to its children in a min-heap. This structure is particularly useful for implementing priority queues and efficient sorting algorithms.

Another important advanced data structure is the trie, which is used for efficient retrieval of strings. Tries store strings in a way that allows for quick prefix-based searching. Implementing a trie involves creating nodes where each node represents a character and maintains links to subsequent characters, facilitating efficient string operations.

In exploring these advanced data structures, one must consider their properties and trade-offs. Trees offer hierarchical data representation and are useful for organizing data in a structured manner. Graphs provide a flexible way to model relationships between entities. Heaps and tries offer specialized functionality for specific use cases, such as priority management and string retrieval.

By understanding and applying these advanced data structures, you can enhance your ability to solve complex problems and optimize algorithms in Racket.

To work with graphs in Racket, you need to understand their basic components and how to represent them. A graph consists of nodes (or vertices) and edges connecting these nodes. There are various ways to represent graphs, but two common methods are adjacency lists and adjacency matrices. Each method has its advantages and use cases depending on the graph's characteristics and the operations you need to perform.

An adjacency list representation of a graph uses a list of lists, where each sublist contains the neighbors of a particular node. This representation is efficient in terms of space when dealing with sparse graphs, where the number of edges is significantly less than the number of nodes squared. In Racket, you can define an adjacency list as follows:

```racket
lang racket

(define graph
 '((A (B C))
   (B (A C D))
   (C (A B D))
   (D (B C))))
```

In this representation, each element of the list represents a node, and the associated list contains the neighboring nodes. For example, node `A` is connected to nodes `B` and `C`, while node `B` is connected to nodes `A`, `C`, and `D`. This structure allows for efficient traversal and neighborhood operations.

In contrast, an adjacency matrix is a 2D array where the cell at row `i` and column `j` indicates the presence or absence of an edge between nodes `i` and `j`. This representation is more suitable for dense graphs where most node pairs are connected. In Racket, you can use a vector of vectors to implement an adjacency matrix:

```racket
lang racket

(define adjacency-matrix
  (vector
   (vector f t t f)
   (vector t f t t)
```

```
(vector t t f t)
(vector f t t f)))
```

Here, `t` indicates the presence of an edge, and `f` indicates the absence. The matrix allows for quick edge lookups but can be less space-efficient for sparse graphs.

Graph algorithms such as depth-first search (DFS) and breadth-first search (BFS) are fundamental for exploring graphs. These algorithms traverse the graph's nodes and edges to discover properties such as connectivity and path lengths. Implementing these algorithms in Racket involves recursive and iterative techniques, making use of the graph's representation.

For instance, a depth-first search can be implemented recursively as follows:

```racket
lang racket

(define (dfs graph start visited)
  (define (explore node)
    (unless (member node visited)
      (set! visited (cons node visited))
      (for-each (lambda (neighbor)
          (explore neighbor))
        (cdr (assoc node graph)))))
  (explore start)
  visited)
```

In this implementation, `dfs` takes a graph, a starting node, and a list of visited nodes. It explores each node's neighbors recursively, adding nodes to the visited list. The `assoc` function retrieves the neighbors from the adjacency list.

In addition to trees and graphs, other advanced data structures include heaps and tries. A heap is a specialized tree-based structure that satisfies the heap property, which ensures that each parent node is either greater than or less than its child nodes, depending on whether it's a max-heap or min-heap. Heaps are used in algorithms such as heap sort and priority queues.

A trie, also known as a prefix tree, is used primarily for efficient retrieval of keys in a dataset of strings. It is particularly useful in applications such as autocomplete and spell-checking. Each node in a trie represents a character, and paths from the root to leaf nodes represent different strings.

Implementing a heap or a trie in Racket involves defining the structure and implementing insertion and retrieval operations. For example, a simple binary heap can be represented as a vector, and heap operations such as insertion and deletion require maintaining the heap property through heapification processes.

By understanding and implementing these advanced data structures, you gain the ability to handle complex data manipulation tasks more efficiently. The choice of data structure impacts both the performance and the clarity of your code, and mastering these structures allows for optimization and improved problem-solving capabilities in your Racket programs.

To delve into trees, another fundamental data structure, it's essential to understand their hierarchical nature. A tree consists of nodes connected in a parent-child relationship, with a single root node from which all other nodes descend. Each node can have zero or more children but only one parent, except for the root node which has no parent. Trees are used extensively in scenarios like file systems, hierarchical data representations, and more.

In Racket, you can represent a tree using nested lists. For

example, consider a simple binary tree where each node has at most two children:

```racket
lang racket

(define binary-tree
  '(A
    (B
     (D () ())
     (E () ()))
    (C
     (F () ())
     (G () ()))))
```

In this representation, each node is a list where the first element is the value of the node, and the subsequent elements are the left and right subtrees, respectively. For instance, node `A` has two children, `B` and `C`, and `B` has two children `D` and `E`. This representation allows for straightforward tree traversal operations.

Traversal algorithms such as in-order, pre-order, and post-order are critical for working with trees. In Racket, you can implement these traversals using recursive functions. For example, the in-order traversal visits the left subtree, then the node, and finally the right subtree:

```racket
lang racket

(define (in-order tree)
  (cond
    [(empty? tree) '()]
    [else
     (append
      (in-order (second tree))
```

```
    (list (first tree))
    (in-order (third tree)))]))
```

In this function, `in-order` processes a tree by recursively visiting the left subtree, processing the node's value, and then recursively visiting the right subtree. The `append` function is used to concatenate the results of these traversals.

Graphs and trees are not the only advanced data structures; there are many others, including heaps, tries, and more. Each of these structures has unique properties and applications. For example, heaps are useful for implementing priority queues, where the highest (or lowest) priority element is always at the root. In Racket, a heap can be represented using vectors, and various heap operations such as insertion and deletion are performed to maintain the heap property.

```racket
lang racket

(define (heap-insert heap value)
  ;; Assume heap is represented as a vector and value is to be inserted
  ;; This is a simplified version and does not include the reheapification
  (vector-append heap (vector value)))
```

Heaps are typically implemented with additional operations to ensure that the heap property is maintained after each insertion or removal. For practical use, one would also need to implement the heapify process to reorganize the heap elements as needed.

Tries, or prefix trees, are another sophisticated structure used primarily for managing strings or sequences of characters. They are particularly efficient for operations such as prefix matching and auto-completion. In Racket, a trie can be implemented using nested hash tables where each node represents a character in a string:

```racket
lang racket

(define (make-trie)
 (make-hasheq))

(define (trie-insert trie key)
 (define (insert-helper node key)
  (cond
   [(empty? key) (hash-set node 'end-of-word t)]
   [else
    (let ([char (first key)]
       [rest (rest key)])
     (hash-update! node char (lambda (subtrie) (insert-helper (or subtrie (make-trie)) rest)) (lambda () (insert-helper (make-trie) rest))))]))
 (insert-helper trie (string->list key)))
```

Here, `trie-insert` adds a key to the trie by iterating through its characters and updating or creating nodes as necessary. The `hash-update!` function is used to manage the trie's structure dynamically.

Understanding and working with these advanced data structures require not only familiarity with their representations and operations but also a grasp of their time and space complexities. By analyzing the efficiency of operations such as insertions, deletions, and lookups, you can select the most appropriate data structure for a given problem.

In summary, mastering advanced data structures such as graphs and trees, and understanding how to implement and manipulate them effectively in Racket, equips you with the tools to tackle complex programming challenges. These structures enable more efficient data management and manipulation, leading to optimized algorithms and more robust applications.

CHAPTER 17: CONCURRENCY AND PARALLELISM

Concurrency and parallelism are critical concepts for developing modern applications that can perform multiple tasks simultaneously. They enhance the efficiency and responsiveness of programs, particularly in scenarios where tasks can be executed independently or require coordination between multiple threads. Racket, as a functional programming language, provides robust support for these concepts, offering a range of tools to handle concurrent operations effectively.

At the heart of concurrency in Racket is the concept of threads. A thread is an independent sequence of execution that can run concurrently with other threads. Racket provides a simple interface for creating and managing threads through its standard library. The basic function for creating a new thread is `thread`, which takes a procedure and runs it concurrently. For instance:

```racket
lang racket

(define (print-message)
  (displayln "Hello from a thread!"))

(thread print-message)
```

```

In this example, the `print-message` procedure is executed in a new thread. This allows the main thread to continue running independently of the new thread. Threads in Racket can be used to perform tasks such as background processing, handling user input, or managing multiple connections.

However, concurrency introduces challenges, particularly when multiple threads need to interact with shared resources. This is where synchronization mechanisms come into play. In Racket, you can use channels for communication between threads, ensuring that data is safely transmitted and received. Channels provide a way to send and receive messages between threads, facilitating coordination and communication without directly sharing mutable state.

To create a channel, you use the `make-channel` function. This function returns a new channel that can be used to send and receive messages. For example:

```racket
lang racket

(define ch (make-channel))

(define (producer)
 (channel-put ch 'message))

(define (consumer)
 (displayln (channel-get ch)))


(thread producer)
(thread consumer)
```

In this code, the `producer` thread sends a message to the channel, while the `consumer` thread retrieves and displays the message. This pattern of using channels allows threads
```

to communicate effectively while avoiding issues related to direct shared state.

Synchronization is another key aspect of concurrency. When multiple threads access shared resources, it's crucial to ensure that these resources are managed safely to avoid conflicts and inconsistencies. Racket provides several synchronization primitives, such as mutexes, which are used to control access to shared resources. A mutex is essentially a lock that can be acquired by one thread at a time, ensuring that other threads must wait until the lock is released.

To use a mutex in Racket, you first create one using `make-mutex`, and then use `mutex-lock` and `mutex-unlock` to control access. For instance:

```racket
lang racket

(define m (make-mutex))

(define (critical-section)
 (mutex-lock m)
 ;; Critical section code here
 (mutex-unlock m))
```

In this example, `critical-section` ensures that only one thread can execute the critical section code at a time by locking and unlocking the mutex. This prevents race conditions and ensures the consistency of shared resources.

Parallelism, while related to concurrency, focuses specifically on performing multiple operations simultaneously to achieve greater computational efficiency. In Racket, parallelism can be achieved through parallel processing constructs and libraries. For example, the `racket/async` library provides support for asynchronous computation, allowing tasks to be executed in parallel without blocking the main thread.

An example of using asynchronous tasks in Racket is shown below:

```racket
lang racket

(require racket/async)

(define (compute-task)
  (sleep 1) ; Simulate a time-consuming task
  (displayln "Task complete"))

(define t (async/enable (lambda () (compute-task))))
```

In this code, `async/enable` runs the `compute-task` procedure asynchronously, allowing it to execute in parallel with other tasks. This approach can be useful for tasks that are I/O-bound or that can benefit from concurrent execution.

As applications become more complex, effectively managing concurrency and parallelism becomes increasingly important. Understanding how to use threads, channels, and synchronization mechanisms in Racket allows developers to build efficient and responsive applications. By leveraging these tools, you can ensure that your programs handle multiple tasks effectively and maintain high performance, even in the face of concurrent execution.

In concurrent programming, synchronization mechanisms are crucial for ensuring that multiple threads can access shared resources without causing data corruption or inconsistencies. Racket provides several tools for managing such synchronization, including mutexes and semaphores. Mutexes, or mutual exclusion locks, are used to prevent multiple threads from accessing a shared resource simultaneously. This is achieved by locking the resource when a thread is using it and unlocking it when the thread is done.

In Racket, you can use the `make-mutex` function to create a mutex. Once created, you can use `mutex-lock` to acquire the lock and `mutex-unlock` to release it. For instance, if you have a shared variable that multiple threads need to modify, you would surround the critical section of code with lock and unlock operations:

```racket
lang racket

(define m (make-mutex))
(define shared-var 0)

(define (increment)
  (mutex-lock m)
  (set! shared-var (+ shared-var 1))
  (mutex-unlock m))

(thread increment)
(thread increment)
```

Here, the `increment` procedure locks the mutex before modifying the shared variable and unlocks it afterward. This ensures that only one thread can modify `shared-var` at a time, preventing race conditions and ensuring data consistency.

In addition to mutexes, Racket also supports semaphores, which are another form of synchronization primitive. Semaphores are particularly useful when you need to control access to a finite number of resources. A semaphore can be initialized with a certain count, and threads can signal or wait on the semaphore. Racket provides functions such as `make-semaphore`, `semaphore-wait`, and `semaphore-post` to work with semaphores.

For example, if you have a resource pool with a limited number of slots, you can use a semaphore to manage access:

```racket
lang racket

(define sem (make-semaphore 3))

(define (access-resource)
  (semaphore-wait sem)
  (displayln "Resource accessed")
  (sleep 1)
  (semaphore-post sem))

(thread access-resource)
(thread access-resource)
(thread access-resource)
(thread access-resource)
```

In this example, the semaphore is initialized with a count of 3, allowing up to three threads to access the resource concurrently. If more than three threads attempt to access the resource, they will be blocked until a slot becomes available.

Beyond synchronization primitives, it is also essential to handle potential deadlocks in concurrent programs. A deadlock occurs when two or more threads are waiting indefinitely for resources held by each other. To avoid deadlocks, you should follow best practices such as acquiring locks in a consistent order and using timeout mechanisms to detect and handle potential deadlocks.

Racket provides facilities for handling timeouts with its `sync` and `timeout` functions. These can be used to manage operations that may block indefinitely. For instance, if you want to ensure that a thread does not wait too long for a resource, you can specify a timeout value:

```racket
```

```
lang racket

(define (safe-operation)
  (with-handlers ([exn:fail:timeout? (lambda (e) (displayln "Operation timed out"))]
                  [exn:fail:resource? (lambda (e) (displayln "Resource failure"))])
    (sync (timeout 5000 (begin (sleep 10) 'done)))))

(safe-operation)
```

In this code, `sync` with `timeout` ensures that if the operation does not complete within 5000 milliseconds, it will be interrupted, and an appropriate message will be displayed.

Understanding and effectively utilizing these concurrency and synchronization mechanisms is key to developing robust and efficient concurrent applications in Racket. By mastering these tools, you can handle complex scenarios involving multiple threads and shared resources while maintaining data integrity and application performance.

To enhance concurrency in Racket, it is also important to understand the concept of channels, which facilitate communication between threads. Channels are particularly useful in scenarios where threads need to exchange data or synchronize their actions. In Racket, the `make-channel`, `channel-put`, and `channel-get` functions are key for working with channels.

A channel can be thought of as a conduit through which threads can send and receive messages. When a thread puts a value into a channel using `channel-put`, it is stored until another thread retrieves it using `channel-get`. This mechanism helps to avoid the complexity of manual synchronization and makes inter-thread communication straightforward.

Here's an example of using channels to coordinate between two threads:

```racket
lang racket

(define ch (make-channel))

(define (producer)
 (for ([i (in-range 5)])
  (channel-put ch i)
  (sleep 1))
 (channel-put ch 'done))

(define (consumer)
 (let loop ()
  (define value (channel-get ch))
  (cond
   [(equal? value 'done) (displayln "Consumer done")]
   [else (displayln (format "Received: ~a" value))
      (loop)])))

(thread producer)
(thread consumer)
```

In this example, the producer thread sends five numbers to the channel and then sends a 'done' signal to indicate that no more data will be sent. The consumer thread continuously retrieves values from the channel and processes them until it receives the 'done' signal.

Concurrency can introduce complexity, particularly when dealing with shared resources and ensuring that operations are performed atomically. To manage this complexity, it is crucial to design programs with a clear understanding of how threads interact and how data is shared and synchronized.

In addition to these basic concurrency constructs, Racket

offers more advanced concurrency tools such as futures and places. Futures provide a way to perform computations asynchronously and retrieve their results once they are ready. The `future` function creates a future task that is executed in parallel, allowing the main thread to continue running while the future computes its result. Here's a brief example:

```racket
lang racket

(define f (future
    (lambda ()
      (sleep 2)
      (* 2 3))))

(displayln "Doing other work...")
(displayln (future-ref f)) ; Waits for the future to complete and returns its result
```

In this snippet, the `future` function executes a computation that multiplies two numbers. The `future-ref` function blocks until the computation is complete and then returns the result. This allows for non-blocking execution where the main thread can continue to perform other tasks while waiting for the future's result.

Places, another advanced concurrency feature, enable the distribution of computation across multiple processes. This is useful for parallelizing tasks that are computationally intensive or require significant memory. Places can be thought of as separate Racket environments that run in parallel, with each place having its own memory space. You communicate between places using message passing. The `place` form creates a new place, and `place-channel-put` and `place-channel-get` functions are used to send and receive messages between places. This feature is particularly valuable for scaling computations that require substantial resources.

Consider this example of using places:

```racket
lang racket

(define p (place
      (lambda ()
        (define ch (make-channel))
        (place-channel-put ch 42)
        (place-channel-get ch))))

(define result (place-channel-get p))
(displayln (format "Result: ~a" result))
```

In this case, a new place is created, which puts a value into a channel and then retrieves it. The main thread communicates with this place using channels to obtain the result.

Concurrency and parallelism are powerful tools for enhancing the efficiency and responsiveness of programs. By understanding and applying Racket's concurrency features—threads, channels, mutexes, semaphores, futures, and places—you can develop applications that perform well and handle multiple tasks simultaneously. As with any advanced programming technique, careful design and testing are essential to ensure correctness and avoid common pitfalls such as race conditions and deadlocks.

CHAPTER 18: BUILDING AND USING LIBRARIES

Creating and utilizing libraries is essential for effective code management and reuse, allowing developers to modularize their code into reusable components. In Racket, libraries are organized into modules, which encapsulate related functions, variables, and other definitions. By understanding how to build and use libraries, you can create robust, maintainable, and easily shareable code.

To begin, let's discuss the structure of a Racket library. A library in Racket is essentially a module that exports a set of functions or values for use in other modules. The `lang` directive at the top of a Racket file specifies the language and module level, such as `lang racket` or `lang typed/racket`. This directive sets up the environment for the module.

For example, to create a simple library, we first define a module with `lang racket` and use the `provide` statement to export the functions or values we want to make available to other modules. Consider a library that provides basic mathematical operations:

```
```racket
lang racket

(provide (rename-out [add add-numbers]
```
```

          [subtract subtract-numbers]))

(define (add-numbers x y)
 (+ x y))

(define (subtract-numbers x y)
 (- x y))
```

In this example, the `provide` statement makes the `add-numbers` and `subtract-numbers` functions available for use in other modules. The `rename-out` clause allows us to export these functions under different names if desired.

Once you have defined a library, you can use it in other modules by requiring it with the `require` statement. For instance, if you have saved the above library in a file named `math-lib.rkt`, you can use it in another file as follows:

```racket
lang racket
(require "math-lib.rkt")

(displayln (add-numbers 5 3))    ; Outputs: 8
(displayln (subtract-numbers 5 3)) ; Outputs: 2
```

Managing dependencies is a crucial aspect of building libraries. In Racket, you can manage dependencies between libraries by using the `require` statement within your module. Dependencies are specified by listing the modules your library depends on. For example:

```racket
lang racket

(require racket/list)

(provide (rename-out [sum list-sum]))

(define (list-sum lst)

```
(apply + lst))
```

In this library, we require the `racket/list` module to use its list functions and provide a function `list-sum` that computes the sum of a list. Properly managing dependencies ensures that your library works correctly with the necessary external code.

Publishing libraries involves making them available for use by others. Racket uses a system called the Racket Package Manager (RPM) to handle packages and libraries. To publish a library, you need to create a package definition file, typically named `info.rkt`, which provides metadata about your library such as its name, version, and dependencies.

Here's an example of a basic `info.rkt` file:

```racket
lang racket

(define meta
 (package
  (name "my-math-lib")
  (version "1.0")
  (description "A library for basic math operations")
  (require
   (file "math-lib.rkt"))))
```

In this file, you define the metadata for your package, including its name, version, and a brief description. The `require` clause specifies the files that are part of the package.

To publish your library, you can use the `raco pkg` command-line tool. This tool helps in creating, managing, and publishing packages. For example, to create a new package, you would use:

```bash
```

```
raco pkg new my-math-lib
```

This command creates a new directory for your package with the necessary files. After you have added your library code and updated the `info.rkt` file, you can build the package using:

```bash
raco pkg install
```

This command installs the package locally. To publish it to a package repository, you would need to use the `raco pkg publish` command, ensuring you have the necessary credentials and repository setup.

When structuring and documenting libraries, it's important to follow best practices to ensure usability and maintainability. Include clear and concise documentation for each function and module, explaining their purpose, usage, and any parameters or return values. Use Racket's built-in documentation tools, such as `raco doc`, to generate and manage documentation for your library. This practice not only aids in code readability but also facilitates easier integration and usage by other developers.

By understanding and applying these principles, you can create effective and reusable libraries in Racket, enhancing your code's modularity and maintainability. Building libraries allows you to share useful components across different projects and contribute to the broader Racket community.

Managing dependencies effectively ensures that your libraries integrate seamlessly with other code and that all required modules are available. In Racket, dependencies are handled through the `require` statement, which imports the necessary modules. To specify dependencies, you include a `require` statement at the top of your module file, listing the modules you depend on. For example, if your library relies on another library for additional functionality, you would include:

```racket
(require (prefix-in other-lib: "path/to/other-lib.rkt"))
```

This line tells Racket to load the `other-lib.rkt` file and makes its functions available with the `other-lib:` prefix. By using prefixes, you can avoid name clashes between functions from different libraries and make your code more organized.

When building libraries, it is also essential to consider how to structure your library files and directories. A well-organized library typically includes a main module file, which provides the core functionality, and additional files for documentation, tests, and any helper modules. For example, you might have a directory structure like:

```
my-library/
 |- main.rkt
 |- utils.rkt
 |- tests/
 |- docs/
 |- setup.rkt
```

In this structure, `main.rkt` contains the primary functionality of the library, `utils.rkt` includes helper functions, and the `tests/` directory contains unit tests for the library. The `docs/` directory holds documentation files, and `setup.rkt` is used for configuring the library's setup when published.

Publishing a Racket library involves creating a package that can be easily shared and installed. Racket uses the `raco` tool for package management, which simplifies the process of distributing libraries. To publish your library, you first need to create a `package` directory with a `package.rkt` file that defines the package metadata, including the name, version, and dependencies. Here's a basic example:

```racket
lang setup/infotab
(define name "my-library")
(define version "1.0")
(define release-notes
 '("Initial release"))
(define categories '(devtools))
(define primary-file "main.rkt")
```

The `package.rkt` file provides essential information about the package and its entry points. You also need to create a `info.rkt` file that includes additional metadata and dependencies:

```racket
lang setup/infotab
(define dependencies
 '((racket "8.0")
   (some-dependency "1.2")))
```

Once you have set up the package directory and files, you can use `raco` to create a `.plt` file, which is a package archive that can be shared and installed. The command for this process is:

```shell
raco pkg install --link /path/to/package-directory
```

This command creates an installable package from your

library's directory, making it easy to distribute and integrate into other projects.

Documentation is another crucial aspect of building and using libraries. Well-documented libraries are easier to use and maintain. Racket provides tools for documenting libraries, such as the `scribble` documentation tool. To create documentation, you write `.scrbl` files that describe the functionality of your library, using the `scribble` syntax to format and organize the content. For instance:

```racket
lang scribble/manual
@(require scribble/core)
@(require (for-label my-library/main))

@(title "My Library Documentation")
@(section "Overview"
  "This library provides ...")

@(section "Functions"
 @(define-sections
   (function (name "Function Name")
    (summary "A brief summary of the function.")
    (description "A detailed description of the function.")
    (example "Usage examples of the function."))))
```

In this documentation, you provide an overview of the library, detail the functions and their usage, and include examples to illustrate how to use them. Proper documentation helps users understand how to integrate and use your library effectively.

By adhering to best practices in structuring, documenting, and publishing your Racket libraries, you ensure that your code is reusable, maintainable, and easy to share. This approach not only improves the quality of your code but also facilitates collaboration and integration with other projects, contributing to a more efficient and productive development process.

To ensure your library is both effective and user-friendly, it's essential to follow best practices for documentation and code organization. Clear documentation not only helps others understand how to use your library but also aids in maintaining and extending it in the future. Racket's `scribble` tool can be employed to generate comprehensive documentation for your library. Using `scribble`, you can create well-structured documentation by including function descriptions, usage examples, and module overviews. For instance, you can write documentation for a function in a `.scrbl` file, which `scribble` will then compile into HTML or PDF formats. Here's an example of how to document a function using `scribble`:

```racket
lang scribble/doc

@title{My Library Documentation}

@section{Function: @tt{add}}
@codeblock{
 (define (add x y)
   (+ x y))
}
@description{
 The @tt{add} function takes two numbers, @tt{x} and @tt{y},
 and returns their sum. It is a simple example to demonstrate
 basic functionality.
}
```

In this example, `@title` specifies the title of the documentation, `@section` introduces a section, and `@codeblock` and `@description` provide the code and its explanation, respectively.

In addition to documentation, unit testing is a crucial aspect of library development. Testing ensures that your library functions as expected and helps catch bugs early. Racket's testing framework provides tools to write and run tests for your library. You can organize your tests in a separate directory within your library project, typically named `tests/`. Here's a simple example of how to use Racket's `rackunit` library to test a function:

```racket
lang racket
(require rackunit)
(require "main.rkt")

(check-equal? (add 2 3) 5)
(check-equal? (add -1 1) 0)
```

This test file checks that the `add` function behaves correctly with various inputs. By running these tests regularly, you can ensure that your library remains reliable and consistent as you make changes.

When integrating your library into other projects, consider the ease of use and integration. Make sure that your library provides a clear and consistent API. Good practice includes providing useful error messages, handling edge cases gracefully, and ensuring that the library's functionality is intuitive and easy to use. If your library relies on other libraries or external resources, document these dependencies clearly in your documentation and ensure they are correctly specified in the `package.rkt` file.

Finally, managing and updating libraries involves maintaining version control and addressing user feedback. Semantic versioning is a recommended practice for versioning your library, where versions are incremented based on changes made—major versions for breaking changes, minor versions for new features, and patch versions for bug fixes. When you publish updates, include detailed release notes to inform users of changes and improvements.

By adhering to these practices—careful management of dependencies, structured documentation, rigorous testing, and thoughtful integration—you can create libraries that are robust, reliable, and easy to use. These efforts not only enhance the quality of your own code but also contribute positively to the broader Racket community by providing valuable tools and resources.

CHAPTER 19: WEB DEVELOPMENT WITH RACKET

To begin our exploration of web development with Racket, we start by understanding the fundamental components of web applications, including HTTP requests, responses, and routing. Racket provides several libraries and frameworks to facilitate web development, one of the most notable being `web-server`, which is a robust and versatile toolset for creating web applications.

We will begin by examining how to handle HTTP requests and responses, which are the cornerstone of web communication. HTTP requests are messages sent from a client (such as a web browser) to a server, and they typically contain information such as the method (e.g., GET, POST), the URL, and any data being sent. Responses, on the other hand, are messages sent back from the server to the client, containing the requested information or a status indicating the result of the request.

In Racket, you can use the `web-server` library to handle these HTTP requests and responses. To get started, you'll need to include this library in your Racket code. Here's a basic example that demonstrates how to set up a simple web server that responds with "Hello, world!" to any HTTP GET request:

```
`racket
lang racket
```

```
(require web-server/servlet
    web-server/servlet-env)

(define (start servlet)
 (serve/servlet
  (lambda (request)
   (response/output :content-type "text/plain"
         :body "Hello, world!"))
  :port 8080
  :servlet-path "/"))

(start t)
```

In this example, `serve/servlet` creates a web server that listens on port 8080 and responds to all requests with a plain text message. The `lambda` function provided to `serve/servlet` handles incoming requests and generates a response.

Next, let's discuss routing, which is the mechanism used to direct HTTP requests to different parts of your application based on the URL or other request parameters. Routing allows you to define different endpoints in your application and associate them with specific functions or handlers.

Racket's `web-server/servlet` library provides mechanisms for routing by allowing you to define different servlet paths. For more advanced routing, you might want to use the `racket/web-server/dispatch` library, which offers a more flexible routing mechanism. Here's an example that demonstrates basic routing with the `dispatch` library:

```racket
lang racket
(require web-server/dispatch
    web-server/servlet
    web-server/servlet-env)

(define (home-handler request)
```

```
(response/output :content-type "text/html"
        :body "<h1>Welcome to the Home Page!</h1>"))

(define (about-handler request)
  (response/output :content-type "text/html"
        :body "<h1>About Us</h1>"))

(define (not-found-handler request)
  (response/output :content-type "text/html"
        :body "<h1>404 Not Found</h1>"))

(define (dispatcher request)
  (case (request-uri request)
    [( "/home" ) (home-handler request)]
    [( "/about" ) (about-handler request)]
    [else (not-found-handler request)]))

(serve/servlet
 (lambda (request)
   (dispatcher request))
 :port 8080)
```

In this example, `dispatcher` routes requests based on the URI. If the URI matches `/home`, it directs the request to the `home-handler`, and similarly for `/about`. Any other request is handled by `not-found-handler`, which returns a 404 error page.

Beyond handling requests and routing, web development often requires interacting with web technologies such as forms and databases. In Racket, handling form submissions involves parsing form data from HTTP POST requests. This is facilitated by the `web-server/servlet` library, which allows you to access form data submitted by the client.

Here is a basic example of handling a form submission:

```racket
```

```racket
lang racket
(require web-server/servlet
    web-server/servlet-env)

(define (form-handler request)
  (let ([form-data (request-bindings request)])
    (response/output :content-type "text/html"
                :body (format "<h1>Form Data Received</h1><p>Name: ~a</p><p>Message: ~a</p>"
                (hash-ref form-data 'name "Unknown")
                (hash-ref form-data 'message "No message")))))

(define (serve-form request)
  (response/output :content-type "text/html"
        :body "<form action'/submit' method'post'>
            <label for'name'>Name:</label><input type'text' name'name'><br>
            <label for'message'>Message:</label><textarea name'message'></textarea><br>
            <input type'submit' value'Submit'>
            </form>"))

(define (dispatcher request)
  (case (request-uri request)
   [( "/submit" ) (form-handler request)]
   [else (serve-form request)]))

(serve/servlet
 (lambda (request)
  (dispatcher request))
 :port 8080)
```
```

In this example, `serve-form` serves an HTML form to the client, and `form-handler` processes the submitted form data. The form data is accessed using `request-bindings`, which returns a hash table containing the form fields.
```

As you build more complex web applications, you may need to integrate with databases for persistent data storage. Racket offers various libraries for database interaction, such as `db`, which provides an interface to SQL databases. Using these libraries, you can perform operations like querying and updating data, allowing your application to interact dynamically with a database.

By combining these techniques—handling HTTP requests and responses, routing, form handling, and database integration—you can leverage Racket's capabilities to build sophisticated web applications. Through careful design and implementation, Racket provides a powerful environment for server-side development, enabling you to create responsive and efficient web applications.

To delve deeper into web development with Racket, we now turn our attention to handling more complex HTTP requests and responses, as well as incorporating dynamic content into our web applications.

In addition to the basic "Hello, world!" example, Racket's `web-server` library allows us to handle more intricate requests and responses. For instance, if you want to process form submissions or handle different types of HTTP methods, you would need to access the request body and query parameters.

Handling form submissions involves extracting data sent by the client. When a user submits a form, the browser sends the form data in the body of the request, typically using the POST method. In Racket, you can access this data using functions provided by the `web-server/servlet` library. For example, to handle a form submission, you might use the following code:

```
```racket
lang racket
(require web-server/servlet
```
```

```
    web-server/servlet-env
    web-server/http)

(define (handle-form request)
 (let ([form-data (request-bindings request)])
  (response/output
   :content-type "text/plain"
   :body (format "Received form data: ~a" form-data))))

(define (start servlet)
 (serve/servlet
  (lambda (request)
   (cond
    [(equal? (request-method request) 'post)
     (handle-form request)]
    [else
     (response/output
      :content-type "text/html"
      :body "<form method'post'>
          <input type'text' name'data'/>
          <input type'submit' value'Submit'/>
          </form>")]))
  :port 8080
  :servlet-path "/"))

(start t)
```
```

In this example, `request-bindings` extracts the form data from the request. The `handle-form` function processes this data and generates a response. The servlet serves different content depending on whether the request method is POST or GET.

In addition to handling form data, you might need to deal with different content types and formats. For instance, you may want to serve JSON responses or handle file uploads. To return JSON data, you would set the `content-type` to `application/
```

json` and serialize your data accordingly. Here's how you might return a JSON response:

```racket
lang racket
(require web-server/servlet
    web-server/servlet-env
    json)

(define (json-response data)
 (response/output
  :content-type "application/json"
  :body (jsexpr->string data)))

(define (start servlet)
 (serve/servlet
  (lambda (request)
   (if (equal? (request-method request) 'get)
     (json-response (list (cons 'message "Hello, world!")))
     (response/output
      :content-type "text/html"
      :body "<p>Only GET requests are supported.</p>")))
  :port 8080
  :servlet-path "/"))

(start t)
```

Here, `jsexpr->string` converts a Racket expression into a JSON string, and `json-response` sends this string as a response.

Another important aspect of web development is managing static files, such as images, CSS, and JavaScript. The `web-server/servlet` library can be configured to serve static files by specifying the appropriate paths and content types. You can use the `serve/servlet` function with additional parameters to handle static file serving, but for more comprehensive static file management, you might prefer using dedicated web servers like Nginx or Apache in conjunction with your Racket application.

Now let us consider routing more advanced scenarios. While the basic servlet paths are sufficient for simple applications, more complex applications often require sophisticated routing mechanisms to handle different URL patterns and parameters. The `racket/web-server/dispatch` library provides a more flexible approach to routing by allowing you to define route patterns and associate them with specific handler functions.

Here's an example of using `racket/web-server/dispatch` to implement more sophisticated routing:

```racket
lang racket
(require web-server/dispatch
    web-server/servlet
    web-server/servlet-env)

(define (home-handler request)
 (response/output
  :content-type "text/html"
  :body "<h1>Welcome to the Home Page!</h1>"))

(define (about-handler request)
 (response/output
  :content-type "text/html"
  :body "<h1>About Us</h1>"))

(define (not-found-handler request)
 (response/output
  :content-type "text/html"
  :body "<h1>404 Not Found</h1>"))

(define (start servlet)
 (serve/servlet
  (dispatch
```

```
  [("/home" home-handler)
   ("/about" about-handler)]
  [else not-found-handler])
 :port 8080
 :servlet-path "/"))

(start t)
```

In this example, `dispatch` routes requests based on the URL path. The `home-handler` and `about-handler` functions handle requests to specific paths, while `not-found-handler` handles any unmatched paths.

Through these examples, you should have a solid foundation in building web applications with Racket. By utilizing Racket's libraries and frameworks effectively, you can create dynamic, efficient, and well-structured web applications.

Building upon our understanding of handling basic HTTP requests and responses, let us now explore how to integrate dynamic content and interact with various web technologies using Racket. The flexibility of Racket allows for sophisticated web application development, including advanced features such as session management and templating.

To begin with, session management is crucial for maintaining state across multiple requests from the same client. This is particularly important for web applications that require user authentication or personalized content. Racket's `web-server/servlet` library offers support for sessions through cookies. Here is a basic example illustrating how to implement session management:

```racket
lang racket
(require web-server/servlet
         web-server/servlet-env
```

```
    web-server/http
    web-server/serve/servlet)

(define (handle-request request)
 (define session (session-get request))
 (define count (if session
          (add1 (session-ref session 'count 0))
          1))
 (session-set! request 'count count)
 (response/output
  :content-type "text/html"
  :body (format "<html><body>
          <h1>Session Count: ~a</h1>
          <form method'post'>
            <input type'submit' value'Increase Count'/>
          </form>
          </body></html>"
         count)))

(define (start servlet)
 (serve/servlet
  (lambda (request)
   (if (equal? (request-method request) 'post)
     (handle-request request)
     (response/output
      :content-type "text/html"
      :body "<form method'post'>
          <input type'submit' value'Start Session'/>
          </form>")))
  :port 8080
  :servlet-path "/"))

(start t)
` ` `
```

In this example, `session-get` and `session-set!` are used to manage session data, such as a count variable. The `session-ref` function retrieves the current count, and `session-set!` updates it. This allows each user to maintain their own session state, which can be crucial for applications requiring user-specific data.

Next, let us consider templating, which is essential for generating dynamic HTML content. Racket supports templating through libraries like `scribble` or external libraries such as `racket/template`. Templating allows you to separate HTML structure from the dynamic content, improving code organization and maintainability.

Here is an example of using `racket/template` to generate HTML dynamically:

```racket
lang racket
(require web-server/servlet
    web-server/servlet-env
    web-server/http
    racket/template)

(define template
 (string->template "<html><body>
      <h1>Welcome, ~a!</h1>
      <p>Your message: ~a</p>
      </body></html>"))

(define (handle-request request)
 (define name (or (request-binding request 'name) "Guest"))
 (define message (or (request-binding request 'message) "No message"))
 (response/output
  :content-type "text/html"
  :body (format-template template name message)))

(define (start servlet)
 (serve/servlet
```

```
  (lambda (request)
    (if (equal? (request-method request) 'post)
      (handle-request request)
      (response/output
       :content-type "text/html"
       :body "<form method'post'>
           <label for'name'>Name:</label>
           <input type'text' name'name'/>
           <br/>
           <label for'message'>Message:</label>
           <input type'text' name'message'/>
           <br/>
           <input type'submit' value'Submit'/>
           </form>")))
  :port 8080
  :servlet-path "/"))

(start t)
```
```

In this example, `string->template` creates a template from a string containing placeholders. The `format-template` function replaces these placeholders with actual values from the form submission. This separation of logic and presentation facilitates easier updates and maintenance of the web application.

Lastly, integrating with external web technologies such as databases or REST APIs can further enhance the functionality of your Racket web applications. Racket offers libraries for interacting with databases like SQLite or MySQL, and for making HTTP requests to external APIs. Using these libraries, you can build applications that retrieve data from a database or interact with other web services.

For instance, to interact with a SQLite database, you might use the `db` library to execute queries and manage database
```

connections. Here's a brief example of querying a database:

```racket
lang racket
(require db
         db/sql)

(define conn (sqlite-connect :database "example.db"))

(define (fetch-data)
  (query [row] (select (from table 'users)
                (where (like (column 'username) "admin%")))))

(define (handle-request request)
  (define data (fetch-data))
  (response/output
   :content-type "text/html"
   :body (format "<html><body>
          <h1>User Data</h1>
          <ul>
          ~a
          </ul>
          </body></html>"
          (apply string-join "\n"
             (map (lambda (row)
                (format "<li>~a</li>" (row 'username)))
                data)))))

(define (start servlet)
  (serve/servlet
   (lambda (request)
     (handle-request request))
   :port 8080
   :servlet-path "/"))

(start t)
```

This example connects to a SQLite database, executes a SQL

query to fetch user data, and generates an HTML response with the results.

By mastering these techniques—handling complex requests, managing sessions, templating, and integrating with databases—you will be well-equipped to develop robust and feature-rich web applications using Racket. Each of these aspects contributes to creating responsive and dynamic web solutions that can handle real-world use cases effectively.

CHAPTER 20: INTEGRATING RACKET WITH OTHER LANGUAGES

In today's diverse development landscape, integrating Racket with other programming languages can significantly enhance the flexibility and power of your applications. This section delves into various methods for interfacing Racket with languages such as C, JavaScript, and Python. By exploring these integration techniques, you will gain insight into how Racket can interoperate with different environments, leveraging their strengths while maintaining the unique features of Racket.

To begin with, integrating Racket with C is a common practice, particularly when performance-critical components need to be written in a lower-level language. Racket provides a Foreign Function Interface (FFI) that allows you to call C functions and use C libraries within Racket code. The FFI mechanism is facilitated by the `ffi/unsafe` and `ffi/unsafe/define` libraries, which enable seamless integration between Racket and C.

For example, suppose you have a simple C function that adds two integers:

```c
// add.c
int add(int a, int b) {
  return a + b;
}
```

To use this C function in Racket, you first need to compile the C code into a shared library, such as `libadd.so` on Linux or `add.dll` on Windows. Then, you can use the `ffi/unsafe` library to interface with this shared library:

```racket
lang racket
(require ffi/unsafe
    ffi/unsafe/define)

(define-lib "libadd.so"
 (define-ffi-func (add _int _int) _int))

(define (add-numbers a b)
 (add a b))

(displayln (add-numbers 5 7)) ; Outputs: 12
```

In this example, `define-lib` is used to specify the shared library, and `define-ffi-func` declares the C function `add` with its argument and return types. The `add-numbers` function in Racket then calls the C function, demonstrating how to integrate low-level C code within Racket programs.

Moving on to integration with JavaScript, Racket can interact with JavaScript through the use of web technologies. The `racket/draw` library provides tools for generating and manipulating graphical content, which can be rendered in a web browser using JavaScript. Additionally, Racket's `web-server` library can serve as a backend to a web application where JavaScript handles client-side interactions.

Consider a scenario where you want to create a web application that uses Racket as the backend and JavaScript for the frontend. Here is a simple example of a Racket web server that serves an HTML page with embedded JavaScript:

```racket
lang racket
(require web-server/servlet
    web-server/servlet-env
    web-server/serve/servlet)

(define (handle-request request)
 (response/output
  :content-type "text/html"
  :body "<html><body>
    <h1>Hello from Racket!</h1>
    <script>
     function showAlert() {
      alert('Hello from JavaScript!');
     }
     showAlert();
    </script>
    </body></html>"))

(serve/servlet handle-request
     :port 8080)
```

In this example, the `handle-request` function serves an HTML page containing JavaScript code that displays an alert box when the page is loaded. This demonstrates how Racket can serve web content and interact with JavaScript in a web application.

Integrating Racket with Python is another valuable technique, especially when leveraging existing Python libraries or utilizing Python's extensive ecosystem. Racket's `racket/python` library provides an interface to execute Python code from within Racket. This integration is particularly useful for incorporating Python's scientific computing or data processing capabilities into a Racket-based project.

Here is a simple example of calling a Python function from Racket:

```racket
lang racket
(require racket/python)

; Initialize the Python interpreter
(python-init)

; Define a Python function in Racket
(define py-sum
  (python-eval
   "def sum(a, b):
      return a + b
    sum"))

; Call the Python function from Racket
(define (sum-numbers a b)
  (python-call py-sum a b))

(displayln (sum-numbers 3 4)) ; Outputs: 7
```

In this example, `python-init` initializes the Python interpreter, and `python-eval` defines a Python function `sum`. The `python-call` function is then used to invoke this Python function from Racket, showcasing the interoperability between these two languages.

By understanding and utilizing these integration techniques, you can effectively combine Racket with other programming languages and systems, expanding your capabilities and leveraging the strengths of each language. This interoperability is particularly beneficial in complex projects where different components are best served by different technologies.

Expanding further on integration techniques, interfacing Racket with JavaScript involves utilizing web technologies for seamless communication between Racket and JavaScript environments. While Racket is primarily known for its server-side capabilities, integrating with JavaScript enables you to bridge the gap between server-side logic and client-side interactions, particularly in web applications.

Racket's approach to JavaScript integration is typically facilitated through the use of the `racket/draw` library or by leveraging the Racket-to-JavaScript compiler, `racket-js`. The `racket/draw` library, while primarily for graphical content creation, can be used to generate code that interacts with JavaScript in a web environment. For more direct interaction with JavaScript, you can use Racket's capabilities to compile Racket code into JavaScript, which allows for the execution of Racket programs within a JavaScript runtime, such as a web browser.

Consider a scenario where you need to create a web application where Racket code interacts with JavaScript for dynamic web content updates. By using the `racket-js` compiler, you can write Racket code that compiles into JavaScript, and then this code can be embedded into HTML for execution in the browser. For instance, to create a simple Racket function that is compiled to JavaScript and used in a web page, you might write:

```racket
lang racket/js

(define (hello-world)
  (js "alert('Hello, world!')"))
```

(hello-world)
```

When compiled to JavaScript, this Racket code generates JavaScript that triggers a browser alert. This integration allows Racket to contribute to web applications by generating JavaScript code that can be executed directly in the client-side environment.

In contrast to JavaScript, integrating Racket with Python is generally achieved using Racket's FFI capabilities to interface with Python libraries or by using interoperability libraries designed for cross-language communication. The `racket/python` library provides a bridge between Racket and Python, allowing you to call Python functions and utilize Python libraries within Racket code. This is particularly useful when leveraging Python's extensive ecosystem of scientific and machine learning libraries alongside Racket's unique programming features.

To illustrate this, let's assume you have a Python function that performs a mathematical computation:

```python
math_ops.py
def square(x):
    return x x
```

To call this Python function from Racket, you would first need to ensure that the Python environment is accessible from Racket. The `racket/python` library can be used to interact with Python, but it requires setting up the appropriate environment and ensuring that Python and Racket are correctly configured to communicate. An example of calling the `square` function from Racket would look like:

```racket

```
lang racket
(require racket/python)

(define py (python-module "math_ops"))

(define (square-number x)
  (python-send py 'square x))

(displayln (square-number 5)) ; Outputs: 25
```

Here, `python-module` loads the Python module, and `python-send` calls the `square` function from the `math_ops` module, passing the argument `5` and receiving the result.

Beyond these specific integrations, interfacing Racket with other programming languages often involves handling data exchange and ensuring compatibility across different runtime environments. When integrating with any language, you must be aware of data format compatibility, memory management issues, and the overall architecture of the interacting systems. For example, when working with C or C++ libraries, it is crucial to manage memory allocation and deallocation carefully to avoid memory leaks and crashes. Similarly, when integrating with JavaScript or Python, ensuring that data formats are correctly translated between languages is essential for smooth operation.

Effective integration not only involves calling functions across languages but also managing state and data exchange efficiently. This often means designing clear interfaces and ensuring that data passed between languages is correctly serialized and deserialized. Techniques such as using JSON or XML for data exchange can help standardize communication between Racket and other systems.

In summary, integrating Racket with C, JavaScript, and Python involves leveraging the language's FFI capabilities, using interoperability libraries, and handling data exchange thoughtfully. These techniques enable you to extend Racket's functionality, incorporate it into diverse environments, and utilize the strengths of different programming languages within a unified application framework. By mastering these integration techniques, you can build more versatile and powerful applications that harness the full potential of Racket alongside other technologies.

When working with Python in conjunction with Racket, the `racket/python` library facilitates calling Python code from Racket and enables data exchange between the two languages. This interoperability can be particularly valuable for projects that leverage Python's powerful data processing libraries while utilizing Racket's functional programming strengths.

For instance, suppose you have a Python function in a file named `math_ops.py` that computes the factorial of a number:

```python
math_ops.py
import math

def factorial(n):
    return math.factorial(n)
```

To call this Python function from Racket, you first need to set up a bridge using the `racket/python` library. This library allows Racket to invoke Python functions and handle data types seamlessly. Here's how you might write Racket code to call the `factorial` function from `math_ops.py`:

```racket
lang racket
(require racket/python)

(define python-env
```

```
(python-eval "import math_ops"))

(define (compute-factorial n)
  (python-call python-env 'factorial n))
```

In this example, `python-eval` is used to import the `math_ops` module into the Racket environment. Then, `python-call` is used to invoke the `factorial` function defined in Python, passing `n` as the argument.

Additionally, for integrating with C, Racket provides a Foreign Function Interface (FFI) that enables interaction with C libraries. This is particularly useful when leveraging existing C code or libraries that offer performance optimizations. To use C libraries in Racket, you need to define C functions in a `.c` file, create a corresponding header file, and then use Racket's FFI to bind these C functions.

Suppose you have a C function defined in a file called `example.c`:

```c
// example.c
include <stdio.h>

void greet(const char name) {
    printf("Hello, %s!\n", name);
}
```

You also need a header file for the C function, `example.h`:

```c
// example.h
ifndef EXAMPLE_H
define EXAMPLE_H

void greet(const char name);
```

endif
```

To interface with this C code from Racket, you would write the following Racket code:

```racket
lang racket
(require ffi/unsafe
    ffi/unsafe/define)

(define-ffi-definer c-definer
 (ffi-lib "path/to/your/library"))

(define greet
 (c-definer 'greet (ffi-arg string) (ffi-return void)))

(greet "World")
```

In this snippet, `ffi-lib` is used to specify the path to the compiled C library. `c-definer` is a macro provided by Racket's FFI to define the C function interface, specifying argument and return types. The `greet` function is then called with the string argument "World", which invokes the C function and prints the greeting.

In summary, integrating Racket with other languages like C, JavaScript, and Python involves using specific libraries and interfaces designed to bridge the gap between different programming environments. The use of FFI with C enables performance-critical code to be utilized within Racket, while libraries like `racket/python` and tools like `racket-js` facilitate interaction with Python and JavaScript, respectively. Each integration approach requires careful attention to data types and method invocations to ensure smooth interoperability and effective utilization of the combined capabilities of Racket and the external
```

languages. By mastering these integration techniques, you can leverage Racket's features alongside the strengths of other programming languages, creating powerful and flexible software solutions.

CHAPTER 21: TESTING AND QUALITY ASSURANCE

Ensuring code quality through rigorous testing is an essential aspect of reliable software development. In the context of Racket, various strategies and tools are available to facilitate comprehensive testing. This section explores these approaches, focusing on unit testing, integration testing, and property-based testing, while also introducing relevant Racket libraries and frameworks that support effective test writing and integration.

Unit testing is a foundational practice in software development where individual components of the codebase are tested in isolation to ensure they function correctly. In Racket, the `rackunit` library provides a straightforward way to write unit tests. This library offers a variety of assertions to verify the correctness of functions and modules.

Consider a simple Racket function that calculates the square of a number:

```racket
(define (square x)
  (* x x))
```

To test this function, you would write unit tests using

`rackunit`. Here's how you could set up a test suite:

```racket
lang racket
(require rackunit)

(define (test-square)
  (check-equal? (square 2) 4)
  (check-equal? (square -3) 9)
  (check-equal? (square 0) 0))

(test-square)
```

In this example, `check-equal?` is an assertion provided by `rackunit` that verifies whether the result of `square` matches the expected value. By running the `test-square` function, you execute the tests, and any failed assertions will indicate issues with the `square` function.

Integration testing involves testing the interaction between different components or modules of a system. This type of testing ensures that the integrated parts of the application work together as expected. In Racket, integration tests can be written similarly to unit tests but focus on scenarios that span multiple functions or modules.

Suppose you have a module with several functions that need to interact:

```racket
;; operations.rkt
lang racket

(define (add x y)
  (+ x y))

(define (subtract x y)
  (- x y))
```

You might have a higher-level function that combines these operations:

```racket
;; calculations.rkt
lang racket
(require "operations.rkt")

(define (compute x y)
  (let ([sum (add x y)]
        [difference (subtract x y)])
    (+ sum difference)))
```

To test the integration of `compute` with `add` and `subtract`, you would write integration tests:

```racket
lang racket
(require rackunit)
(require "calculations.rkt")

(define (test-compute)
  (check-equal? (compute 5 3) 10)
  (check-equal? (compute -1 4) 6))

(test-compute)
```

These tests ensure that `compute` correctly utilizes `add` and `subtract` and produces the expected results.

Property-based testing is another advanced testing strategy that focuses on verifying that a function adheres to certain properties or invariants rather than testing specific examples. This type of testing is useful for ensuring that a function behaves correctly across a wide range of inputs.

In Racket, the `racket/prop` library facilitates property-based testing. For example, suppose you want to verify that a function that calculates the absolute value of a number always returns a non-negative result. You would use `racket/prop` as follows:

```racket
lang racket
(require racket/prop)

(define (absolute x)
  (if (negative? x) (- x) x))

(define absolute-prop
  (prop:for-all [x (in-naturals)]
    (> (absolute x) 0)))

(prop:check absolute-prop)
```

In this property-based test, `prop:for-all` generates a wide range of natural numbers to test the `absolute` function, ensuring that it consistently returns a non-negative value. The `prop:check` function evaluates the property and reports if any test cases fail.

Integrating testing into your development workflow is crucial for maintaining code quality. Continuous integration (CI) systems can be configured to automatically run tests whenever code changes are made. In Racket, this involves setting up a CI pipeline that executes your test suites and reports results. Tools like Travis CI or GitHub Actions can be used to automate this process, ensuring that your tests are run consistently across different environments.

Additionally, adopting a test-driven development (TDD) approach, where tests are written before the code itself, can help in designing robust and reliable software. By starting with tests, you ensure that your code meets the desired requirements and behaves correctly from the outset.

In summary, effective testing in Racket encompasses various strategies including unit testing, integration testing, and property-based testing. Leveraging the `rackunit` library for unit tests, writing integration tests for complex interactions, and applying property-based tests for broader verification help ensure that your Racket applications are reliable and maintainable. Integrating these testing practices into your development workflow, along with automated CI systems, will contribute significantly to the quality and robustness of your software projects.

Testing strategies are crucial for ensuring the robustness and reliability of software, and Racket provides a rich set of tools and methodologies to support these practices. Beyond unit and integration testing, property-based testing is an advanced technique that can significantly enhance the reliability of your code by testing a wide range of input cases and ensuring that your functions adhere to certain properties or invariants.

Property-based testing differs from unit testing in that it focuses on testing the properties or characteristics of functions rather than specific input-output pairs. This approach can be particularly useful for discovering edge cases or unexpected behaviors that might not be covered by standard unit tests. In Racket, the `racket/test` library supports property-based testing through the use of the `check-property` function, which allows you to define and verify properties of your functions.

To illustrate property-based testing, consider a function that sorts a list of numbers:

```racket
lang racket

(define (sort-list lst)
  (sort lst <))
```

A property-based test for this function might check that the output list is always sorted. We can write such a test using `check-property`:

```racket
lang racket
(require rackunit)

(define (sorted? lst)
  (or (null? lst)
      (not (member f (map (lambda (i)
                            (if (null? (cdr i))
                                t
                                (< (car i) (cadr i))))
                          (map list lst (cdr lst)))))))

(check-property "sort-list should produce a sorted list"
  (lambda (lst)
    (sorted? (sort-list lst))))
```

In this example, `sorted?` is a helper function that checks whether a list is sorted. The `check-property` function then verifies that for any given list `lst`, the result of `sort-list` is always a sorted list. This test will automatically generate a variety of input lists and check that the property holds for all of them.

Effective testing not only involves writing tests but also integrating them into your development workflow to ensure that they are executed regularly and that their results are used to guide development. Continuous integration (CI) is a practice that automates the running of tests and other quality assurance processes whenever changes are made to the codebase. In Racket, you can set up CI to run your tests automatically using tools like Travis CI or GitHub Actions.

To set up CI for a Racket project, you typically create a configuration file that specifies the environment in which your tests will be run and the commands to execute them. For example, a `.travis.yml` file for Travis CI might look like this:

```yaml
language: racket
script:
 - raco test
```

This configuration tells Travis CI to use the Racket language environment and run the `raco test` command, which executes all tests defined in your project. Similarly, GitHub Actions uses a workflow file, such as `.github/workflows/test.yml`, to specify the CI process:

```yaml
name: Racket Tests

on: [push, pull_request]

jobs:
 test:
  runs-on: ubuntu-latest

   steps:
  - uses: actions/checkout@v2
  - name: Set up Racket
   uses: Racket-lang/setup-racket@v1
  - name: Run tests
   run: raco test
```

This GitHub Actions workflow runs on every push or pull request, setting up the Racket environment and executing tests to ensure code quality is maintained.

In addition to traditional testing methods, code quality can be further enhanced by incorporating static analysis tools. These tools analyze your code without executing it, providing insights into potential issues such as code complexity, style violations, or unused variables. Racket's `racket` command-line tool can be used to run some of these checks, but more advanced static analysis and linting tools may be integrated into your development process as needed.

By employing a combination of unit testing, integration testing, property-based testing, and continuous integration, you can ensure that your Racket projects maintain high standards of quality and reliability. These practices not only help identify and fix issues early in the development process but also facilitate ongoing improvements and adaptations as your codebase evolves.

To ensure effective testing and quality assurance, it's crucial to integrate testing practices into your development workflow systematically. This means not only writing tests but also adopting a structured approach to manage and execute them. Racket provides several tools and practices that help in embedding testing deeply into the software development lifecycle, enhancing the reliability and maintainability of your codebase.

One key practice in maintaining code quality is adopting continuous testing. Continuous testing is a practice where tests are executed frequently, often as part of the continuous integration (CI) process. This approach helps in detecting issues early, before they become critical problems. In Racket, you can use tools like `raco test` to run your test suites automatically. This tool allows you to define test files that group your tests and execute them in a batch. By integrating `raco test` into your CI pipeline, you ensure that every code change is validated by your tests.

Here's an example of how you might set up a test file using `raco test`. Suppose you have several test cases defined in various files, such as `test-sorting.rkt`, `test-math.rkt`, and `test-io.rkt`. Each of these files contains tests relevant to their respective modules:

```racket
lang racket
(require rackunit)
(require "sorting.rkt") ; The module under test

(define (test-sort)
 (check-equal? (sort-list '(3 1 2)) '(1 2 3))
 (check-equal? (sort-list '()) '())
 (check-equal? (sort-list '(5 3 5 2)) '(2 3 5 5)))
```

You would include similar tests in the other files, and then you can run all these tests together using:

```shell
raco test
```

This command will execute all the tests in the current directory and its subdirectories, giving you a comprehensive view of your code's stability.

Another important aspect of testing in Racket is ensuring that your code handles edge cases and behaves correctly under various conditions. For example, when writing tests for functions that interact with external systems or user input, you should include tests that simulate different scenarios. This might involve creating mock objects or using dependency injection to isolate the function under test from its external dependencies. This practice ensures that your tests are both reliable and reproducible.

When dealing with integration testing, you need to test how different modules or components of your system work together. This kind of testing often requires setting up a test environment that mirrors the production environment as closely as possible. In Racket, you might create integration tests that involve multiple modules interacting with each other, and validate that the interactions produce the expected results. For instance, if you have a module that processes data and another that stores it, you would write integration tests to ensure that data flows correctly from one module to the other and is stored as expected.

Moreover, quality assurance encompasses more than just testing; it includes practices like code reviews and static analysis. Code reviews involve having other developers examine your code for potential issues, design flaws, or deviations from coding standards. Racket, being a Lisp dialect, benefits from code reviews to catch errors that might not be apparent from static analysis alone. Static analysis tools can help identify potential problems in your code without actually executing it. Tools like `raco lint` can check your Racket code for common issues and adherence to best practices.

Finally, documenting your tests and the testing process is essential for maintaining quality assurance in the long term. Clear documentation helps other developers understand the purpose and scope of each test, how to run them, and what the expected outcomes are. This transparency ensures that the testing process is robust and that future modifications to the codebase do not inadvertently introduce regressions or break existing functionality.

In conclusion, integrating Racket's testing tools and practices into your development workflow helps ensure code quality and reliability. By employing unit tests, integration tests, and property-based tests, and by using tools like `raco test` and `raco lint`, you can create a robust testing framework that supports continuous integration and fosters high-quality software development. Coupled with practices like code reviews and comprehensive documentation, these techniques contribute to a sustainable and effective quality assurance process.

CHAPTER 22: PERFORMANCE OPTIMIZATION

In software development, performance optimization is crucial for delivering efficient and responsive applications. Optimizing Racket programs involves a comprehensive understanding of performance bottlenecks and applying targeted techniques to address them. This process includes profiling your code to identify performance issues, improving execution speed, and optimizing memory usage.

Profiling is the first step in performance optimization. It involves analyzing a program to determine where time is spent and how resources are used. Racket provides tools like `racket/profile` and `racket/trace` that are instrumental in profiling and debugging performance issues. The `racket/profile` module allows you to collect detailed information about the time spent in different functions, which is essential for identifying hotspots in your code.

To start profiling, you would typically use the `racket/profile` module to instrument your code. For example, if you have a function `compute-heavy-task` that you suspect is causing performance issues, you can profile it as follows:

```racket
lang racket
(require racket/profile)
```

```
(define (compute-heavy-task n)
 (if ( n 0)
   0
   (+ n (compute-heavy-task (sub1 n)))))

(profile (compute-heavy-task 10000))
```

When you run this code, `racket/profile` will produce a report showing how much time was spent in `compute-heavy-task` and its recursive calls. This report helps pinpoint which parts of the function are the most time-consuming.

Once you identify performance bottlenecks, the next step is to optimize execution speed. This process often involves revisiting algorithms and data structures used in your program. For instance, if you find that a particular function is slow due to inefficient algorithms, consider alternative approaches that reduce time complexity. If your code uses a lot of list operations, switching to more efficient data structures like vectors or hash tables may lead to performance improvements.

To illustrate, suppose you have a function that performs a linear search on a list to find an element. If the list is large, this operation can be costly. Replacing the list with a hash table can improve performance, as hash tables offer average constant-time complexity for lookups. Here's a simple comparison:

```racket
lang racket
(require racket/set)

;; Linear search
(define (linear-search lst target)
 (cond [(empty? lst) f]
    [(equal? (first lst) target) t]
    [else (linear-search (rest lst) target)]))
```

```
;; Hash table search
(define (hash-table-search ht target)
  (hash-has-key? ht target))

(define my-list '(1 2 3 4 5 6 7 8 9 10))
(define my-hash-table (make-hasheq))
(for ([i my-list]) (hash-set! my-hash-table i t))

(time (linear-search my-list 5))
(time (hash-table-search my-hash-table 5))
```

In this example, the `linear-search` function performs a linear search on a list, while `hash-table-search` uses a hash table. The time measurements will reveal that the hash table search is faster, especially for larger data sets.

Memory optimization is another critical aspect of performance improvement. Efficient memory usage can be achieved by minimizing allocations and deallocations and by using data structures that are appropriate for your needs. For instance, when dealing with large data sets, consider using Racket's built-in data structures like `bytevector` for binary data, which can be more memory-efficient than lists or strings.

Additionally, memory profiling tools can help identify memory leaks or excessive memory usage. Racket provides memory profiling tools such as `racket/memory-profile` to help you analyze memory consumption and identify objects that are not being collected by the garbage collector. This can be especially useful for applications that use a lot of dynamic memory or create many temporary objects.

Here's an example of how to use `racket/memory-profile`:

```racket
lang racket
(require racket/memory-profile)
```

```
(define (generate-large-list n)
  (build-list n (lambda (i) i)))

(memory-profile (generate-large-list 1000000))
```

In this code, `memory-profile` provides insights into how much memory is used by the `generate-large-list` function. By analyzing the output, you can determine if memory usage is excessive and take steps to reduce it, such as by using more compact data structures or by optimizing algorithms.

In summary, performance optimization in Racket involves a combination of profiling, improving execution speed, and optimizing memory usage. By employing Racket's profiling tools and carefully analyzing your code, you can identify and address performance bottlenecks, leading to more efficient and responsive applications.

Performance optimization not only involves improving execution speed but also entails careful management of memory usage. Efficient memory management is crucial in ensuring that your application does not consume excessive resources, which can lead to performance degradation or even system crashes. In Racket, optimizing memory usage involves understanding garbage collection and how to write code that minimizes unnecessary memory allocations.

Racket employs a garbage collector (GC) to manage memory automatically. However, understanding how garbage collection works and how it interacts with your code can help you write more memory-efficient programs. The primary goal is to minimize the creation of unnecessary objects and to manage the lifespan of objects effectively.

For instance, if your program frequently creates and discards large data structures, this can put a significant strain on the garbage collector. One strategy to mitigate this issue is to reuse objects whenever possible. Instead of creating new objects each time a function is called, consider using existing objects or data structures.

A concrete example involves optimizing functions that generate lists. If you are frequently appending to a list, using a functional approach that constructs lists incrementally can be more memory-efficient than repeatedly creating new lists. For example:

```racket
lang racket

;; Inefficient list appending
(define (append-to-list lst elem)
  (append lst (list elem)))

;; More efficient list building
(define (build-list n)
  (let loop ([i n] [lst '()])
    (if (zero? i)
        lst
        (loop (sub1 i) (cons i lst)))))

(build-list 10000)
```

In the above example, the `build-list` function uses `cons` to build a list incrementally, avoiding the need for repeated list concatenations, which can be inefficient.

Another important aspect of memory optimization is understanding the trade-offs between different data structures. For instance, using immutable data structures in Racket can sometimes lead to higher memory usage compared to mutable structures due to the need for copying when changes are made. However, immutable structures offer benefits in terms of safety and simplicity, particularly in concurrent programming scenarios. Balancing the choice of data structures with your application's performance requirements is key.

Profiling tools in Racket can help monitor memory usage and identify areas where optimization is needed. The `racket/metrics` module provides functionality for tracking memory consumption and can help diagnose issues related to excessive memory use. For example:

```racket
lang racket
(require racket/metrics)

(define (memory-usage-example)
  (let ([data (make-list 1000000 0)])
    (collect-garbage)
    (metrics-report)))

(memory-usage-example)
```

The `metrics-report` function provides an overview of memory usage that can help you identify if certain operations or data structures are consuming more memory than expected.

Optimizing I/O operations is another critical area for performance enhancement. In many applications, especially those involving large datasets or network interactions, I/O operations can become a bottleneck. To optimize I/O performance in Racket, consider using buffered I/O and asynchronous operations where possible. Buffered I/O can reduce the overhead of frequent disk or network accesses by accumulating data in memory before performing I/O operations. Asynchronous I/O allows your program to continue processing while waiting for I/O operations to complete, thus improving responsiveness.

For example, using the `racket/file` module for file I/O with buffering:

```racket
lang racket
(require racket/file)

(define (read-large-file file-path)
  (with-input-from-file file-path
    (lambda ()
      (let ([in (open-input-file file-path)])
        (let loop ([line (read-line in)])
          (unless (eof-object? line)
            (process-line line)
            (loop (read-line in))))))))

(read-large-file "large-file.txt")
```

Here, `with-input-from-file` is used to ensure proper handling of file resources, while buffered operations through `open-input-file` manage large files efficiently.

Lastly, optimizing concurrency and parallelism involves ensuring that your code is well-structured for multi-threaded execution. This includes minimizing contention for shared resources and ensuring that threads are effectively balanced. Racket's concurrency primitives, such as channels and places, can help manage parallel tasks and data exchanges, but proper synchronization and coordination are essential to avoid issues like deadlocks or race conditions.

By applying these strategies and utilizing Racket's profiling and optimization tools, you can enhance the performance of your applications. Efficient memory management, careful choice of data structures, effective I/O handling, and proper concurrency practices are all crucial for developing high-performance Racket programs.

Profiling is a critical step in identifying performance

bottlenecks within your Racket programs. The goal is to understand where the most time is being spent and which parts of your code are most resource-intensive. Racket offers several tools for profiling, including the built-in `racket/profile` library. This library enables you to collect and analyze data about function call frequencies and execution times, providing valuable insights into the performance of your program.

To use the `racket/profile` library, you first need to include it in your program. By wrapping the code you want to profile with `profile`, you can gather performance metrics. For instance:

```racket
lang racket
(require racket/profile)

(define (slow-function n)
  (if (zero? n)
      0
      (+ n (slow-function (sub1 n)))))

(profile (slow-function 1000))
```

The output from this profiling will show you the time taken by `slow-function` and how often it was called, allowing you to pinpoint where optimizations might be needed. After identifying the performance hotspots, you can apply various optimization strategies to improve execution speed.

CHAPTER 23: ALGORITHMIC OPTIMIZATION

ONE EFFECTIVE APPROACH TO OPTIMIZATION IS ALGORITHMIC IMPROVEMENTS. BY SELECTING MORE EFFICIENT ALGORITHMS, YOU CAN OFTEN ACHIEVE SIGNIFICANT

PERFORMANCE GAINS. FOR EXAMPLE, IF YOU ARE WORKING WITH SORTING OPERATIONS, USING QUICKSORT OR MERGESORT INSTEAD OF BUBBLE SORT CAN DRASTICALLY REDUCE EXECUTION TIME. THE CHOICE OF ALGORITHM DEPENDS ON THE problem you are solving and the characteristics of your data. In Racket, the `sort` function is optimized for performance, but understanding the underlying algorithms can help you make informed decisions about when to use it

OR IMPLEMENT A CUSTOM SORTING FUNCTION.

Another important technique is reducing redundant computations. This can be achieved through memoization, where the results of expensive function calls are cached and reused when the same inputs occur again. Memoization can be particularly beneficial in scenarios where a function is called repeatedly with the same arguments. In Racket, memoization can be implemented using the `racket/match` library, which provides a convenient way to create memoized functions:

```racket
lang racket
(require racket/match)

(define (slow-function n)
  (if (zero? n)
      0
      (+ n (slow-function (sub1 n)))))

(define memoized-slow-function
  (memoize slow-function))

(memoized-slow-function 1000)
```

By replacing `slow-function` with `memoized-slow-function`, repeated calls with the same arguments will be much faster due to cached results.

Additionally, optimizing I/O operations can lead to performance improvements. I/O operations, such as reading from or writing to files, can be slow and block other computations. Using asynchronous I/O or buffering can help mitigate these issues. For instance, reading large files in chunks rather than loading the entire file into memory at once can improve performance and reduce memory usage.

When dealing with concurrent or parallel processing, it is essential to manage synchronization and communication between threads effectively. Racket provides constructs for managing concurrency, such as channels and mutexes. Efficient use of these constructs can prevent issues like race conditions and deadlocks, which can adversely affect performance. For example, using a channel to pass data between threads can be more efficient than using shared variables with explicit locking:

```racket
lang racket
(require racket/async)

(define channel (make-channel))

(define (producer)
  (for ([i (in-range 100)])
    (channel-put channel i)))

(define (consumer)
  (for ([i (in-range 100)])
    (define value (channel-get channel))
    (printf "Received: ~a\n" value)))

(async-run
  (let ([p (async/launch producer)]
        [c (async/launch consumer)])
    (async/wait p)
    (async/wait c)))
```

In this example, the `producer` function puts values into a channel, while the `consumer` function retrieves them. The use of channels allows for clean and efficient communication between threads.

In summary, optimizing performance in Racket involves a combination of profiling, choosing efficient algorithms, reducing redundant computations, and optimizing I/O operations. By using profiling tools to identify bottlenecks, applying algorithmic improvements, and implementing techniques like memoization and asynchronous I/O, you can significantly enhance the performance of your Racket applications. Additionally, understanding concurrency constructs and managing synchronization effectively can further contribute to improved performance.

Building user interfaces is a fundamental aspect of application development, enabling users to interact with software in intuitive and effective ways. In Racket, graphical user interfaces (GUIs) are constructed using a variety of libraries and tools that facilitate the creation of interactive elements and management of user interactions. This discussion delves into the primary libraries available for GUI development in Racket, focusing on window management, event handling, and widget creation.

To begin with, Racket provides the `racket/gui` library, which serves as the primary toolset for creating graphical user interfaces. This library allows for the construction of windows, dialog boxes, and various widgets, providing a robust foundation for GUI applications. The core concept in this library is the notion of frames, which act as the top-level containers for GUI applications.

A basic example of creating a window in Racket involves using the `frame` function from the `racket/gui` library. Here is a simple example:

```
```racket
lang racket
```
```

```
(require racket/gui)

(define my-frame (new frame% [label "Hello, Racket!"]))

(send my-frame show t)
```

In this example, a new frame is created with the label "Hello, Racket!" and is made visible using the `show` method. This creates a basic window with a title, but it does not yet include any interactive elements or event handling capabilities.

To create more complex interfaces, you will need to incorporate widgets such as buttons, text fields, and labels. These widgets are added to the frame using various classes provided by the `racket/gui` library. For instance, adding a button to the frame can be done as follows:

```racket
lang racket
(require racket/gui)

(define my-frame (new frame% [label "Button Example"]))

(define my-button
  (new button%
    [label "Click Me!"]
    [parent my-frame]
    [callback (lambda (button-event)
        (send button-event get-event-object)
        (message "Button clicked!"))]))

(send my-frame show t)
```

In this snippet, a button is created with the label "Click Me!" and added to the frame. The `callback` parameter specifies a function to be executed when the button is clicked. The `lambda` function defined here demonstrates a simple interaction where a message is printed to the console when the button is clicked.

Event handling is a critical aspect of GUI programming, enabling your application to respond to user actions such as button clicks, text input, and window resizing. In Racket, event handling is managed through event handlers, which are functions or methods that react to specific types of events.

The `racket/gui` library provides various classes for event handling, including `button%`, `text-field%`, and `frame%`. Each of these classes has methods for setting up event handlers. For example, handling a text input event can be done as follows:

```racket
lang racket
(require racket/gui)

(define my-frame (new frame% [label "Text Input Example"]))

(define my-text-field
  (new text-field%
    [parent my-frame]
    [callback (lambda (text-field-event)
        (send text-field-event get-event-object)
        (message "Text input received!"))]))

(send my-frame show t)
```

In this code, a text field is added to the frame, and a callback function is specified to handle text input events. When the user types into the text field, the callback function is invoked, allowing the application to process the input accordingly.

Widgets in Racket's GUI library can be combined and arranged within frames to create more complex interfaces. Layout management is an important part of this process, involving the arrangement of widgets within the frame to achieve the desired user interface design. The `racket/gui` library provides several layout managers, such as `horizontal-panel%`, `vertical-panel%`, and `grid-panel%`, which help in organizing widgets within the frame.

For instance, you can use a `vertical-panel%` to stack widgets vertically within a frame:

```racket
lang racket
(require racket/gui)

(define my-frame (new frame% [label "Vertical Layout Example"]))

(define my-panel
  (new vertical-panel%
    [parent my-frame]))

(new button%
    [label "Button 1"]
    [parent my-panel])

(new button%
    [label "Button 2"]
    [parent my-panel])

(send my-frame show t)
```

In this example, a vertical panel is used to arrange two buttons vertically within the frame. This layout manager simplifies the process of aligning widgets and ensures a consistent and visually appealing user interface.

In addition to the standard widgets and layout managers, Racket's `racket/gui` library also supports advanced features such as custom widget creation and interaction with other graphical systems. By extending the base classes provided by the library, you can create specialized widgets tailored to your application's needs. This capability allows for the development of highly interactive and visually dynamic interfaces.

To summarize, Racket's GUI capabilities, encapsulated in the `racket/gui` library, provide a comprehensive toolkit for building graphical user interfaces. By leveraging frames, widgets, event handling, and layout managers, you can create intuitive and interactive applications that meet user needs and enhance the overall user experience. The examples provided illustrate fundamental concepts and practices, serving as a foundation for more complex GUI development tasks.

In extending the creation of user interfaces in Racket, one must delve into the aspects of event handling and layout management, which are crucial for building functional and visually appealing applications. Event handling, in particular, involves responding to user actions such as button clicks, key presses, and mouse movements. This allows for dynamic interaction within the application, making it more responsive and engaging.

To effectively manage events, Racket uses an event-driven programming model, where events are captured and handled by specific callbacks or handlers. In the `racket/gui` library, this is achieved through event handlers that can be associated with various GUI components. For example, handling a button click involves defining a callback function that specifies the actions to be performed when the button is interacted with. This function is tied to the button's event, enabling the application to respond to user input appropriately.

Here's a practical example illustrating event handling in Racket:

```racket
lang racket
(require racket/gui)
```

```
(define my-frame
 (new frame%
   [label "Event Handling Example"]
   [width 300]
   [height 200]))

(define my-button
 (new button%
   [label "Click Me!"]
   [parent my-frame]
   [callback (lambda (button-event)
       (send (new message-dialog%
          [message "Button clicked!"]
          [parent my-frame])
          show t))]))

(send my-frame show t)
```

In this example, when the button is clicked, a message dialog is displayed, indicating that the button has been clicked. The `callback` function creates a new `message-dialog%` object and shows it with a message. This demonstrates a simple yet effective way of providing feedback to the user based on their actions.

In addition to handling events, layout management is essential for organizing the visual components within the window. Racket provides several layout managers to arrange GUI elements in a structured manner. The most commonly used layout managers are the `horizontal-panel%` and `vertical-panel%`, which arrange components horizontally and vertically, respectively. For more complex layouts, `grid-panel%` allows for a grid-based arrangement of components.

Consider the following example, where a vertical layout is used to arrange a label and a button within a frame:

```racket
lang racket
(require racket/gui)

(define my-frame
  (new frame%
    [label "Layout Management Example"]
    [width 300]
    [height 200]))

(define my-panel
  (new vertical-panel%
    [parent my-frame]))

(define my-label
  (new message%
    [label "This is a label"]
    [parent my-panel]))

(define my-button
  (new button%
    [label "Click Me!"]
    [parent my-panel]
    [callback (lambda (button-event)
        (send (new message-dialog%
           [message "Button clicked!"]
           [parent my-frame])
           show t))]))

(send my-frame show t)
```

Here, the `vertical-panel%` is used to stack a label and a button vertically within the frame. The layout manager ensures that these components are arranged in a clear and orderly manner. Using layout managers effectively helps in creating user interfaces that are both aesthetically pleasing and functionally organized.

Beyond basic widgets and layouts, Racket also supports more advanced GUI features, including custom drawing and complex interactions. For custom drawing, you can override the `on-paint` method of a canvas or other drawable component to perform custom graphics operations. This allows for creating more sophisticated visual elements, such as custom charts or interactive graphics.

For example, the following snippet demonstrates custom drawing in a canvas:

```racket
lang racket
(require racket/gui)

(define my-frame
  (new frame%
    [label "Custom Drawing Example"]
    [width 400]
    [height 300]))

(define my-canvas
  (new canvas%
    [parent my-frame]
    [paint-callback (lambda (canvas dc)
          (send dc draw-text "Hello, Racket!"
            100 100)
          (send dc set-pen "red" 3 'solid)
          (send dc draw-line 50 50 150 150))]))

(send my-frame show t)
```

In this example, the `paint-callback` function uses the drawing context `dc` to render text and lines on the canvas. Custom drawing allows for a high degree of flexibility in creating unique and interactive visual elements.

In conclusion, building user interfaces in Racket involves understanding and utilizing its graphical libraries effectively. By mastering window management, event handling, layout management, and custom drawing, you can create sophisticated and user-friendly interfaces. These skills are crucial for developing applications that not only function well but also provide an engaging and intuitive user experience. As you continue to explore and apply these concepts, you will enhance your ability to design and implement high-quality interfaces for a variety of applications.

As we delve further into building user interfaces with Racket, it is essential to address the creation and customization of widgets, which are the building blocks of any GUI application. Widgets such as buttons, labels, text fields, and sliders are fundamental components that users interact with, and their proper management can significantly impact the usability of an application.

Widgets in Racket are encapsulated as classes within the `racket/gui` library. Each widget class provides a set of methods to control its appearance and behavior. For instance, the `button%` class allows for the creation of buttons with customizable labels and actions, while the `text-field%` class creates input fields where users can enter text.

Consider the following code snippet that demonstrates creating and customizing several widgets in a Racket application:

```racket
lang racket
(require racket/gui)

(define my-frame
  (new frame%
    [label "Widget Example"]
```

```
    [width 400]
    [height 300]))

(define my-button
  (new button%
    [label "Submit"]
    [parent my-frame]
    [callback (lambda (button-event)
        (send (new message-dialog%
            [message "Submitted!"]
            [parent my-frame])
          show t))]))

(define my-label
  (new message%
    [label "Enter your name:"]
    [parent my-frame]))

(define my-text-field
  (new text-field%
    [parent my-frame]
    [init-value "Type here"]))

(send my-frame show t)
```
```

In this example, a `frame%` is created as the main window, containing a button, a label, and a text field. The button is associated with a callback function that displays a message dialog when clicked. The label provides a prompt for the user, and the text field allows for user input. This setup demonstrates the basic customization of widgets and their integration into a cohesive interface.

Another important aspect of GUI development is managing the layout and responsiveness of the application. Effective layout management ensures that widgets are positioned correctly and maintain their arrangement across different
```

screen sizes and resolutions. Racket's `racket/gui` library offers several layout managers to handle different arrangements.

For instance, the `horizontal-panel%` and `vertical-panel%` classes provide horizontal and vertical layouts, respectively. These panels can be used to arrange widgets in a row or column, making it easy to create organized and aesthetically pleasing interfaces. The `grid-panel%` class offers more flexibility, allowing for a grid-based layout where widgets can be placed in specific rows and columns.

Here is an example illustrating the use of `grid-panel%` for arranging widgets:

```racket
lang racket
(require racket/gui)

(define my-frame
  (new frame%
    [label "Grid Layout Example"]
    [width 300]
    [height 200]))

(define my-grid-panel
  (new grid-panel%
    [parent my-frame]
    [columns 2]
    [rows 3]))

(define my-label1
  (new message%
    [label "Name:"]
    [parent my-grid-panel]))

(define my-text-field1
  (new text-field%
    [parent my-grid-panel]
```

```
    [init-value ""]))
(define my-label2
  (new message%
    [label "Age:"]
    [parent my-grid-panel]))
(define my-text-field2
  (new text-field%
    [parent my-grid-panel]
    [init-value ""]))
(define my-button
  (new button%
    [label "Submit"]
    [parent my-grid-panel]
    [callback (lambda (button-event)
        (send (new message-dialog%
            [message "Form Submitted!"]
            [parent my-frame])
            show t))]))

(send my-frame show t)
```
```

In this example, the `grid-panel%` is used to arrange labels, text fields, and a button in a grid layout. Each widget is placed in a specific cell of the grid, ensuring an orderly and systematic arrangement. This layout is particularly useful for forms and data entry applications, where a structured presentation of input fields is essential.

Lastly, it is important to consider user experience and accessibility when building GUIs. Ensuring that interfaces are intuitive and easy to navigate is crucial for creating effective applications. Accessibility features such as keyboard shortcuts, screen reader support, and responsive design should be incorporated to accommodate users with various
```

needs and preferences.

In conclusion, building user interfaces in Racket involves creating and customizing widgets, managing layouts, and considering user experience and accessibility. By leveraging Racket's graphical libraries and understanding the principles of event handling and layout management, you can develop interactive and user-friendly applications that meet a wide range of needs and requirements.

CHAPTER 24: DEBUGGING TECHNIQUES

Debugging is an indispensable skill in software development, crucial for ensuring that code functions correctly and efficiently. In Racket, effective debugging involves a blend of understanding the tools available, leveraging debugging techniques, and applying systematic problem-solving strategies. This section delves into these aspects, providing practical guidance on identifying, diagnosing, and fixing issues in Racket programs.

A primary tool for debugging in Racket is the built-in `DrRacket` IDE, which integrates several debugging features that facilitate code examination and error correction. One of the most basic yet powerful features is setting breakpoints. A breakpoint allows developers to pause program execution at a specific line of code. This pause enables inspection of the current program state, including variable values, which is crucial for understanding how data flows through the application and where it may be going awry.

To set a breakpoint in DrRacket, one simply clicks on the left margin next to the line of code where the breakpoint should be placed. Once the program execution reaches this line, it will pause, and the developer can examine the state of the program at that point. This process is invaluable for pinpointing where logic errors or incorrect data manipulations occur.

For example, consider a function that is not behaving as expected. By setting a breakpoint within this function, a developer can inspect the values of the parameters when the function is invoked, ensuring that they are what the function expects. Additionally, examining local variables and the call stack during the breakpoint can provide insights into how the function is being used and how control is passing through the code.

DrRacket also offers a set of debugging commands and tools accessible via the Debugger window. These tools include step-over, step-into, and step-out commands. The step-over command allows execution to proceed line-by-line, but without stepping into function calls, which is useful for observing how control moves from one part of the code to another. Conversely, the step-into command delves into the function being called, which helps in understanding its internal workings and detecting issues within nested functions. The step-out command resumes execution until the current function completes, which is useful for exiting from a function once its behavior has been inspected.

Moreover, DrRacket provides an interactive REPL (Read-Eval-Print Loop) that is extremely useful for debugging. The REPL allows developers to execute Racket expressions and functions interactively, making it possible to test small code snippets or validate specific assumptions about the program's behavior without running the entire program. This feature is particularly beneficial for experimenting with different solutions to problems and verifying that changes produce the desired effects.

In addition to using integrated tools, another effective debugging technique is the use of `printf` statements. These statements can be inserted into the code to output variable values, function calls, and execution flow information. While this method is less sophisticated than using breakpoints and stepping commands, it can provide immediate feedback and is often used in conjunction with other debugging methods. For example, inserting a `printf` statement before and after a critical computation can help determine if the computation is producing the expected results and identify where discrepancies might arise.

For systematic bug diagnosis, a structured approach to problem-solving is essential. This approach typically involves the following steps: reproduce the issue consistently, isolate the problematic code, simplify the problem by removing unrelated parts, and then test potential fixes. Reproducing the issue is crucial because it ensures that the problem can be observed and tested under controlled conditions. Isolating the problematic code involves narrowing down the part of the program where the issue occurs, often by commenting out sections or using smaller test cases.

Simplification involves reducing the complexity of the code to understand the core issue better. By removing extraneous details and focusing on the minimal code that reproduces the problem, developers can more easily identify the source of the issue. Once a potential fix is identified, it should be tested thoroughly to confirm that it resolves the problem without introducing new issues.

Finally, effective debugging requires a good understanding of common types of errors and issues. In Racket, as in other programming languages, errors can be syntactical, logical, or runtime-related. Syntax errors occur when the code does not adhere to the language's grammar rules and are usually caught by the compiler or interpreter. Logical errors, on the other hand, arise when the code executes without syntax errors but produces incorrect results due to faulty logic. Runtime errors occur during program execution and can include issues such as division by zero or invalid array indices.

Understanding these different types of errors and knowing how to approach them systematically will enhance your ability to debug Racket programs efficiently. By combining the use of debugging tools, interactive testing, and a methodical problem-solving approach, you can identify and resolve issues more effectively, leading to more reliable and robust Racket applications.

In addition to using breakpoints and debugging commands, the interactive REPL (Read-Eval-Print Loop) in DrRacket plays a crucial role in the debugging process. This feature allows developers to evaluate expressions and inspect their results in real time, providing immediate feedback and facilitating rapid experimentation. The REPL can be used to test individual functions or expressions outside the main program flow, making it an excellent tool for isolating and understanding specific issues.

When debugging with the REPL, you can incrementally test and modify parts of your code. For instance, if you suspect a particular function is causing an issue, you can call it directly in the REPL with various inputs to observe its behavior and output. This approach helps in verifying if the function behaves correctly in isolation before reintegrating it into the larger application context. This isolation technique is especially useful when dealing with complex or multifaceted problems where issues might not be immediately apparent.

Another valuable feature provided by DrRacket is the `check-expect` mechanism, which is part of the Racket testing framework. This tool allows for writing and running test cases to validate that functions produce expected results. While primarily used for testing, `check-expect` can also assist in debugging by ensuring that functions maintain their correctness over time. By writing comprehensive test cases that cover various input scenarios, developers can detect regressions or unintended changes in behavior as they modify their code.

Beyond the tools within DrRacket, understanding and applying general debugging principles are equally important. One such principle is the practice of simplifying the problem. When faced with a bug, reducing the complexity of the code to the smallest reproducible example can be immensely helpful. By isolating the problematic code from other components, developers can more easily identify the root cause of the issue. This might involve creating minimal versions of functions or removing unrelated code to see if the problem persists.

Moreover, maintaining a systematic approach to debugging can prevent confusion and wasted effort. Start by reproducing the bug consistently to understand under what conditions it occurs. Next, gather as much information as possible about the error, including any error messages or unusual behavior. From there, use debugging tools and techniques to examine the state of the program and trace the problem's origin. Finally, implement a fix and verify its effectiveness by retesting the application.

Documenting the debugging process is another effective strategy. Keeping a record of the steps taken, observations made, and solutions implemented can provide insights into recurring issues and help streamline future debugging efforts. This documentation also serves as a reference for understanding complex bugs and their resolutions, contributing to a more efficient development workflow.

In addition to these strategies, leveraging Racket's profiling tools can provide insights into performance-related issues that might not be immediately obvious through standard debugging techniques. Profiling tools help identify performance bottlenecks by measuring how much time is spent in various parts of the code. This information can guide optimization efforts and improve the overall efficiency of the application.

Finally, collaboration and code review play a significant role in debugging. Engaging with peers or seeking feedback from other developers can bring new perspectives and solutions to challenging problems. Code reviews often uncover issues that might be overlooked by the original author and provide opportunities for learning and improvement.

In conclusion, mastering debugging techniques in Racket involves a combination of using the available tools effectively, applying systematic problem-solving approaches, and integrating best practices. By leveraging features like breakpoints, the REPL, and testing frameworks, and by adhering to debugging principles and documentation practices, developers can enhance their ability to identify, diagnose, and resolve issues in their Racket code.

Documenting the debugging process is also a critical practice. By keeping detailed notes on the problems encountered, the steps taken to diagnose and address them, and the outcomes of those efforts, you create a valuable resource for future reference. This documentation can help in identifying recurring issues and provide insight into the effectiveness of different debugging strategies. Additionally, it serves as a reference for understanding complex bugs and their solutions, which can be particularly useful for teams or when revisiting old projects.

Another important aspect of debugging is the use of version control systems. Tools like Git allow developers to track changes in their codebase, which can be incredibly useful for identifying when a particular issue was introduced. By reviewing commit history, you can pinpoint modifications that might have led to the bug. This practice not only aids in debugging but also supports a more structured and organized development workflow.

In Racket, you can leverage specific libraries and functions to assist in debugging. For example, the `racket/trace` library can be used to trace function calls and monitor their execution. This tool allows developers to insert tracing statements into their code, providing a detailed log of function invocations, arguments, and return values. Analyzing this trace information can reveal discrepancies between expected and actual behavior, helping to identify problematic areas in the code.

When dealing with memory-related issues, such as leaks or excessive usage, Racket's `racket/collects` library includes tools for monitoring memory consumption. The `racket/match` library also offers advanced pattern matching capabilities that can simplify complex data structures and improve code readability, reducing the likelihood of bugs related to data manipulation.

Another technique worth discussing is the practice of code reviews. Peer reviews can be an effective way to catch errors that might be missed during individual debugging efforts. By having another set of eyes examine the code, you can benefit from different perspectives and potentially identify issues that were overlooked. Code reviews also foster a collaborative environment where team members can share debugging techniques and best practices.

In addition to these tools and practices, it is crucial to adopt a mindset geared towards proactive problem-solving. Anticipating potential issues and addressing them before they manifest can significantly reduce debugging time. This approach involves writing clean, maintainable code and incorporating rigorous testing and error-handling mechanisms from the outset.

Consider incorporating design patterns and principles that promote robustness and reliability. For instance, using the principle of fail-fast programming, where errors are detected and reported as soon as they occur, can prevent issues from escalating and make debugging easier. Similarly, adhering to principles like separation of concerns and single responsibility can lead to more modular and testable code, reducing the likelihood of complex bugs.

Finally, it's important to stay updated with the latest debugging techniques and tools available in Racket. The programming landscape is continually evolving, and new debugging methods and utilities are regularly developed. Engaging with the Racket community, reading documentation, and experimenting with new tools can enhance your debugging skills and keep your practices current.

In conclusion, debugging is a multifaceted process that involves a combination of tools, techniques, and practices. Mastery of debugging in Racket requires a thorough understanding of available tools, the application of systematic approaches, and continuous learning and adaptation. By effectively leveraging debugging tools, adopting best practices, and maintaining a proactive mindset, you can significantly enhance the reliability and performance of your Racket applications.

CHAPTER 25: ADVANCED MACRO TECHNIQUES

Macros in Racket offer a powerful means to extend the language and tailor it to specific needs, significantly improving programming efficiency and flexibility. Building on foundational macro concepts, this section delves into more advanced techniques that can transform how you write and manage code. We will explore macro hygiene, macro expansion, and custom syntax extensions, providing detailed examples to illustrate each concept.

Macro hygiene is a critical concept when dealing with advanced macros. It ensures that macros behave predictably and avoid unintended interactions with their surrounding environment. In essence, macro hygiene prevents name collisions by properly managing variable bindings. Without hygiene, macros could inadvertently alter or clash with existing variables, leading to subtle bugs and unpredictable behavior. In Racket, hygiene is enforced through the use of `define-syntax` and `syntax-rules`, which abstract away the complexity of scope management. By leveraging these tools, you can create macros that operate in a controlled environment, minimizing the risk of unintended consequences.

To illustrate macro hygiene, consider a macro that generates code for defining a new function with specified parameters and body. For instance, you might define a macro `define-func` that simplifies the syntax for function definitions:

```racket
(define-syntax define-func
  (syntax-rules ()
    [(_ (name params ...) body ...)
     (define (name params ...)
       body ...)]))
```

Using `define-func`, you can create functions more succinctly:

```racket
(define-func add (x y)
  (+ x y))
```

This macro ensures that the function name and parameters are correctly scoped and do not interfere with other parts of the program. The hygiene provided by `syntax-rules` guarantees that the macro expansion does not unintentionally alter or clash with existing variables or definitions.

Next, we delve into macro expansion, a process where macros are transformed into Racket code before compilation. Understanding macro expansion is crucial for debugging and optimizing macros. The `syntax/parse` library in Racket offers a more advanced approach to macro expansion compared to `syntax-rules`. It provides a mechanism for defining macros with complex patterns and custom syntax, allowing for greater flexibility in macro creation.

For example, using `syntax/parse`, you can define a macro that creates a conditional expression based on the number of arguments provided:

```racket
(require syntax/parse)

(define-syntax-rule (conditional (test expr1 expr2 ...))
  (if test
      expr1
      (cond
        [else expr2 ...])))
```

Here, `syntax/parse` allows you to define macros that handle various input patterns more robustly. This approach enables more sophisticated macros that can adapt to different usage scenarios.

Custom syntax extensions offer another layer of advanced macro functionality. They allow you to define new syntactic constructs that can enhance the expressiveness of Racket. By extending the syntax, you can create domain-specific languages or integrate new language features seamlessly into your codebase.

Consider a scenario where you want to introduce a new control structure, such as a `while` loop, into Racket. You could create a macro that extends Racket's syntax to support this construct:

```racket
(define-syntax while
  (syntax-rules ()
    [(_ test body ...)
     (let loop ()
       (when test
         body ...
         (loop)))]))
```

This macro defines a `while` loop that repeatedly executes

the body while the test condition holds true. By using `while` in your code, you gain access to a familiar control structure without modifying the core language or its existing constructs.

Another example of custom syntax extension is defining a domain-specific language for a particular application. Suppose you are working on a configuration management system and want to introduce a concise syntax for defining configuration options. You could create a macro that translates this syntax into standard Racket code:

```racket
(define-syntax config
 (syntax-rules ()
  [(_ (option value ...))
   (define option value ...)]))
```

With this macro, you can define configuration options using a streamlined syntax that is easier to read and write. The macro expands to the underlying Racket code, allowing for a more intuitive configuration process.

In summary, mastering advanced macro techniques in Racket can greatly enhance your programming capabilities. By understanding and applying macro hygiene, macro expansion, and custom syntax extensions, you can create more robust, flexible, and efficient code. These techniques enable you to define new language constructs, streamline repetitive tasks, and tailor Racket to fit your specific needs. As you continue to explore and experiment with macros, you will discover new ways to leverage their power and integrate them seamlessly into your development workflow.

To extend the discussion on macro expansion, it is vital to comprehend how macros interact with the code they generate. One of the most compelling aspects of Racket's macro system is its ability to handle complex syntax transformations through custom expansion. Unlike `syntax-rules`, which is suitable for simpler macro definitions, `syntax/parse` offers a more granular approach to parsing and expanding macros.

For instance, consider a macro that creates a specialized logging function depending on the verbosity level of the logging. Using `syntax/parse`, you can define a macro that parses different verbosity levels and generates appropriate logging code:

```racket
(require syntax/parse)

(define-syntax-rule (define-logger name)
 (begin
   (define (name msg) (displayln (string-append "LOG: " msg)))
     (define (name-verbose msg) (displayln (string-append "VERBOSE LOG: " msg)))))

(define-logger my-logger)

(my-logger "This is a log message.")
(my-logger-verbose "This is a verbose log message.")
```

In this example, the `define-logger` macro generates two functions: `my-logger` and `my-logger-verbose`. The `syntax/parse` library allows you to handle different patterns and provide more complex macro transformations. By using custom parsing rules, you can create macros that cater to various syntactic needs, making your macros more powerful and flexible.

Moreover, custom syntax extensions are another advanced technique that can be employed to create domain-specific languages (DSLs) or extend the syntax of Racket itself. These extensions enable you to design new syntactic constructs tailored to your specific application requirements. For example, you might want to create a DSL for describing data transformations in a more expressive manner than what is available with standard Racket syntax.

To illustrate, let's define a macro that extends Racket with a new control structure for conditional logging. This control structure could look something like `when-verbose`, which only logs messages if a verbosity flag is set:

```racket
(require syntax/parse/define)

(define-syntax (when-verbose stx)
  (syntax-parse stx
   [(_ flag body ...)
    (with-syntax ([flag (if (syntax-e flag) (format "~a" (syntax-e flag)) t)])
      `(when flag
         body ...))]))

(define verbose? t)

(when-verbose verbose?
  (displayln "This message is logged only if verbose? is true."))
```

In this macro, `when-verbose` checks if the verbosity flag is set and only executes the body of the code if it is. The use of `syntax-parse` allows for sophisticated handling of input patterns, ensuring that the macro operates correctly in various contexts.

Another important aspect of advanced macros is understanding and managing macro expansion traces. Debugging macro expansions can be challenging, as the generated code might not always be immediately clear. Tools such as the `racket/match` library can be instrumental in inspecting and debugging macro expansions.

By incorporating the `racket/match` library, you can use pattern matching to analyze and understand the generated code from macros. This can help identify and resolve issues in macro definitions, leading to more reliable and maintainable macros.

```racket
(require racket/match)

(define-syntax (trace-macro-expansion stx)
  (syntax-case stx ()
    [(_ expr)
     (displayln (format "Expanding: ~a" (syntax-e expr)))
     (syntax/loc stx expr)]))

(trace-macro-expansion (define x 10))
```

In this example, `trace-macro-expansion` outputs the code that is being expanded, which can be invaluable for diagnosing issues with macro definitions.

Lastly, the ability to create macros that interact seamlessly with other language features is crucial for leveraging Racket's full potential. Advanced macros can encapsulate complex behavior, abstract repetitive patterns, and create higher-level constructs that streamline development. Mastery of these techniques requires not only a deep understanding of Racket's macro system but also practical experience in applying these techniques to real-world problems.

By developing sophisticated macros, you can significantly enhance your programming productivity, create cleaner and more expressive code, and build robust applications that leverage Racket's powerful metaprogramming capabilities. This advanced knowledge of macros will equip you with the tools to push the boundaries of what is possible with Racket, enabling you to tackle complex programming challenges with greater ease and effectiveness.

When advancing to more sophisticated macro techniques, the concept of macro hygiene becomes increasingly crucial. Macro hygiene ensures that macros do not inadvertently interfere with the identifiers in the code where they are used. This principle helps avoid common pitfalls such as name collisions and unintended variable capture, which can lead to subtle and difficult-to-debug errors.

Macro hygiene is fundamentally about controlling how macro expansions interact with the environment in which they are expanded. In Racket, this is typically handled through the use of `syntax` and `syntax-e` operations, which encapsulate and manipulate code during macro expansion. When defining macros, it is essential to carefully manage how identifiers are introduced and ensure they do not clash with existing names in the surrounding scope.

Consider a scenario where you are designing a macro to create a new kind of loop structure that abstracts over different looping constructs. Suppose you want to create a macro that generates a loop depending on the provided iteration count and a body of code to execute. You might write something like:

```racket
(define-syntax (repeat-macro stx)
  (syntax-parse stx
   [(_ count body ...)
    (with-syntax ([count (syntax-e count)])
     '(begin
        (for ([i (in-range count)])
         body ...)))]))
```

In this macro, `repeat-macro` generates a `for` loop based on the iteration count and the body provided. By using `syntax-parse`, the macro can ensure that the `count` is safely extracted and used within the generated code. This approach preserves hygiene by keeping the macro's identifiers distinct from those in the surrounding code.

Another key aspect of advanced macros is understanding how to handle macro expansion. Macros in Racket can be expanded in multiple stages, and the sequence of these expansions can influence the final behavior of the generated code. To explore this further, consider the use of `define-syntax` to create a macro that abstracts over different data structure operations. For example, you might create a macro to define a set of operations for a custom data structure:

```racket
(define-syntax (define-data-structure stx)
 (syntax-parse stx
  [(_ name (fields ...))
   (with-syntax ([name (syntax-e name)])
    '(begin
      (define-struct name (fields ...))
      (define (name-operation1 x) ...)
      (define (name-operation2 x) ...)))])
```

This macro, `define-data-structure`, generates a data structure definition along with associated operations. By encapsulating the operations and the structure definition within the macro, you create reusable and clean abstractions. This approach not only improves code readability but also simplifies maintenance.

Custom syntax extensions further illustrate the power of macros in Racket. These extensions allow you to create entirely new syntactic constructs, enhancing the expressiveness of the language for specific use cases. To achieve this, you might define a macro that adds a new control flow construct, such as a conditional block that executes only if a certain condition is met:

```racket
(define-syntax (when-true stx)
  (syntax-parse stx
    [(_ cond body ...)
     (with-syntax ([cond (syntax-e cond)])
       '(if cond
          (begin
            body ...)))]))
```

In this example, `when-true` acts as a conditional construct that executes the body if the condition evaluates to true. By defining this syntax extension, you extend the language with a new control structure tailored to your specific needs.

Finally, it is essential to test and debug macros carefully. Given that macros operate at the syntactic level, errors in macro definitions can lead to complex issues that are not always immediately apparent. Using Racket's built-in tools such as the `syntax/parse` library helps in ensuring that macros are correctly defined and expand as expected. Additionally, incorporating macro testing strategies, such as creating unit tests for macro-generated code, can greatly aid in validating their correctness.

By mastering these advanced macro techniques, you can significantly enhance your ability to write efficient, flexible, and robust Racket code. The skills you develop in managing macro hygiene, understanding macro expansion, and creating custom syntax extensions will empower you to create powerful abstractions and streamline your programming process.

CHAPTER 26: ERROR HANDLING AND EXCEPTIONS

Effective error handling is a cornerstone of robust software development. In Racket, managing errors gracefully and ensuring that your application can handle unexpected conditions is essential for creating reliable and resilient programs. This segment will delve into Racket's error handling mechanisms, including exception handling and custom error types, with a focus on constructs like `try`, `catch`, and others to help manage errors effectively.

Error handling in Racket relies on a few key constructs: `raise`, `with-handlers`, `try`, and `catch`. The primary tool for error handling in Racket is the `raise` function, which allows you to signal that an error condition has occurred. When you invoke `raise`, you pass an instance of an exception, which is a value representing an error. This value is then propagated up the call stack until it is caught by an appropriate handler.

For instance, suppose you are working on a function that performs division. You need to handle the case where the denominator might be zero, which would result in a division error. Here's how you might use `raise` to manage this:

```racket
(define (safe-divide x y)
```

```
  (if (zero? y)
    (raise (exn:fail:contract "Division by zero"))
    (/ x y)))
```

In this code, `raise` is used to signal an exception if the denominator is zero. The exception created is of type `exn:fail:contract`, a standard type used for contract failures in Racket.

To handle exceptions raised during the execution of your program, you use the `with-handlers` construct. This construct allows you to specify one or more handlers for different types of exceptions. When an exception is raised within the `with-handlers` body, Racket will attempt to match it with the provided handlers. Here's an example of how to use `with-handlers`:

```racket
(define (safe-divide x y)
    (with-handlers ([exn:fail:contract? (lambda (e) "Error: Division by zero")])
    (if (zero? y)
      (raise (exn:fail:contract "Division by zero"))
      (/ x y))))
```

In this example, if an exception of type `exn:fail:contract` is raised, it is caught by the handler specified in `with-handlers`, which returns a string indicating the error. This mechanism allows you to handle errors in a controlled manner and provide meaningful feedback to the user or logging system.

Beyond handling specific types of exceptions, you might need to define your own custom error types to represent application-specific error conditions. Racket allows you to create custom exceptions by using the `define-syntax` and `raise` constructs. You can define a custom error type like this:

```racket
(define-syntax (define-custom-error stx)
  (syntax-parse stx
   [(_ name)
    (with-syntax ([name (syntax-e name)])
     '(define (name msg) (raise (exn:fail:custom msg))))]))
```

In this snippet, `define-custom-error` is a macro that creates a custom error type. When you use this macro, it generates a function that raises an exception of type `exn:fail:custom` with the provided message. This approach allows you to create meaningful and descriptive error types that can be tailored to the specific needs of your application.

Another useful construct in error handling is `try`, which simplifies exception handling by providing a more streamlined approach to catching exceptions. Here's an example of how `try` can be used:

```racket
(define (safe-divide x y)
  (try (lambda ()
         (if (zero? y)
             (raise (exn:fail:contract "Division by zero"))
             (/ x y)))
       [exn:fail:contract? (lambda (e) "Error: Division by zero")]))
```

In this code, `try` is used to encapsulate the code that may raise an exception. If an exception occurs, the specified handler is invoked. This pattern helps in writing more concise and readable error-handling code.

Additionally, Racket supports error handling for more

complex scenarios involving asynchronous operations or multiple possible sources of errors. For instance, you might use `with-handlers` in conjunction with concurrency constructs like threads, where each thread may need its own error handling logic.

To summarize, effective error handling in Racket involves understanding and utilizing constructs like `raise`, `with-handlers`, and `try`, along with creating and managing custom error types. By carefully employing these techniques, you can ensure that your programs handle unexpected conditions gracefully, providing robust and user-friendly error management.

In Racket, another important mechanism for error handling is the `try` construct, which is part of the `racket/try` library. This construct provides a way to handle errors that occur during the execution of a block of code, allowing you to specify both the code to be executed and the code to handle any exceptions that may be raised. The `try` construct is useful when you want to encapsulate error-prone operations and handle exceptions in a structured manner.

Here's a basic example of how `try` can be used:

```racket
(require racket/try)

(define (safe-divide x y)
  (try
    (/ x y)
    (catch exn:fail:contract? (lambda (e) "Error: Division by zero"))))
```

In this example, the `try` block attempts to perform the division. If an exception is raised during this operation, the `catch` clause handles it, providing a message indicating the error. This approach is particularly useful when you have multiple error-prone operations within a single block and want to handle exceptions in a unified way.

Beyond basic error handling, Racket allows you to define custom error types. Custom errors are useful when you need to represent specific error conditions that are not covered by standard exception types. You can create custom error types using the `define-struct` construct in combination with `exn:fail` to define your own error objects. Here's an example of defining and using a custom error type:

```racket
(define-struct custom-error (message))

(define (safe-divide x y)
  (if (zero? y)
    (raise (make-custom-error "Division by zero"))
    (/ x y)))

(define (handle-error)
  (with-handlers ([custom-error? (lambda (e) (format "Custom Error: ~a" (custom-error-message e)))])
    (safe-divide 10 0)))
```

In this code, `define-struct` is used to create a `custom-error` struct with a `message` field. The `raise` function is then used to create an instance of this custom error type if a division by zero is detected. The `with-handlers` construct is employed to handle this custom error, displaying a formatted error message.

Error handling in Racket also involves understanding the different categories of exceptions and how to manage them effectively. The `exn` family of types includes several specific exception types such as `exn:fail:contract`, `exn:fail:network`, and `exn:fail:syntax`. Each of these types represents different kinds of errors, and handling them appropriately requires knowing which type of exception to expect. For example, `exn:fail:network` would be used for errors related to network operations, while `exn:fail:syntax` would be used for syntax errors.

For debugging and logging purposes, Racket provides utilities for inspecting and managing exception data. The `exn-message` function extracts the error message from an exception, while `exn:fail:contract?` is used to check if an exception is a contract failure. These functions can be instrumental in diagnosing issues and improving error handling strategies.

When working with asynchronous operations or multi-threaded code, error handling becomes even more critical. Racket's concurrency primitives, such as `thread` and `place`, introduce additional complexities for error management. In multi-threaded environments, exceptions raised in one thread do not automatically propagate to other threads. Instead, you need to explicitly handle exceptions within each thread and potentially communicate errors back to the main thread or the thread that initiated the operation.

Here's a basic example of handling exceptions in a multi-threaded context:

```racket
(define (threaded-operation)
    (define th (thread (lambda () (try (/ 1 0) (catch exn:fail:contract? (lambda (e) "Thread error"))))))
  (thread-wait th))
```

In this example, a new thread is created to perform a division operation. The `try` construct is used within the thread to handle any exceptions that might occur, ensuring that the thread does not terminate abruptly without proper error handling.

As you develop more complex applications, it is essential to build a robust error handling strategy that covers all potential failure points. This involves not only handling exceptions but also designing your code to fail gracefully and recover from errors whenever possible. By leveraging Racket's error handling constructs and custom error types, you can create more reliable and user-friendly applications that effectively manage unexpected conditions.

In addition to the constructs already discussed, Racket provides a suite of error handling utilities that further enhance your ability to manage and recover from errors. One such utility is the `with-handlers` form, which allows you to specify a set of handlers for different types of exceptions. This is particularly useful when you want to handle errors in a more granular manner, responding differently based on the type of error encountered.

Here's an illustrative example of using `with-handlers` to manage different types of errors:

```racket
(define (safe-operation x y)
    (with-handlers ([exn:fail:contract? (lambda (e) (format "Contract Error: ~a" (exn-message e)))])
    (with-handlers ([exn:fail? (lambda (e) (format "General Error: ~a" (exn-message e)))])
      (/ x y))))
```

In this example, `with-handlers` is nested to handle different types of exceptions. The outer `with-handlers` clause catches errors related to contract violations, while the inner clause catches general exceptions. This approach enables you to tailor your error responses based on specific conditions, providing more detailed feedback and allowing for more refined error recovery strategies.

Another important aspect of error handling in Racket is the ability to inspect and manipulate exception objects directly. This can be valuable for debugging and understanding the context in which an error occurred. Exception objects in Racket are structured with several fields, including the message and the condition that caused the error. By examining these fields, you can gain insights into what went wrong and why.

Consider the following example where we inspect an exception to provide a more detailed error report:

```racket
(define (detailed-error-report x y)
  (with-handlers ([exn:fail? (lambda (e)
              (format "Error: ~a\nCondition: ~a\nStack Trace: ~a"
                      (exn-message e)
                      (exn-condition e)
                      (exn-stacktrace e)))])
    (/ x y)))
```

Here, the `with-handlers` form captures general exceptions and generates a detailed error report that includes the exception message, condition, and stack trace. This detailed reporting can be crucial for diagnosing complex issues and ensuring that errors are addressed appropriately.

Additionally, Racket supports error propagation through its `raise` mechanism, which allows exceptions to be passed up the call stack until they are caught by an appropriate handler. This feature is useful when you want to handle errors at a higher level in your application, after they have been processed or partially handled at a lower level. By raising exceptions, you can delegate error management to components that are better equipped to handle them, adhering to the principle of separation of concerns.

For example, if you have a function that performs a series of operations, you might choose to raise an exception when a critical error occurs, allowing the caller to decide how to respond:

```racket
(define (perform-critical-operation x y)
  (if (zero? y)
     (raise (exn:fail:contract "Critical error: Division by zero"))
     (/ x y)))

(define (main)
   (with-handlers ([exn:fail:contract? (lambda (e) (format "Caught critical error: ~a" (exn-message e)))])
   (perform-critical-operation 10 0)))
```

In this example, the `perform-critical-operation` function raises an exception if a division by zero is detected. The `main` function catches this exception and provides a meaningful message, demonstrating how error propagation and handling can be combined to manage errors effectively across different layers of an application.

Moreover, error handling in Racket extends beyond exceptions and custom error types to encompass debugging practices that can aid in diagnosing and resolving issues. Tools such as the `racket/trace` library enable you to trace function calls and monitor the flow of execution, which can be invaluable when trying to pinpoint the source of an error. By incorporating these debugging tools into your development workflow, you can enhance your ability to understand and fix issues that arise during runtime.

In summary, Racket offers a comprehensive set of

tools for handling errors and exceptions, including `try`, `with-handlers`, custom error types, and error propagation mechanisms. By mastering these techniques and incorporating detailed error reporting and debugging practices into your development process, you can build robust applications that are resilient to unexpected conditions and easier to maintain and troubleshoot.

CHAPTER 27: METAPROGRAMMING AND REFLECTION

Metaprogramming is a powerful paradigm that allows programs to generate, analyze, and transform code dynamically. In Racket, this capability is not only a fundamental aspect of the language but also a critical tool for enhancing flexibility and reducing redundancy in code. To understand metaprogramming in Racket, one must first grasp the concept of reflection and how it intersects with code generation.

Reflection in Racket involves examining and modifying the program's own structure at runtime. This feature allows developers to introspect the types, values, and even the behavior of their code, facilitating a deeper level of interaction and manipulation. For instance, Racket's `syntax` and `define-syntax` forms enable the creation and evaluation of code that generates or modifies other code. This allows for sophisticated metaprogramming techniques that can lead to more concise and adaptable codebases.

Consider the use of `syntax-rules`, a macro system in Racket, which provides a means to create new syntactic constructs. `syntax-rules` operates by pattern matching against the syntax of the code, enabling developers to write macros that transform code based on predefined patterns. This approach abstracts away the complexities of code manipulation, allowing programmers to define new language constructs that can simplify their programming tasks.

For example, one can define a simple macro that generates a sequence of arithmetic operations:

```racket
(define-syntax (make-adder stx)
 (syntax-case stx ()
  [(_ n)
   (with-syntax ([add (datum->syntax stx '+)])
    '(lambda (x) (add x n)))]))
```

In this example, the `make-adder` macro creates a function that adds a specific number to its argument. By using `syntax-case`, the macro pattern matches the input and generates a lambda function with the desired arithmetic operation. This demonstrates how Racket's metaprogramming facilities can be used to produce reusable and modular code components.

Reflection in Racket also extends to the ability to examine and manipulate the program's runtime environment. Functions like `eval` allow for the execution of code that is constructed as data at runtime. This dynamic execution capability can be leveraged to build flexible applications that adapt to varying conditions or inputs.

For instance, consider a scenario where you need to evaluate user-generated code safely:

```racket
(define (safe-eval expr)
    (with-handlers ([exn:fail? (lambda (e) (format "Error: ~a" (exn-message e)))])
     (eval expr)))
```

In this function, `safe-eval` attempts to evaluate an expression while handling potential errors gracefully. By incorporating error handling within the evaluation process, you can mitigate the risks associated with executing arbitrary code, thus enhancing the robustness of your application.

Furthermore, Racket's metaprogramming capabilities extend to code generation, where you can write code that generates other code. This feature is particularly useful for creating domain-specific languages (DSLs) or for automating repetitive coding tasks. For example, if you are developing a library that needs to handle multiple data formats, you can use metaprogramming to generate code that adapts to each format without manually writing redundant code.

Consider a DSL for defining mathematical operations:

```racket
(define-syntax (define-operation stx)
  (syntax-case stx ()
   [(_ name op)
    (with-syntax ([name (datum->syntax stx name)])
     '(define (name a b) (op a b)))]))
```

In this macro, `define-operation` generates functions for various mathematical operations based on the provided operator. By using this macro, you can define functions like addition and subtraction succinctly:

```racket
(define-operation add +)
(define-operation subtract -)
```

Here, `define-operation` automates the creation of functions for different operations, showcasing how metaprogramming can streamline the development process and reduce boilerplate code.

Another advanced aspect of Racket's metaprogramming is the use of `syntax-parse`, which provides a more powerful and flexible macro system compared to `syntax-rules`. `syntax-parse` allows for more complex pattern matching and transformation, enabling the creation of highly customizable macros that can adapt to a wide range of programming needs.

For example, you can define a macro using `syntax-parse` that handles optional arguments:

```racket
(define-syntax (optional-args stx)
 (syntax-parse stx
  [(_ (optional a b) ... )
   '(begin
     (displayln "Optional argument processing:")
     (displayln a)
     (displayln b))]))
```

This macro processes optional arguments and generates code accordingly. The use of `syntax-parse` enables sophisticated parsing and code generation, illustrating the advanced capabilities of Racket's macro system.

Through these examples, it becomes clear that metaprogramming and reflection in Racket provide a robust set of tools for dynamic code manipulation and generation. By leveraging these capabilities, developers can write more flexible, reusable, and maintainable code, ultimately enhancing their programming efficiency and effectiveness.

To effectively leverage metaprogramming in Racket, it's essential to understand the nuances of code generation and manipulation. In Racket, macros and reflection provide powerful tools for creating flexible and dynamic programs.

Code generation, a crucial aspect of metaprogramming, allows us to construct and execute code based on varying conditions or inputs. This technique is particularly useful when dealing with repetitive or boilerplate code, as it enables developers to automate and generalize code patterns.

One prominent feature of Racket for code generation is the `define-syntax` construct, which provides a means to define new syntactic constructs by specifying patterns and transformations. This construct utilizes Racket's macro system, which operates by pattern matching and transforming code snippets. For example, the `syntax-parse` library offers an advanced way to define and handle macros with complex patterns and contextual information. This library is an extension of Racket's macro system, providing enhanced capabilities for parsing and manipulating syntax.

Consider a situation where you need to create multiple similar data structures with slight variations. Instead of manually defining each structure, you can use macros to generate them dynamically. For instance, suppose you need to define several record types with similar fields but different names. You can use a macro to automate this process:

```racket
lang racket
(require syntax/parse/define)

(define-syntax (define-record stx)
 (syntax-parse stx
  [(_ (name field1 field2 ...))
   (with-syntax ([record-name (datum->syntax stx name)])
    '(define-record-type record-name
       [field1 field2 ...]))]))

(define-record (Person name age))
(define-record (Address street city))
```

In this example, the `define-record` macro generates definitions for multiple record types, reducing redundancy and improving maintainability. The `syntax-parse` library facilitates pattern matching and context-aware transformations, making it easier to define complex macros.

Another critical aspect of metaprogramming in Racket is reflection, which allows a program to introspect and manipulate its own structure and behavior. Racket provides several functions for reflection, such as `eval`, which evaluates code represented as data, and `dynamic-require`, which loads modules dynamically at runtime. These functions are invaluable for creating flexible and adaptive systems.

For example, you can use `eval` to construct and execute code snippets dynamically based on user input or runtime conditions:

```racket
(define (dynamic-expression expr)
  (eval expr (current-module)))

(dynamic-expression '(+ 1 2)) ; Evaluates to 3
```

In this example, the `dynamic-expression` function takes a list representing an expression and evaluates it using `eval`. This allows the code to be constructed and executed dynamically, providing a high degree of flexibility.

Reflection also plays a significant role in debugging and testing. By inspecting and manipulating the program's runtime state, developers can gain insights into the program's behavior and identify issues more effectively. For example, Racket's `trace` function can be used to monitor function calls and their arguments, helping to diagnose performance bottlenecks or logic errors:

```racket
(require racket/trace)

(define (add x y)
  (+ x y))

(trace add)
(add 1 2) ; Traced output will show the function call and its arguments
```

In this example, `trace` is used to monitor the `add` function, providing information about its invocation and arguments. This can be particularly useful for understanding complex interactions and ensuring that the program behaves as expected.

Finally, metaprogramming in Racket also involves custom syntax extensions, which enable the creation of new language constructs tailored to specific needs. By defining custom syntax rules and transformations, developers can extend Racket's syntax to support domain-specific languages or other specialized constructs. For instance, you can create a domain-specific language for querying databases or defining custom control structures, enhancing the expressiveness and usability of your code.

In summary, metaprogramming in Racket offers a rich set of tools and techniques for creating flexible, dynamic, and efficient programs. By mastering reflection and code generation, developers can automate repetitive tasks, adapt to changing conditions, and extend the language to suit their needs. Whether through macros, reflective functions, or custom syntax extensions, Racket provides powerful mechanisms for enhancing programming efficiency and capability.

Exploring the depths of Racket's reflective capabilities reveals a potent toolkit for creating highly adaptable and dynamic software systems. At the heart of reflection is the ability to inspect and modify a program's structure and behavior at runtime, which can significantly enhance the flexibility and expressiveness of your code.

A key function for reflection in Racket is `eval`, which executes code that is represented as data. This function allows you to construct and evaluate code snippets dynamically, making it possible to generate code based on runtime conditions. For instance, if you need to build a function that can handle various data types or operations based on user input or external data, you can use `eval` to construct and run the necessary code on-the-fly. Here's an example illustrating how `eval` can be used to define a function dynamically:

```racket
lang racket

(define (create-adder n)
  (eval `(define (adder x) (+ x ,n))))


(create-adder 10)
(adder 5) ; This will output 15
```

In this example, `create-adder` uses `eval` to generate a function `adder` that adds a specific value to its input. By passing different values to `create-adder`, you can create various adder functions without manually writing each one.

Another powerful reflective feature in Racket is `dynamic-require`, which allows you to load and use modules at runtime. This capability is particularly useful for applications that need to load plugins or modules based on user configuration or other runtime factors. By dynamically requiring modules, you can build extensible systems where the functionality can be extended or modified without altering the core application code. Here's a basic example:

```racket
lang racket

(define my-module (dynamic-require '("path/to/module.rkt") 'module-function))

(my-module) ; Call the function from the dynamically loaded module
```

In this code, `dynamic-require` loads a module from a specified path and retrieves a function from that module, allowing you to invoke it. This approach enables your program to remain flexible and modular, as it can adapt to new modules or changes in configuration without needing a recompilation or restart.

The integration of macros with reflection further enhances the power of metaprogramming in Racket. Macros can generate code that includes reflective operations, allowing you to create highly specialized and efficient code constructs. For instance, you can design macros that automate common patterns of code involving reflection or dynamic behavior. This capability is particularly useful for building domain-specific languages (DSLs) or for implementing advanced programming paradigms.

Consider a scenario where you want to create a macro that generates functions with dynamic behavior based on parameters passed to it. You can combine macros and reflection to achieve this:

```racket
lang racket

(require (for-syntax syntax/parse/define))
```

```
(define-syntax (define-dynamic-function stx)
 (syntax-parse stx
  [(_ (name arg) body)
   (with-syntax ([func-name (datum->syntax stx name)])
    '(define (func-name arg)
      (eval `(lambda (x) ,body))))]))

(define-dynamic-function (dynamic-adder x)
 (+ x 10))

(dynamic-adder 5) ; This will output 15
```

Here, `define-dynamic-function` is a macro that generates a function with dynamic behavior. The generated function uses `eval` to execute the code provided in its body. This pattern allows you to create functions with complex behavior determined at runtime, enhancing the flexibility and expressiveness of your code.

In summary, Racket's support for metaprogramming through reflection and macros provides powerful mechanisms for developing dynamic and adaptable software. By utilizing reflective capabilities like `eval` and `dynamic-require`, along with sophisticated macro techniques, you can create highly flexible and efficient programs. These tools not only streamline the development process but also enable you to build complex and responsive systems that can evolve with changing requirements and conditions.

CHAPTER 28: INTERACTING WITH DATABASES

Interacting with databases is a crucial skill in software development, especially when dealing with applications that require persistent data storage and complex data retrieval. Racket provides several mechanisms for connecting to both SQL and NoSQL databases, executing queries, and managing transactions. This exploration into Racket's database interaction capabilities will guide you through the process of integrating databases into your applications effectively.

To start with, connecting to SQL databases in Racket typically involves using external libraries that provide the necessary functionality for database communication. One commonly used library for this purpose is `db` from the Racket package repository. This library supports a range of SQL databases, including SQLite, PostgreSQL, and MySQL.

First, you need to install the required database driver. For instance, if you are working with SQLite, you can install the `db` package using Racket's package manager:

```racket
(require db)
```

Once the library is included, you can establish a connection to your SQLite database using the `sqlite3` function. Here's a basic example of how to connect to a database and execute a simple query:

```racket
lang racket

(require db)

(define conn (sqlite3-connect :database "example.db"))

(define (create-table)
  (send conn exec "CREATE TABLE IF NOT EXISTS users (id INTEGER PRIMARY KEY, name TEXT)"))

(define (insert-user name)
  (send conn exec "INSERT INTO users (name) VALUES (?)" name))

(define (get-users)
 (query conn "SELECT FROM users"))
```

In this example, `sqlite3-connect` establishes a connection to the SQLite database file `example.db`. The `create-table` function creates a `users` table if it does not already exist. The `insert-user` function inserts a new user into the table, and `get-users` retrieves all users from the table.

For other SQL databases like PostgreSQL or MySQL, you would use similar functions provided by the respective database libraries, with minor adjustments for connection parameters and query syntax.

When it comes to interacting with NoSQL databases, Racket offers libraries for various systems such as MongoDB. The `racket-mongodb` package, for example, provides an interface for working with MongoDB. To use this package, you first need to install it and then establish a connection as follows:

```racket
(require mongodb)

(define conn (mongodb-connect :host "localhost" :port 27017))

(define (insert-doc collection doc)
  (mongodb-insert conn "mydb" collection doc))

(define (find-documents collection query)
  (mongodb-find conn "mydb" collection query))
```

In this code snippet, `mongodb-connect` connects to a MongoDB instance running on `localhost` at port `27017`. The `insert-doc` function inserts a document into a specified collection, while `find-documents` retrieves documents that match a given query.

Managing transactions is another critical aspect of database interaction, particularly in SQL databases where atomicity and consistency are essential. Transactions allow you to execute a sequence of operations as a single unit, which can be committed or rolled back depending on whether the operations succeed or fail.

In Racket, transactions with SQL databases can be managed using the `transaction` function provided by the `db` library. Here's an example demonstrating how to use transactions to ensure that a series of database operations are executed atomically:

```racket
(define (perform-transaction)
  (with-transaction
    (lambda ()
      (send conn exec "UPDATE accounts SET balance  balance - 100 WHERE id  ?" 1)
      (send conn exec "UPDATE accounts SET balance  balance +
```

100 WHERE id ?" 2))))
```

In this example, the `with-transaction` macro ensures that the updates to the `accounts` table are treated as a single transaction. If an error occurs during one of the operations, the entire transaction is rolled back, ensuring that no partial updates are committed.

Effective error handling during database interactions is also important. You should anticipate and handle exceptions that may arise from database operations, such as connectivity issues or query syntax errors. Racket's error handling mechanisms, such as `with-handlers` and `raise`, can be employed to manage such scenarios gracefully.

```racket
(define (safe-query query)
    (with-handlers ([exn:fail:database? (lambda (e) (printf "Database error: ~a\n" e))])
    (query conn query)))
```

In this example, `with-handlers` is used to catch and handle any database-related exceptions that occur during the execution of the `safe-query` function. This approach helps in providing informative error messages and ensuring that your application can recover from unexpected conditions.

Understanding and utilizing these techniques for interacting with SQL and NoSQL databases in Racket allows you to build robust applications that can efficiently handle data storage and retrieval. Whether you're managing simple relational data or complex document-based structures, Racket's database libraries and error handling features equip you with the tools necessary to develop reliable and performant database-driven applications.
```

When working with NoSQL databases like MongoDB in Racket, the approach differs from SQL databases due to the schema-less nature of NoSQL systems. MongoDB is a document-oriented database, which means it stores data in JSON-like documents rather than in structured tables. The `racket-mongodb` package provides the necessary tools to interact with MongoDB databases. To begin using this package, you must first install it and then establish a connection to your MongoDB server.

Here is an example of how to connect to a MongoDB database and perform basic operations such as inserting and querying documents:

```racket
lang racket

(require mongo)

(define db (mongo-connect :host "localhost" :port 27017 :db "example"))

(define (insert-document collection document)
  (mongo-insert db collection document))

(define (find-documents collection query)
  (mongo-find db collection query))
```

In this example, `mongo-connect` connects to a MongoDB instance running on `localhost` at port `27017`, using the database named `example`. The `insert-document` function inserts a document into a specified collection, while the `find-documents` function retrieves documents that match a query from a specified collection. The flexibility of NoSQL databases like MongoDB allows for dynamic schemas, meaning that you can store documents with different structures in the same collection.

Another important aspect of database interaction is managing transactions. Transactions ensure that a series of operations are executed atomically, meaning either all operations succeed, or none of them do. This is particularly important in SQL databases to maintain data integrity. In Racket, transaction management is often handled through the database library's API.

For example, when using SQL databases with Racket, you can manage transactions by explicitly starting and committing or rolling back transactions. Here's how you might handle transactions using the `db` package with SQLite:

```racket
lang racket

(require db)

(define conn (sqlite3-connect :database "example.db"))

(define (begin-transaction)
  (send conn exec "BEGIN TRANSACTION"))

(define (commit-transaction)
  (send conn exec "COMMIT"))

(define (rollback-transaction)
  (send conn exec "ROLLBACK"))

(define (perform-transaction)
  (begin-transaction)
  (let ([result (try
          (insert-user "Alice")
          (insert-user "Bob")
          (commit-transaction)
          (values 'success)
          (catch exn:fail?
            (lambda (e)
              (rollback-transaction)
```

```
        (values 'failure)))]))
  (if (equal? result 'success)
    (displayln "Transaction successful")
    (displayln "Transaction failed"))))
```

In this script, `begin-transaction`, `commit-transaction`, and `rollback-transaction` functions are used to manage transactions. The `perform-transaction` function demonstrates a typical transaction workflow where multiple operations are attempted within a transaction. If any operation fails, the transaction is rolled back to maintain data consistency.

For NoSQL databases, transaction management varies depending on the database system. MongoDB, for example, supports multi-document transactions starting from version 4.0, allowing you to ensure atomicity across multiple documents within a single database.

Error handling is another crucial aspect of interacting with databases. When dealing with database operations, errors can occur due to various reasons such as connectivity issues, query syntax errors, or data constraints violations. Racket's error handling mechanisms, such as `try` and `catch`, can be employed to gracefully handle such exceptions.

For example, in the context of interacting with a SQL database, you might use `try` and `catch` to handle errors during query execution:

```racket
lang racket

(require db)

(define conn (sqlite3-connect :database "example.db"))

(define (safe-query query)
```

```
(try
 (lambda ()
  (send conn exec query))
 (catch exn:fail?
  (lambda (e)
   (displayln (format "Error: ~a" (exn-message e))))))
```
```

In this code snippet, `safe-query` attempts to execute a SQL query, and if an error occurs, it catches the exception and displays an appropriate error message. This approach allows you to handle database-related errors without terminating the application abruptly.

In summary, interacting with databases in Racket involves using various libraries and techniques tailored to different types of databases. SQL databases require managing connections, executing queries, and handling transactions, while NoSQL databases like MongoDB offer flexible data storage and querying capabilities. Effective error handling and transaction management are crucial for ensuring data integrity and application reliability. By leveraging Racket's database libraries and handling mechanisms, you can build robust applications that efficiently manage data storage and retrieval.

When interacting with databases in Racket, managing connections and transactions effectively is crucial to ensure data consistency and integrity. This section explores how to handle transactions and connection pooling, which are essential for robust database interactions.

To handle transactions in Racket using SQL databases, such as SQLite, you need to manage the transaction lifecycle explicitly. Transactions ensure that a sequence of operations either all succeed or all fail, maintaining the database's consistency. In practice, this involves beginning a transaction, executing a series of operations, and then either committing the
```

transaction if all operations succeed or rolling it back if any operation fails.

Here's an example of managing transactions using SQLite with Racket:

```racket
lang racket

(require db)

(define conn (sqlite3-connect :database "example.db"))

(define (begin-transaction)
  (send conn exec "BEGIN TRANSACTION"))

(define (commit-transaction)
  (send conn exec "COMMIT"))

(define (rollback-transaction)
  (send conn exec "ROLLBACK"))

(define (perform-transaction)
  (begin-transaction)
  (let ([success t])
    (try
      (send conn exec "INSERT INTO users (name, age) VALUES ('Alice', 30)")
      (send conn exec "UPDATE users SET age 31 WHERE name 'Alice'")
      (if success
        (commit-transaction)
        (rollback-transaction))
    (catch exn
      (rollback-transaction)))))
```

In this example, `perform-transaction` starts a transaction, performs two operations (inserting and updating data), and commits the transaction if both operations succeed. If an exception occurs, the transaction is rolled back to ensure no partial updates are applied. This pattern helps maintain the integrity of the database, especially in scenarios involving multiple related updates.

When dealing with NoSQL databases like MongoDB, transaction management can be a bit different. MongoDB supports multi-document transactions, but they require careful handling to ensure consistency. For example, using the `mongodb` package, transactions are managed as follows:

```racket
lang racket

(require mongo)

(define db (mongo-connect :host "localhost" :port 27017 :db "example"))

(define (perform-mongo-transaction)
  (define session (mongo-start-session db))
  (mongo-start-transaction session)
  (let ([success t])
    (try
      (mongo-insert db "users" :session session '((name . "Alice") (age . 30)))
      (mongo-update db "users" :session session :query '((name . "Alice"))
                    :update '((set (age . 31))))
      (if success
          (mongo-commit-transaction session)
          (mongo-abort-transaction session))
      (catch exn
        (mongo-abort-transaction session)))))
```

In this example, `perform-mongo-transaction` initiates a transaction session, performs operations within the transaction, and commits or aborts the transaction based on whether the operations succeed. MongoDB transactions are more complex due to their support for multi-document operations, which must be managed carefully to ensure consistency across documents.

Connection pooling is another crucial aspect of interacting with databases, especially in applications with high concurrency. Connection pooling allows for the reuse of database connections, which reduces the overhead associated with establishing new connections for each database operation.

In Racket, connection pooling for SQL databases can be managed using libraries that support connection pooling. For example, with the `db` package, connection pooling is not directly supported, but you can implement a simple pooling mechanism manually. Here's a basic example:

```racket
lang racket

(require db)

(define pool (make-parameter '()))

(define (initialize-pool size)
  (set! pool (make-parameter (for/list ([i (in-range size)])
               (sqlite3-connect :database "example.db")))))

(define (get-connection)
  (parameterize ([pool (lambda () (first (pool)))])
   (parameterize ([pool (lambda () (rest (pool)))])
    (first (pool)))))

(define (return-connection conn)
  (parameterize ([pool (lambda () (append (pool) (list conn)))])
     (set! pool (parameterize ([pool (lambda () (list conn))])
(pool)))))
```

```

In this code, `initialize-pool` creates a pool of database connections, while `get-connection` and `return-connection` manage the allocation and deallocation of connections. This simple pooling mechanism helps manage database connections more efficiently in applications with multiple concurrent requests.

By understanding and implementing these techniques, you can effectively manage database interactions in Racket, ensuring that your applications handle data storage and retrieval efficiently while maintaining the integrity and performance of your database systems.
```

CHAPTER 29: BUILDING COMMAND-LINE TOOLS

Creating command-line tools is an essential skill for automating tasks, scripting, and integrating various components of a system. In Racket, building such tools involves several key aspects: parsing command-line arguments, formatting output, and interacting with the operating system. This section delves into each of these aspects, providing a comprehensive guide to creating robust and user-friendly command-line applications.

The first step in building a command-line tool in Racket is to parse command-line arguments. Racket provides a simple yet powerful way to handle command-line arguments using the `racket/argparse` library. This library facilitates the definition of options and arguments for your command-line application, making it easier to process user inputs and configure the tool's behavior. Here's an example of how to use this library to define and parse arguments:

```racket
lang racket

(require racket/argparse)
```

```
(define parser
  (new command-line-parser%
    [args '("program" "--option VALUE")]
    [description "A simple command-line tool."]
    [options (list
          (make-option
           [name '--input]
           [type 'string]
           [description "Input file"]
           [default "default.txt"])
          (make-option
           [name '--verbose]
           [type 'boolean]
           [description "Enable verbose output"]
           [default f])])]))

(define (main args)
  (define-values (input verbose) (parse-command-line parser args))
  (if verbose
      (printf "Verbose mode enabled.\n"))
  (printf "Input file: ~a\n" input))

(main (current-command-line-arguments))
```
```

In this code, `command-line-parser%` is used to define the command-line options `--input` and `--verbose`. The `parse-command-line` function is then used to process these options and retrieve their values. This setup allows the tool to handle various inputs and configurations specified by the user.

Next, formatting output is a crucial aspect of building command-line tools. Racket provides several functions for output formatting, including `printf`, `display`, and `write`. Depending on the needs of your tool, you might use `printf` for formatted strings, `display` for simple text
```

output, or `write` for more complex data representations. Here's an example of how to format output for a command-line tool:

```racket
lang racket

(define (format-output data verbose)
 (if verbose
   (printf "Verbose Output:\n~a\n" data)
   (printf "Output: ~a\n" data)))

(define (main args)
  (define-values (input verbose) (parse-command-line parser args))
  (format-output (file->string input) verbose))

(main (current-command-line-arguments))
```

In this example, the `format-output` function is used to control the output format based on the `verbose` flag. If `verbose` is `t`, a more detailed output is provided; otherwise, a simpler output is displayed. This approach enhances the usability of the command-line tool by allowing different levels of verbosity.

Finally, integrating with the operating system is often necessary for command-line tools, especially when interacting with files, directories, or environment variables. Racket's standard library provides functions for these tasks. For example, you can use `file->string` to read the contents of a file, `directory-list` to list files in a directory, and `getenv` to retrieve environment variables. Here's a demonstration of these functions in a command-line tool context:

```racket
lang racket
```

```
(require racket/file)

(define (process-file file-path)
  (if (file-exists? file-path)
    (let ([content (file->string file-path)])
      (printf "File content:\n~a\n" content))
    (printf "File does not exist: ~a\n" file-path)))

(define (main args)
  (define-values (input verbose) (parse-command-line parser args))
  (process-file input))

(main (current-command-line-arguments))
```
` ` `

In this code snippet, `process-file` checks if a file exists and reads its content if it does. This functionality is crucial for tools that need to work with file systems. By incorporating these features, you can build command-line tools that are both powerful and user-friendly.

In summary, building command-line tools in Racket involves defining and parsing command-line arguments, formatting output appropriately, and integrating with the operating system for tasks such as file handling and environment interaction. By leveraging Racket's libraries and functions, you can create robust command-line applications that automate tasks and streamline workflows effectively.

When creating command-line tools, another important consideration is how to interact with the operating system. This involves performing tasks such as reading and writing files, executing external commands, and managing system processes. Racket offers several libraries and functions to facilitate these interactions, making it easier to integrate your command-line tools with the underlying operating system.

One of the fundamental tasks in command-line tools is file manipulation. Racket's `racket/file` library provides functions to handle file operations such as reading, writing, and checking file existence. For example, to read the contents of a file and process them, you might use the `file->string` function:

```racket
lang racket

(require racket/file)

(define (read-file filename)
  (with-input-from-file filename
    (lambda ()
      (let loop ([line (read-line)])
        (unless (eof-object? line)
          (printf "Read line: ~a\n" line)
          (loop (read-line)))))))

(read-file "example.txt")
```

In this snippet, `with-input-from-file` is used to open the file, and `read-line` reads each line until the end of the file is reached. This approach is useful for processing text files line by line.

Similarly, writing to files can be accomplished using `with-output-to-file` and `fprintf`:

```racket
lang racket

(require racket/file)

(define (write-file filename content)
  (with-output-to-file filename
    (lambda ()
```

```
  (fprintf (current-output) "~a\n" content))
 :append t))

(write-file "example.txt" "New content to append")
```

Here, `with-output-to-file` opens the file for writing, and `fprintf` formats and writes the content. The `:append t` argument ensures that content is added to the file without overwriting existing data.

Executing external commands is another critical functionality for command-line tools. Racket's `subprocess` function allows you to run shell commands and capture their output. This can be useful for invoking system utilities or other programs from within your tool:

```racket
lang racket

(require racket/system)

(define (run-command cmd)
  (define-values (in out err) (subprocess f f f cmd))
  (define result (port->string in))
  (printf "Command output: ~a\n" result))

(run-command "ls -l")
```

In this example, `subprocess` executes the `ls -l` command, capturing its output and printing it. You can adapt this approach to run any command-line utility or script, making your tool versatile and capable of leveraging existing system capabilities.

Managing system processes is also a key aspect of integrating with the operating system. Racket provides functions for handling processes, such as `process` and `kill-process`, which allow you to start and terminate processes programmatically. For instance, to start a process and wait for it to complete, you could use:

```racket
lang racket

(require racket/system)

(define (start-process cmd)
  (define proc (process cmd))
  (printf "Process started: ~a\n" cmd)
  (process-wait proc)
  (printf "Process completed.\n"))

(start-process "sleep 5")
```

In this code, `process` starts a new process with the given command, and `process-wait` blocks until the process finishes. This setup is useful for managing long-running tasks or coordinating multiple processes.

To create effective and user-friendly command-line tools, consider incorporating error handling to manage unexpected conditions gracefully. Racket's `with-handlers` provides a mechanism for dealing with errors by specifying how to handle exceptions. For example:

```racket
lang racket

(require racket/error)

(define (safe-read-file filename)
  (with-handlers ([exn:fail? (lambda (e)
            (printf "Error reading file: ~a\n" (exn-message e)))])
    (file->string filename)))

(safe-read-file "nonexistent-file.txt")
```

Here, `with-handlers` is used to catch exceptions raised during file reading, allowing the program to continue running even if an error occurs. This approach ensures that your tool can handle issues like missing files or permission errors gracefully.

Finally, documentation and user support are crucial for any command-line tool. Providing clear help messages and usage instructions can significantly enhance the user experience. Racket's `racket/argparse` library, mentioned earlier, can be used to generate help messages automatically based on the options and arguments defined for your tool. Additionally, consider including examples and explanations of common use cases in your tool's documentation.

By integrating these techniques—argument parsing, output formatting, file manipulation, external command execution, and error handling—you can build powerful and reliable command-line tools in Racket. Whether for automation, scripting, or system integration, these tools will enhance your programming capabilities and efficiency.

When developing command-line tools, a crucial aspect is managing how the tool interacts with the operating system. This involves executing system commands, handling file operations, and managing processes. Racket provides robust support for these tasks through its standard libraries, allowing you to build comprehensive command-line utilities.

To execute external commands and capture their output, Racket's `subprocess` function is highly effective. This function allows you to run shell commands and interact with their input and output streams. For instance, you might want to execute a command like `ls` to list directory contents and capture the output for further processing:

```racket
```

```racket
lang racket

(require racket/system)

(define (run-command cmd)
  (define-values (in out err) (subprocess f f f
                  (string->list cmd)))
  (let loop ([line (read-line out)])
   (unless (eof-object? line)
    (printf "Output: ~a\n" line)
    (loop (read-line out)))))

(run-command "ls -l")
```

In this example, `subprocess` creates a new process to execute the command specified by `cmd`. The `f` arguments indicate that we are not providing custom input or error handling for the subprocess. We then read from the standard output stream of the subprocess and print each line. This approach can be adapted for various commands and can handle complex interactions with external programs.

In addition to executing commands, handling files is a fundamental part of command-line tools. Racket's file manipulation functions, such as `with-input-from-file` and `with-output-to-file`, make it straightforward to read from and write to files. For example, if you need to process a file's contents and then write results to a new file, you can combine these functions as follows:

```racket
lang racket

(require racket/file)

(define (process-file input-filename output-filename)
  (with-input-from-file input-filename
    (lambda ()
```

```
  (define contents (port->string (current-input-port)))
  (with-output-to-file output-filename
    (lambda ()
      (fprintf (current-output) "Processed content: ~a\n" contents))))))
(process-file "input.txt" "output.txt")
```

Here, `port->string` reads the entire contents of `input-filename` into a string, which is then written to `output-filename` after processing. This example demonstrates basic file operations and how they can be used to develop more complex file-handling routines.

Another important aspect of command-line tools is argument parsing. Racket offers various ways to handle command-line arguments, including the use of the `racket/cmdline` library. This library simplifies argument parsing and helps in creating user-friendly command-line interfaces. Here's an example of how to parse arguments and handle them in a command-line application:

```racket
lang racket

(require racket/cmdline)

(define (main)
  (define args (current-command-line-arguments))
  (match args
    [(list "--help")
     (printf "Usage: program [options]\n")]
    [(list "--version")
     (printf "Version 1.0\n")]
    [(list "--file" filename)
     (printf "Processing file: ~a\n" filename)]
    [else
```

```
      (printf "Unknown argument: ~a\n" (first args))]))
(main)
```
```

In this snippet, `current-command-line-arguments` retrieves the list of arguments passed to the program. The `match` form is used to handle different cases based on the provided arguments. This approach allows for flexible command-line interfaces and can be expanded to support additional options and arguments as needed.

Formatting output is another essential feature of command-line tools. Racket provides powerful output formatting functions through `format` and `fprintf`. These functions allow you to create well-structured and readable output. For example, you might use `fprintf` to produce a formatted report based on user input or command results:

```racket
lang racket

(require racket/format)

(define (generate-report data)
  (with-output-to-file "report.txt"
    (lambda ()
      (fprintf (current-output) "Report\n")
      (for ([item data])
        (fprintf (current-output) "~a\n" item)))))

(generate-report '("Item 1" "Item 2" "Item 3"))
```

In this case, `fprintf` is used to write a formatted report to `report.txt`. The `for` loop iterates over a list of items, each of which is printed on a new line in the report. This approach demonstrates how to structure and format output to create readable and useful reports.
```

Integrating command-line tools with the operating system also involves managing processes and handling errors. Racket's subprocess functions can be used to start and control external processes, and its error handling mechanisms ensure that your tools can gracefully manage issues that arise during execution.

Through these examples, you can see how Racket's capabilities enable the creation of powerful and efficient command-line tools. By leveraging its file manipulation functions, subprocess handling, argument parsing, and output formatting features, you can build tools that are both effective and user-friendly.

CHAPTER 30: WORKING WITH NETWORKING

In the realm of modern application development, networking stands as a fundamental component, enabling applications to communicate over various networks, including local area networks and the internet. Mastering networking concepts and implementing them effectively is crucial for building robust, scalable applications. This discussion delves into networking fundamentals and the use of Racket's libraries to handle networking tasks. We will cover socket programming, client-server architecture, and data transmission with detailed examples to illustrate how to build networked applications and services.

To begin with, understanding socket programming is essential as it forms the backbone of network communication. In Racket, socket programming is facilitated through the `racket/tcp` and `racket/udp` libraries, which provide the tools needed to create and manage network connections. Sockets are endpoints for sending or receiving data across a network, and they are integral to both client and server applications.

A socket connection can be established using either Transmission Control Protocol (TCP) or User Datagram Protocol (UDP). TCP is connection-oriented, ensuring reliable data transmission with error-checking and acknowledgment mechanisms. UDP, on the other hand, is connectionless and offers faster communication with less overhead but without guaranteed delivery.

To create a simple TCP server in Racket, you can use the following code:

```racket
lang racket

(require racket/tcp)

(define server
  (tcp-listen 12345 t))

(define (handle-client in out)
  (printf "Client connected: ~a\n" (tcp-address in))
  (let loop ()
    (when (not (eof-object? (read-line in)))
      (fprintf out "Received: ~a\n" (read-line in))
      (flush-output out)
      (loop))))

(let ([client (tcp-accept server)])
  (define-values (in out) client)
  (handle-client in out)
  (close-input-port in)
  (close-output-port out))
```

In this example, `tcp-listen` creates a TCP server that listens for incoming connections on port `12345`. The `tcp-accept` function waits for a client to connect and returns a pair of ports for reading from and writing to the client. The `handle-client` function processes client data, echoes received messages, and maintains the connection until the client disconnects. This example demonstrates basic TCP server functionality, which can be expanded to include more complex features as needed.

Conversely, a TCP client in Racket can be implemented with the following code:

```racket
lang racket

(require racket/tcp)

(define client
  (tcp-connect "localhost" 12345))

(define-values (in out) client)
(printf "Connected to server\n")
(printf out "Hello, Server!\n")
(flush-output out)
(let ([response (read-line in)])
  (printf "Server response: ~a\n" response))
(close-input-port in)
(close-output-port out)
```

Here, `tcp-connect` establishes a connection to a server at "localhost" on port `12345`. The client sends a greeting message and waits for a response from the server, which is then printed out. This code shows the basic process of connecting to a server, sending data, and receiving a response.

For UDP, which does not establish a connection but sends datagrams to a specified address and port, you can use the `racket/udp` library. Here's an example of a UDP server:

```racket
lang racket

(require racket/udp)

(define server
  (udp-listen 12345))
```

```
(define (handle-client in)
  (let loop ([datagram (udp-receive server)])
    (when (not (eof-object? datagram))
      (printf "Received: ~a\n" (udp-datagram-data datagram))
      (loop))))

(handle-client server)
```

This code creates a UDP server that listens on port `12345` and processes incoming datagrams. Unlike TCP, there is no persistent connection; instead, the server receives individual packets, which are processed and then discarded.

On the client side for UDP, you can use:

```racket
lang racket

(require racket/udp)

(define client
  (udp-open))

(define (send-message message)
  (udp-send client "localhost" 12345 message))

(send-message "Hello, UDP Server!")
```

In this example, `udp-open` opens a UDP socket, and `udp-send` sends a datagram to the server at "localhost" on port `12345`.

Building networked applications also involves handling errors and managing network resources effectively. Error handling is crucial for dealing with unexpected issues such as connection failures or timeouts. In Racket, you can use standard error-handling techniques, such as conditionals and exceptions, to manage these issues gracefully.

Effective resource management, including closing sockets and freeing up resources, is essential to avoid memory leaks and ensure the stability of networked applications. Using Racket's built-in functions for closing ports and handling exceptions will help you build reliable and efficient networked services.

As you develop your command-line tools and networked applications, integrating with the operating system and managing various aspects of networking will be key to creating robust and effective solutions. Understanding and applying these principles will enhance your ability to develop applications that leverage network communication effectively.

Continuing with the exploration of networking in Racket, let us delve into client-server architecture, which is crucial for understanding how networked applications communicate. The client-server model divides the network into two distinct components: servers, which provide resources or services, and clients, which request and use those resources. This architecture is prevalent in many applications, ranging from web servers to database systems.

To build a TCP client in Racket, you use the `tcp-connect` function from the `racket/tcp` library. This function establishes a connection to a specified server. The following example demonstrates how to create a simple client that connects to the server created previously:

```racket
lang racket

(require racket/tcp)

(define-values (in out)
  (tcp-connect "localhost" 12345))

(printf "Sending message to server...\n")
(displayln "Hello, Server!" out)
```

```
(flush-output out)

(printf "Receiving response from server...\n")
(let ([response (read-line in)])
 (printf "Server response: ~a\n" response))

(close-input-port in)
(close-output-port out)
```

In this client example, `tcp-connect` is used to connect to the server running on `localhost` at port `12345`. After establishing the connection, the client sends a message to the server and waits for a response. The `displayln` function sends data to the server through the output port, and `read-line` reads the server's response from the input port. Finally, both the input and output ports are closed to terminate the connection.

This basic client-server interaction illustrates how clients can send requests and receive responses. For more complex scenarios, such as handling multiple clients concurrently, servers typically use threading or asynchronous I/O to manage simultaneous connections. Racket supports concurrency through the `racket/async-channel` and `racket/future` libraries, enabling non-blocking operations and parallel processing.

For example, a server that handles multiple clients can use Racket's threading support to create a new thread for each incoming client connection. This allows the server to manage multiple clients without blocking. Here is a modified version of the earlier server code that demonstrates handling multiple clients:

```racket
lang racket

(require racket/tcp racket/thread)
```

```
(define server
 (tcp-listen 12345 t))

(define (handle-client in out)
 (printf "Client connected: ~a\n" (tcp-address in))
 (let loop ()
  (when (not (eof-object? (read-line in)))
   (fprintf out "Received: ~a\n" (read-line in))
   (flush-output out)
   (loop))))

(define (start-server)
 (let loop ()
  (define-values (in out) (tcp-accept server))
  (thread (lambda () (handle-client in out)))
  (loop)))

(start-server)
```
```

In this example, the `thread` function is used to create a new thread for each client connection. The `start-server` function continuously accepts new client connections and starts a new thread to handle each client, allowing multiple clients to be processed in parallel.

Moving on to data transmission, it is essential to handle the format and integrity of data being sent and received. When transmitting data over a network, data can be serialized into various formats, such as text or binary, depending on the application's requirements. Racket provides functions to handle different data formats and ensure correct encoding and decoding of data.

For instance, to send and receive binary data, you might use the `write-bytes` and `read-bytes` functions. These functions handle raw byte data, which can be useful for applications that need to transmit binary files or other non-
```

textual data.

Consider the following example, where a server and client exchange binary data:

```racket
lang racket

(require racket/tcp)

(define server
  (tcp-listen 12345 t))

(define (handle-client in out)
  (printf "Client connected: ~a\n" (tcp-address in))
  (let ([data (read-bytes 1024 in)])
    (printf "Received binary data: ~a\n" data)
    (write-bytes data out)
    (flush-output out)))

(define (start-server)
  (let loop ()
    (define-values (in out) (tcp-accept server))
    (handle-client in out)
    (close-input-port in)
    (close-output-port out)
    (loop)))

(start-server)
```

In this server example, `read-bytes` reads up to 1024 bytes of binary data from the client, and `write-bytes` sends the same data back to the client. The handling of binary data is straightforward and follows a similar approach to handling text data, with attention paid to the data format and size.

In summary, building networked applications in Racket involves understanding and applying socket programming principles, client-server architecture, and data transmission techniques. By using Racket's networking libraries and features, you can create efficient, scalable, and reliable networked applications tailored to a variety of use cases.

Expanding further on networking in Racket, we must consider various aspects of data transmission and handling networked applications robustly. Data transmission between a client and a server is central to networking and involves ensuring that data is sent and received accurately and efficiently.

When dealing with data transmission, it's essential to understand how to serialize and deserialize data to ensure it can be sent over the network and interpreted correctly by the recipient. Serialization is the process of converting data structures into a format that can be easily transmitted or stored, while deserialization is the reverse process of converting serialized data back into a usable format.

In Racket, the `write` and `read` functions can be used for serialization and deserialization. For instance, if a server needs to send a complex data structure to a client, it can use `write` to serialize the data, and the client can use `read` to deserialize it. Here's an example demonstrating how to serialize a list of messages on the server side and deserialize them on the client side:

On the server side:

```racket
lang racket

(require racket/tcp)

(define-values (in out)
  (tcp-listen 12345 t))

(define (handle-client in out)
  (let ([messages '("Hello" "World" "From" "Server")])
    (write messages out)
```

```
   (flush-output out)
   (close-output-port out)
   (close-input-port in)))

(while t
  (define-values (client-in client-out) (tcp-accept server))
  (thread (lambda () (handle-client client-in client-out))))
```

In this server example, the server listens for incoming connections, and when a client connects, it spawns a new thread to handle the client. It serializes a list of messages using `write` and sends it to the client.

On the client side:

```racket
lang racket

(require racket/tcp)

(define-values (in out)
  (tcp-connect "localhost" 12345))

(printf "Receiving messages from server...\n")
(let ([messages (read in)])
  (printf "Received messages: ~a\n" messages))

(close-input-port in)
(close-output-port out)
```

In this client example, the client connects to the server and uses `read` to deserialize the received data. The list of messages sent by the server is printed to the console.

Additionally, error handling during data transmission is critical. Network communication is prone to various issues such as connection timeouts, data corruption, and server failures. In Racket, you can use exception handling to manage such errors gracefully. For instance, wrapping network operations in a `with-handlers` block allows you to catch and respond to exceptions that may occur during data transmission. Here's how you might handle exceptions in a client application:

```racket
lang racket

(require racket/tcp)

(define-values (in out)
  (tcp-connect "localhost" 12345))

(with-handlers ([exn:fail? (lambda (e)
              (printf "An error occurred: ~a\n" e)
              (exit))])
  (printf "Receiving messages from server...\n")
  (let ([messages (read in)])
    (printf "Received messages: ~a\n" messages)))

(close-input-port in)
(close-output-port out)
```

In this example, if an exception occurs during the `read` operation, it is caught by the `with-handlers` block, and an appropriate message is displayed. This ensures that the program can handle network errors without crashing.

Finally, it's essential to consider security when developing networked applications. Data transmitted over the network can be intercepted or tampered with, so implementing encryption and secure protocols is vital. For example, using Transport Layer Security (TLS) can help protect data during transmission. Racket supports TLS through external libraries, enabling you to encrypt data and establish secure connections between clients and servers.

In conclusion, working with networking in Racket involves understanding client-server architecture, implementing robust data transmission mechanisms, handling errors gracefully, and ensuring security. By leveraging Racket's networking libraries and exception handling features, you can build efficient, reliable, and secure networked applications. As you gain more experience, you'll find that mastering these concepts will significantly enhance your ability to develop complex and scalable networked systems.

CHAPTER 31: PERFORMANCE BENCHMARKING

Performance benchmarking is a critical aspect of software development, providing valuable insights into how well applications perform under various conditions. In Racket, as with other programming languages, measuring execution time, memory usage, and resource consumption is essential for identifying bottlenecks and optimizing code. This section will guide you through the process of benchmarking in Racket, including the tools and techniques available for effective performance measurement.

To begin with, understanding execution time is fundamental to performance benchmarking. Execution time refers to the duration it takes for a program or a specific piece of code to run. In Racket, you can measure execution time using the `time` function. This function is part of the `racket/base` library and provides a straightforward way to get insights into how long a particular operation takes. Here's an example of how to use `time` to measure the execution time of a function:

```racket
lang racket

(define (slow-function n)
  (for ([i (in-range n)])
```

```
  (sleep (/ 1 1000)))
'done)

(time (slow-function 1000))
```

In this example, `slow-function` simulates a delay by sleeping for a small fraction of a second repeatedly. The `time` function wraps around the call to `slow-function`, and it prints out the time taken to execute the function. This simple approach gives a quick overview of how execution time varies with different inputs or function implementations.

However, execution time alone does not provide a complete picture of performance. Memory usage is another crucial metric. Memory usage measures how much memory an application consumes during its execution. In Racket, the `collect-garbage` function can be used to manually invoke garbage collection, which can help in measuring the memory footprint of a program more accurately. To get detailed memory usage information, you can use the `gc-stats` function from the `racket/gc` library:

```racket
lang racket

(require racket/gc)

(define (memory-intensive-function n)
  (define list (build-list n (λ (i) (make-vector 1000 'a))))
  (gc-stats))

(displayln (memory-intensive-function 1000))
```

In this example, `memory-intensive-function` creates a list of large vectors and then uses `gc-stats` to collect and display memory usage statistics. By examining the output, you can gauge how different operations or data structures impact memory consumption.

Resource consumption extends beyond execution time and memory usage. It encompasses factors such as CPU usage, disk I/O, and network bandwidth. In Racket, while direct measurement of CPU usage and other system resources might not be built into the language, you can leverage external tools and libraries. For instance, you might use system-specific commands or third-party libraries that provide performance metrics. In Unix-like systems, commands such as `time`, `top`, or `htop` can offer insights into CPU and memory usage from outside the Racket environment.

Benchmarking also involves running multiple tests and comparing results to understand performance characteristics thoroughly. For rigorous benchmarking, it is important to ensure consistency and accuracy by isolating variables and controlling the environment in which benchmarks are run. Factors such as system load, background processes, and hardware differences can significantly impact performance measurements.

To facilitate consistent benchmarking, you can automate your tests and use statistical methods to analyze results. Racket's support for scripting and automation can be employed to create benchmarking scripts that repeatedly run your tests, collect data, and produce reports. Here's a simplified approach to automate benchmarking:

```racket
lang racket

(define (benchmark-function func args)
  (define start-time (current-inexact-milliseconds))
  (apply func args)
  (define end-time (current-inexact-milliseconds))
  (- end-time start-time))
```

```
(define (benchmark-tests)
 (for ([n (in-range 1000 10000 1000)])
  (printf "Time for size ~a: ~a ms\n"
      n
      (benchmark-function slow-function (list n)))))

(benchmark-tests)
```

In this script, `benchmark-function` measures the execution time of a given function with specified arguments. `benchmark-tests` runs a series of benchmarks with varying input sizes, and it prints out the time taken for each size. By running such tests multiple times and analyzing the results, you can gain a deeper understanding of how your code performs under different conditions.

In summary, effective performance benchmarking in Racket requires a combination of measuring execution time, memory usage, and resource consumption. By using built-in functions like `time` and `gc-stats`, along with external tools for broader metrics, you can gain valuable insights into the efficiency of your code. Automating benchmarks and analyzing results statistically can help in optimizing performance and ensuring that your applications run efficiently in real-world scenarios.

Analyzing resource consumption is another critical aspect of performance benchmarking. Resource consumption encompasses not just memory and execution time but also other resources like CPU usage and I/O operations. For a more comprehensive performance analysis, it is important to profile how your application utilizes these resources during its execution. In Racket, while specific libraries for profiling CPU usage are limited, you can still use external tools and strategies to gather and analyze this data.

For instance, using system monitoring tools can provide insights into CPU and I/O usage while running Racket programs. Tools such as `top` or `htop` on Unix-based systems or Task Manager on Windows can help you monitor the CPU and memory usage of your Racket applications. To integrate this with your benchmarking efforts, you might run your Racket application and monitor the system's resource usage simultaneously.

Profiling tools are also beneficial in examining the performance of specific parts of your code. Racket provides a `profiler` tool in the `racket/profiling` library, which helps identify hotspots and bottlenecks in your application. This tool gives detailed reports on function call frequencies, execution times, and memory usage, helping you pinpoint which parts of your code are consuming the most resources. To use the profiler, you would instrument your code with profiling hooks and analyze the generated data:

```racket
lang racket

(require racket/profiling)

(define (compute-intensive-function n)
  (for ([i (in-range n)])
    (sqrt i)))

(profiler-start)
(compute-intensive-function 10000)
(profiler-stop)

(profiler-report)
```

In this code snippet, `profiler-start` begins collecting profiling data, and `profiler-stop` ends the data collection. The `profiler-report` function then outputs the profiling results, which include metrics on function execution times and call counts. This allows you to examine the efficiency of different parts of your program and make targeted optimizations.

Benchmarking is not solely about measuring performance; it also involves interpreting the results to guide optimization decisions. For effective optimization, you need to understand how changes in your code affect performance metrics. After identifying performance bottlenecks using the profiler, you can experiment with different optimizations and re-run the benchmarks to compare their impact. This iterative process helps refine your approach to achieving the best performance.

It is also important to consider the impact of different data structures and algorithms on performance. For instance, choosing an appropriate data structure can significantly affect both time and space complexity. Racket provides various data structures, such as lists, vectors, and hash tables, each with different performance characteristics. Understanding these characteristics and selecting the most efficient data structure for your specific use case is crucial for optimizing performance.

In addition to profiling and monitoring, benchmarking should be integrated into your development workflow. Regular benchmarking during development helps ensure that performance issues are identified and addressed early. Automated tests that include performance benchmarks can be set up to monitor performance continuously and detect regressions before they become significant problems.

When benchmarking, it's also essential to consider the impact of the runtime environment on performance. Factors such as the hardware specifications, operating system, and runtime configuration can all influence performance metrics. Running benchmarks under consistent conditions and understanding the environment's role can provide more reliable and actionable performance data.

Ultimately, effective performance benchmarking involves a combination of accurate measurement, thoughtful analysis, and iterative optimization. By leveraging Racket's profiling tools and integrating external monitoring solutions, you can gain a deep understanding of your application's performance characteristics. This knowledge enables you to make informed decisions about optimizations and improvements, ensuring that your application runs efficiently and effectively.

In summary, mastering performance benchmarking in Racket involves understanding how to measure execution time, memory usage, and resource consumption accurately. By utilizing tools for profiling and monitoring, analyzing the results, and applying iterative optimization strategies, you can enhance the performance of your Racket applications significantly.

Once you've collected and analyzed performance data, it's crucial to understand how various factors influence benchmarking results. For instance, execution time measurements can be affected by factors such as the system's current load, background processes, and hardware variations. To mitigate these effects and ensure more accurate benchmarking, you should run multiple iterations of your benchmarks and use statistical methods to aggregate the results. This approach helps smooth out anomalies and provides a clearer picture of your application's performance characteristics.

When dealing with memory usage, it's also important to consider the different types of memory your application utilizes. For example, Racket, like many languages, manages both heap and stack memory. Tools like the `gc-stats` library can provide insights into garbage collection behavior and memory allocation patterns. Analyzing garbage collection logs can reveal how frequently and how long garbage collection pauses occur, which can be indicative of memory pressure or inefficiencies in memory management.

For advanced memory profiling, you might use the `racket/trace` module to track memory allocation and deallocation in your program. This module can help identify parts of the code that contribute to excessive memory usage, such as objects that are not being properly de-referenced or large data structures that are retained longer than necessary. Here is an example of how to use tracing to analyze memory usage:

```racket
lang racket

(require racket/trace)

(define (large-list n)
  (build-list n (lambda (i) (make-list 1000 i))))

(trace large-list)
(define my-list (large-list 1000))
```

In this snippet, `trace` is used to monitor calls to the `large-list` function and observe its impact on memory. By examining the trace output, you can gain insights into how the function's memory usage evolves over time.

Another important aspect of performance benchmarking is understanding the trade-offs involved in optimization. Improving execution time or reducing memory usage in one part of your application might come at the expense of increased complexity or slower performance in another part. Therefore, it is essential to evaluate not only the quantitative performance metrics but also the qualitative aspects of code maintainability and readability.

To make informed decisions about where to focus

your optimization efforts, consider using profiling and benchmarking tools in combination with code review and design principles. For example, before diving into low-level optimizations, assess whether algorithmic changes or higher-level architectural improvements might yield better overall performance. Often, optimizing algorithms or adjusting data structures can lead to more significant performance gains than micro-optimizations at the code level.

In summary, performance benchmarking in Racket involves a multifaceted approach that includes measuring execution time, memory usage, and resource consumption. Using tools like the `racket/profiling` library, system monitoring utilities, and memory profiling techniques can provide valuable insights into your application's performance. By running multiple benchmarks, analyzing the data carefully, and considering the trade-offs of various optimizations, you can enhance your application's efficiency and ensure it meets your performance requirements.

CHAPTER 32: CREATING AND MANAGING PROJECTS

Effective project management is essential for successful software development, and this holds true for projects written in Racket as well. Properly managing a Racket project involves a systematic approach to project structure, version control, and dependency management. By adhering to best practices in these areas, you can enhance the organization, maintainability, and overall efficiency of your projects.

When setting up a Racket project, the initial structure is critical. A well-organized project layout helps in maintaining clarity and simplicity as the project grows. Typically, a Racket project should include the following directories and files:

1. `src/`: This directory contains the source code for the project. It is common to structure this directory further into subdirectories for different modules or components of the application.
2. `tests/`: A directory dedicated to unit tests and other testing scripts. Organizing tests in a separate directory keeps them distinct from the application code and facilitates easier test management.
3. `docs/`: Documentation for the project, including design

documents, API references, and user guides. Maintaining comprehensive documentation helps in understanding and maintaining the project over time.

4. `build/`: This directory is used for build artifacts, such as compiled files or generated documentation. Keeping build outputs separate from source code prevents clutter and makes it easier to manage the build process.

5. `README.md`: A markdown file that provides an overview of the project, instructions for setup and usage, and any other pertinent information. This file serves as the first point of reference for anyone new to the project.

6. `Makefile` or `raco` scripts: Automation scripts for building, testing, and managing the project. These scripts simplify repetitive tasks and ensure consistency in the build and deployment processes.

Once the project structure is established, version control becomes a crucial aspect of project management. Git is a popular version control system that integrates seamlessly with Racket projects. It allows you to track changes, manage branches, and collaborate with others effectively. Setting up a Git repository involves initializing the repository, creating a `.gitignore` file to exclude unnecessary files, and regularly committing changes with meaningful messages.

Here is a basic workflow for using Git with a Racket project:

1. Initialize the Repository: Use the `git init` command to create a new Git repository in your project directory.
2. Create a `.gitignore` File: Specify files and directories that should be ignored by Git. Common entries include build artifacts, temporary files, and IDE-specific configurations.
3. Commit Changes: Regularly commit changes to capture the state of the project at different points in time. Use descriptive commit messages to document the purpose of each change.
4. Branch Management: Create and switch between branches to work on new features or bug fixes. Use `git branch` to list

branches and `git checkout` to switch between them.
5. Merge and Resolve Conflicts: Merge changes from different branches and resolve any conflicts that arise. Use `git merge` to combine changes and `git status` to identify and resolve conflicts.

Dependency management is another critical aspect of project management. In Racket, managing dependencies ensures that your project can easily incorporate and work with external libraries. The `raco` tool is used to manage packages and dependencies in Racket projects. Here's how you can manage dependencies effectively:

1. Define Dependencies: Use the `package` form in your Racket source code or a `pkg` file to specify required libraries. This ensures that anyone working on the project can easily install the necessary packages.
2. Use `raco pkg` Commands: The `raco pkg` commands provide tools for installing, updating, and removing Racket packages. For example, `raco pkg install` is used to install a package, and `raco pkg update` updates installed packages to their latest versions.
3. Lock Dependencies: Use a `deps` file or `package` definition file to lock the versions of dependencies. This helps maintain consistency across different environments and ensures that the project works as expected with specific versions of libraries.

To further streamline project management, consider using continuous integration (CI) tools and automated testing frameworks. CI tools automatically build, test, and deploy your project whenever changes are pushed to the repository. This practice helps in identifying issues early and ensures that the project remains in a deployable state.

By following these best practices for project structure, version control, and dependency management, you can effectively manage Racket projects and enhance their maintainability and robustness. Remember that the key to successful project management lies in consistency and attention to detail throughout the project's lifecycle.

When managing dependencies in Racket, utilizing the built-in package management system, `raco`, is fundamental. This system helps you manage libraries and packages essential for your project, ensuring that your project remains consistent and up-to-date with its dependencies. You start by declaring your dependencies in a `package` file or within your `project` file, which should be located at the root of your project directory. This file lists all the external packages your project relies on, along with their versions.

To add a dependency, you can use the `raco pkg install` command, followed by the package name. This command downloads and installs the package and any required dependencies. Managing updates to these packages is also streamlined through `raco`, which allows you to keep your project up to date with the latest versions of the libraries you use. It is essential to regularly update your dependencies and review changes in their release notes to avoid compatibility issues.

Furthermore, setting up a continuous integration (CI) system can significantly enhance the management of your Racket project. CI tools automate the process of building, testing, and deploying your project, which helps catch issues early and ensures that your codebase remains in a deployable state. By configuring CI pipelines, you can automate tasks such as running unit tests, linting code, and building documentation, which contributes to maintaining code quality and consistency.

Effective project management also involves defining clear and consistent coding standards. Adopting a coding style guide helps maintain readability and consistency throughout your codebase. In Racket, adhering to conventions such as naming conventions for functions and variables, and consistent use of indentation and spacing, ensures that your code is easy to read and understand by others. Tools like `racket-mode` in Emacs or `DrRacket` provide support for enforcing these style conventions, which aids in maintaining code quality.

Documentation is another critical aspect of managing a Racket project. Comprehensive documentation facilitates understanding and using your code effectively. This includes inline comments explaining complex logic, as well as external documentation such as API references and user guides. Utilizing tools like `scribble`, Racket's documentation tool, allows you to generate professional-looking documentation from annotated source code. By integrating documentation generation into your build process, you ensure that your documentation remains current with your codebase.

In addition to documentation, you should also consider implementing robust error handling and logging mechanisms within your project. Effective error handling ensures that your application can gracefully handle unexpected situations without crashing or producing misleading results. Logging provides insights into the application's behavior and can be invaluable for diagnosing issues. Using libraries like `racket/logging` allows you to capture and manage logs effectively, aiding in the debugging and monitoring of your application.

As your project evolves, maintaining an organized issue tracker is essential. An issue tracker helps manage bugs, feature requests, and other tasks related to your project. Tools like GitHub Issues or GitLab Issues provide platforms for tracking and managing issues, allowing you to prioritize and assign tasks, track progress, and communicate with collaborators. Properly managing issues helps ensure that development efforts are focused and that progress is visible and trackable.

When preparing for deployment, it is important to consider the deployment environment and the packaging of your application. Racket provides various tools and techniques for packaging applications for different platforms. For instance, you can use `raco exe` to create standalone executables, which simplifies distribution and deployment. Additionally, testing your application in environments that mimic production conditions helps identify potential issues before deployment.

Finally, as you work on your Racket project, regularly revisiting and refining your project management practices is crucial. Continuous improvement ensures that your project remains manageable and that you adapt to new tools, techniques, and best practices as they become available. This iterative process involves reflecting on what works well, identifying areas for improvement, and making adjustments to your project management approach.

By focusing on these aspects of project management, you can enhance the organization, maintainability, and overall effectiveness of your Racket projects. Whether you are starting a new project or managing an existing one, adhering to these practices will help you build robust and well-managed software applications.

In the realm of Racket project management, understanding how to handle project structure effectively is paramount. The organization of files and directories within your project not only impacts the ease of development but also influences maintainability and scalability. A well-structured Racket project typically follows a conventional layout that separates concerns clearly.

At the root of your project, you should find essential files such as `README.md`, which provides a concise overview of the project, including setup instructions, usage guidelines, and contribution notes. Additionally, a `project.rkt` file or similar configuration file may be present, defining project-specific settings and dependencies. This file serves as the central point of reference for your project's configuration.

Within the project directory, it's common to have subdirectories such as `src` for source code, `tests` for unit tests, and `docs` for documentation. The `src` directory should contain your Racket modules and libraries, organized into a logical hierarchy that reflects the structure of your application. For instance, if your project is a web application, you might have subdirectories for models, views, and controllers. This separation helps in isolating different parts of the application and making the codebase easier to navigate.

The `tests` directory is crucial for maintaining code quality. Here, you should place all your test cases, which might be organized by the module they test. Employing a testing framework, such as Racket's `rackunit`, allows you to write automated tests that validate the functionality of your code. By integrating these tests into your continuous integration pipeline, you ensure that every change to the codebase is tested, helping to catch regressions and ensure stability.

Managing version control with Git or a similar system is another integral aspect of project management. Proper version control practices involve not only committing code changes regularly but also writing clear and meaningful commit messages. This practice helps in tracking the history of changes and understanding the rationale behind each modification. Utilizing branches effectively allows you to work on new features or bug fixes in isolation from the main codebase, thereby reducing the risk of introducing instability.

When working with Git, it's beneficial to adhere to a branching strategy. For instance, a common approach is the Git Flow model, which defines branches for development, features, releases, and hotfixes. This strategy helps in managing different stages of development and ensures a structured workflow. Merging branches should be done cautiously, often requiring a code review process to maintain code quality and consistency.

Dependency management extends beyond simply listing dependencies in configuration files. It involves ensuring that your project uses compatible versions of libraries and that those libraries are up-to-date. Tools such as `raco pkg` play a critical role here, providing commands to install, update, and manage packages. It's also advisable to periodically review and update dependencies to address security vulnerabilities and take advantage of improvements in the libraries.

Handling project documentation and ensuring it remains comprehensive and relevant is crucial for effective project management. Good documentation provides context, explains how to use the project, and offers guidelines for contributing. This includes writing clear API documentation, which describes the functionality and usage of each function and module. Tools like `scribble` in Racket help in generating documentation directly from source code, integrating seamlessly into the development process.

In addition to API documentation, user guides and developer notes contribute to a well-rounded documentation suite. User guides offer instructions on how to use the software, including setup and configuration details. Developer notes, on the other hand, provide insight into the architecture, design decisions, and coding standards employed in the project. Keeping these documents up to date ensures that new contributors can quickly get up to speed and that users have access to accurate information.

Moreover, project management involves setting up and adhering to development practices that enhance productivity and code quality. This includes code reviews, where peers examine code changes before they are merged into the main branch. Code reviews help in identifying potential issues early, ensuring adherence to coding standards, and fostering knowledge sharing among team members. Implementing linters and formatters also contributes to maintaining a consistent code style, which enhances readability and reduces errors.

Effective project management in Racket also requires planning for scalability and maintainability. As your project grows, consider how to refactor code and organize it to handle increased complexity. Adopting design patterns and architectural principles can aid in building a robust and adaptable codebase. Regularly revisiting and revising your project's structure and practices helps in addressing evolving needs and ensuring long-term success.

In conclusion, managing a Racket project involves a combination of best practices for project structure, version control, dependency management, and documentation. By adhering to these practices, you set a strong foundation for developing, maintaining, and scaling your project effectively. Implementing structured workflows and utilizing tools designed for Racket will aid in navigating the complexities of software development and contribute to the overall success of your projects.

CHAPTER 33: EXTENDING RACKET WITH PLUGINS

Racket's design philosophy embraces extensibility, making it an ideal candidate for customizing and enhancing its environment through plugins. This chapter delves into the intricacies of creating and using plugins to extend Racket's functionality, focusing on plugin architectures, integration techniques, and practical examples for developing custom plugins.

Understanding the fundamental concept of plugins in Racket begins with recognizing how the language's modular and flexible nature facilitates their integration. At its core, a plugin in Racket is a collection of code that extends the functionality of the base system, providing new features or capabilities. The architecture of Racket plugins generally involves defining a set of functions or modules that interact with the core system, adhering to specific protocols and interfaces.

To create a plugin, you first need to define its purpose and the functionality it will add to the Racket environment. Plugins can range from simple utilities that enhance the development workflow to complex extensions that introduce entirely new language constructs or tools. The development of a plugin typically starts with creating a new Racket module that encapsulates the plugin's functionality. This module should follow Racket's conventions for defining and exporting functions, ensuring that it can be integrated smoothly with other modules.

One critical aspect of developing a plugin is adhering to Racket's plugin architecture, which includes defining a clear and consistent interface. This interface is crucial for ensuring that the plugin can be integrated with Racket's core system and other plugins seamlessly. For example, if you are developing a plugin that adds a new feature to the Racket REPL (Read-Eval-Print Loop), you will need to provide functions that interact with the REPL environment, such as commands or hooks that extend its capabilities.

Integration techniques involve ensuring that your plugin can be loaded and used within the Racket environment effectively. This often requires setting up the plugin to be discovered by Racket's module system. One common approach is to use Racket's package manager, which allows you to distribute and manage plugins as packages. By defining your plugin as a package, you enable users to install and update it easily using Racket's package management tools. Additionally, you can specify dependencies and configuration options within the package definition to streamline the installation process.

Another integration technique is defining hooks and callbacks that allow your plugin to interact with existing Racket tools and libraries. For instance, if your plugin provides new debugging capabilities, you might need to hook into Racket's existing debugging infrastructure, allowing your plugin to enhance or modify the debugging process. This often involves using Racket's built-in support for extending existing libraries or tools, ensuring that your plugin integrates seamlessly with the existing ecosystem.

Practical examples of plugin development illustrate the breadth of possibilities when extending Racket's functionality.

Consider a plugin that introduces a new syntax extension for Racket, enabling a more concise and expressive way to define certain constructs. To develop such a plugin, you would need to define the new syntax using Racket's macro system, ensuring that it integrates smoothly with the existing language features. This might involve creating a new module that defines the syntax and provides functions for transforming and evaluating code written using the new syntax.

Another example might involve creating a plugin that adds a new visualization tool for data analysis. This plugin could provide functions for generating custom plots or graphs, integrating with existing data analysis libraries to offer enhanced visualization capabilities. Developing this type of plugin would require understanding both the data analysis needs and the visualization tools available in Racket, ensuring that your plugin provides meaningful enhancements.

As with any software development process, testing and debugging are crucial for ensuring the reliability and functionality of your plugin. Developing a robust testing strategy involves writing test cases that cover the various aspects of your plugin's functionality, ensuring that it behaves as expected in different scenarios. This might include unit tests for individual functions, integration tests for interactions with other modules, and user tests to validate the plugin's usability and effectiveness.

Additionally, documenting your plugin is essential for helping users understand how to use it and integrate it into their Racket environment. This documentation should include a clear description of the plugin's features, installation instructions, and usage examples. Providing comprehensive documentation not only helps users get started with your plugin but also ensures that they can leverage its full capabilities effectively.

In conclusion, extending Racket with plugins involves a combination of defining clear interfaces, integrating with existing tools and libraries, and providing practical functionality that enhances the Racket environment. By following best practices for plugin development, including defining consistent interfaces, ensuring seamless integration, and providing thorough documentation, you can create powerful and flexible plugins that significantly enhance the capabilities of Racket.

The practical development of Racket plugins involves several nuanced considerations that align with the language's extensibility features and its ecosystem's needs. As we delve further into creating and managing plugins, it becomes essential to explore specific techniques for developing robust, efficient, and well-integrated plugins.

One foundational aspect is defining the plugin's interface. This involves specifying how other components or plugins can interact with your plugin. In Racket, this is often achieved through the creation of module exports and function definitions that conform to expected protocols. For instance, if your plugin is intended to provide new functionality within a Racket web server, you will need to define functions that integrate with the server's existing API. This integration may require defining new request handlers or middleware functions that adhere to the server's interface specifications.

Another significant consideration is managing plugin dependencies. As plugins can rely on other packages or modules, it is crucial to define these dependencies clearly within your plugin's package specification. Racket's package system facilitates this by allowing you to declare dependencies in the package definition file. This ensures that when users install your plugin, all necessary dependencies are resolved and installed automatically. Proper dependency management not only streamlines the installation process but also helps prevent conflicts between different plugins and packages.

Handling version compatibility is another critical factor. As Racket evolves, changes to the core system or other packages may affect your plugin. To mitigate these issues, it is advisable to test your plugin with various versions of Racket and its dependencies. Additionally, employing semantic versioning for your plugin can help users understand the nature of updates and compatibility changes. Semantic versioning involves specifying version numbers in a way that reflects changes in functionality, bug fixes, and compatibility, helping to ensure that users can manage plugin upgrades more effectively.

Testing and debugging are integral to the development process of a Racket plugin. Creating a robust test suite for your plugin helps ensure that it behaves as expected and integrates well with other components. Unit tests can be written to validate individual functions or modules within your plugin, while integration tests can assess how your plugin interacts with the broader Racket environment. Leveraging Racket's testing libraries, such as `rackunit`, can streamline the process of writing and executing tests.

Moreover, debugging plugins involves a similar approach to debugging Racket programs. You can use Racket's built-in debugging tools to step through code, inspect variables, and identify issues. Additionally, including comprehensive logging within your plugin can provide valuable insights during development and troubleshooting. Proper logging helps track the plugin's behavior and can be especially useful for diagnosing issues in complex interactions between your plugin and the Racket environment.

Documentation is an essential part of plugin development. Clear and thorough documentation not only helps users understand how to use your plugin but also aids in maintaining and updating it over time. Good documentation should include an overview of the plugin's functionality, installation instructions, usage examples, and information about any configuration options. Additionally, providing examples of common use cases or integration scenarios can be highly beneficial to users who are trying to leverage your plugin in their projects.

Distributing your plugin involves packaging it in a way that makes it accessible and easy to install. Racket's package manager, `raco`, plays a crucial role in this process. By creating a `.pkg` file and submitting it to the Racket package repository, you can make your plugin available to a broad audience. Additionally, you can use the `raco` tool to test the installation and ensure that your plugin works correctly when installed via the package manager.

To summarize, extending Racket with plugins involves several critical steps, from defining the plugin's interface and managing dependencies to testing, debugging, and documenting the plugin. Each of these steps contributes to creating a robust and functional plugin that integrates seamlessly with Racket's environment. By adhering to best practices and leveraging Racket's extensibility features, you can develop plugins that enhance the language's capabilities and provide valuable tools and functionality for the Racket community.

Developing Racket plugins involves more than just coding and integrating functionality; it also requires thoughtful design and consideration of user experience. A well-designed plugin not only adds value through its features but also integrates seamlessly into the Racket environment, enhancing overall usability.

User documentation and support play crucial roles in the success of your plugin. Clear, concise documentation helps users understand the plugin's functionality, installation process, and configuration options. Providing examples of usage and explaining the plugin's integration with Racket's ecosystem can significantly improve user experience. Documentation should be comprehensive, covering both the basic setup and advanced features. Additionally, including troubleshooting guides and FAQs can address common issues and enhance user satisfaction.

When it comes to deployment and distribution, Racket offers several mechanisms to share your plugin with the community. The primary method is through the Racket package repository, where plugins can be published and made available for installation via Racket's package manager, `raco`. Before publishing, it is essential to ensure that your plugin is thoroughly tested and documented. Submitting your plugin involves creating a package definition that includes metadata such as the plugin's name, version, dependencies, and a brief description of its functionality. Once submitted, users can easily find and install your plugin using `raco` commands, making distribution straightforward.

Maintaining and updating plugins is an ongoing process that requires regular attention. As Racket evolves and new versions are released, it is important to test your plugin with these updates to ensure compatibility. Addressing bugs and incorporating feedback from users can also drive improvements. By providing updates and patches, you can keep your plugin relevant and functional, adapting to changes in the Racket environment and user needs.

Version control systems, such as Git, are invaluable for managing the development and maintenance of plugins. Version control allows you to track changes, collaborate with others, and manage different versions of your plugin. It also facilitates the handling of issues and feature requests from users. By hosting your code repository on platforms like GitHub or GitLab, you can leverage additional tools for issue tracking, code reviews, and continuous integration, further enhancing the development process.

In summary, extending Racket with plugins involves a multifaceted approach that includes designing a plugin architecture, managing dependencies, ensuring compatibility, and providing thorough documentation and support. By focusing on these aspects, you can create plugins that not only enhance the functionality of Racket but also offer a smooth and intuitive experience for users. Effective management practices, such as version control and regular updates, are crucial for maintaining the quality and relevance of your plugin over time.

CHAPTER 34: FUTURE DIRECTIONS AND ADVANCED TOPICS

As we conclude our exploration of Racket programming, it is essential to consider the evolving landscape of the language and the advanced topics that are shaping its future. The trajectory of Racket is deeply intertwined with ongoing research, innovations in programming languages, and emerging technologies that influence how we think about and use programming languages.

One of the most exciting areas of development for Racket is its continued evolution through research and innovation. Racket's research community is actively engaged in enhancing the language and its ecosystem. This includes the development of new language features, improvements in performance, and extensions that broaden the language's applicability. Recent research has focused on enhancing Racket's macro system to support more advanced metaprogramming techniques, which allows for greater flexibility and abstraction in code generation and manipulation.

Another significant area of interest is the integration of Racket with new and emerging technologies. For example, as the Internet of Things (IoT) continues to grow, there is a push to develop libraries and frameworks that enable Racket to interface with various IoT devices and protocols. This requires adapting Racket's concurrency model to handle the demands of real-time data processing and integration with hardware interfaces.

Furthermore, advancements in compiler design are another critical focus. Racket's compiler is built on the principles of functional programming and language design, but ongoing research aims to optimize compilation processes and improve the efficiency of generated code. This includes efforts to enhance just-in-time (JIT) compilation and support for multiple target architectures, which can lead to more efficient execution of Racket programs across diverse platforms.

Language theory also plays a crucial role in shaping Racket's future. As a language designed with a strong emphasis on language theory, Racket continues to explore new paradigms and concepts that influence its design and implementation. Research into type systems, formal semantics, and language integration informs the development of new features and improvements. For instance, advancements in type inference and type checking can lead to more robust and expressive type systems, enhancing Racket's ability to catch errors and support advanced programming techniques.

In addition to theoretical advancements, practical applications of Racket are expanding. The language's unique features make it suitable for various domains, including web development, educational tools, and scripting. As the needs of these domains evolve, Racket must adapt to support new paradigms and use cases. For example, integrating Racket with modern web technologies and frameworks can open new possibilities for building web applications and services that leverage the language's strengths in abstraction and metaprogramming.

The exploration of Racket's potential applications also includes considerations of its role in educational contexts.

Racket is widely used as a teaching language due to its clear syntax and powerful abstractions. Future directions in education might involve developing new teaching materials and tools that leverage Racket's features to teach advanced programming concepts and language design principles. This could include creating interactive environments and educational platforms that make use of Racket's capabilities to engage students in learning about programming and computer science.

Moreover, the integration of Racket with other programming languages and tools is an area of ongoing development. As the software development ecosystem becomes increasingly polyglot, the ability to interface with other languages and tools becomes more critical. Research into language interoperability, including foreign function interfaces (FFIs) and cross-language libraries, enables Racket to work alongside other languages and integrate with existing systems more effectively. This broadens the scope of Racket's applications and makes it a more versatile tool in the software development toolkit.

Looking ahead, the future of Racket is filled with opportunities for innovation and growth. By staying informed about advancements in language design, compiler technology, and emerging applications, developers can contribute to and benefit from the ongoing evolution of Racket. Embracing these future directions will ensure that Racket remains a relevant and powerful tool for a wide range of programming tasks, from theoretical research to practical software development. As we explore these advanced topics, it becomes clear that Racket's journey is just beginning, with many exciting developments on the horizon that promise to expand its capabilities and applications even further.

As we delve deeper into the future directions for Racket, it's essential to consider how the language is adapting to meet the challenges posed by new technologies and evolving user needs. One area of significant potential is Racket's role in advanced parallel and distributed computing. The rise of multicore processors and distributed systems has heightened the need for languages that can effectively manage concurrency and parallelism. Racket's current concurrency model, while robust, may evolve to incorporate more sophisticated abstractions and optimizations to leverage parallelism more effectively. This includes research into more fine-grained control over parallel execution and enhancements to its existing concurrency primitives.

Another exciting area of development is Racket's integration with emerging web technologies. With the proliferation of WebAssembly, there is an opportunity for Racket to bridge the gap between traditional server-side applications and client-side web applications. Integrating Racket with WebAssembly could enable developers to write Racket code that runs efficiently in the browser, opening up new possibilities for client-side programming. This would require adaptations to Racket's runtime system to ensure compatibility with WebAssembly's execution model and constraints.

In terms of educational applications, Racket continues to be a popular choice due to its pedagogical design and the tools it offers for learning programming concepts. Future enhancements might focus on improving educational resources and integrating with modern educational platforms. For instance, developing more interactive tools and environments that support Racket's unique features could enhance its use in teaching programming concepts, making it more accessible to beginners and more powerful for educators.

Moreover, Racket's ecosystem is likely to see growth in the development of libraries and frameworks that cater to specific domains such as data science, machine learning, and system programming. These domains have specific requirements and challenges, and the development of specialized libraries could make Racket more competitive in these fields. For example, integrating with popular data processing libraries or providing efficient interfaces for machine learning frameworks could expand Racket's applicability and utility.

Furthermore, the evolution of Racket's support for language-oriented programming is worth noting. As programming paradigms continue to shift, there is an increasing emphasis on creating languages and tools that are tailored to specific domains. Racket's flexibility in defining new syntactic constructs and abstractions makes it an ideal candidate for domain-specific languages (DSLs). The development of new DSLs and extensions could enhance Racket's capability to address niche requirements and improve productivity in specialized areas.

On the technical front, advancements in Racket's tooling and infrastructure will be crucial. Improvements in development environments, debugging tools, and performance profiling capabilities will enhance the developer experience and productivity. Efforts to create more intuitive and powerful IDEs, better integration with existing tools, and enhanced support for debugging and performance analysis will be key areas of focus. This also includes exploring new ways to visualize and analyze code execution, which can provide deeper insights into program behavior and performance.

Additionally, as the field of software engineering evolves, so too must the approaches to managing and deploying Racket applications. Innovations in deployment strategies, containerization, and cloud integration are increasingly relevant. The development of tools and practices that facilitate the deployment of Racket applications in modern cloud environments and containerized setups will be vital for ensuring that Racket remains a viable option for contemporary software development practices.

Overall, the future of Racket is poised to be shaped by ongoing research and advancements across various domains of computer science and software engineering. As new challenges and opportunities arise, Racket's adaptability and extensibility will play a crucial role in its continued relevance and growth. By focusing on improving concurrency models, integrating with emerging technologies, expanding educational resources, and enhancing tooling and infrastructure, Racket is well-positioned to continue its journey as a powerful and versatile programming language.

As we explore further into advanced topics such as language theory and compiler design, Racket's role in these areas provides rich opportunities for innovation and experimentation. One of Racket's distinguishing features is its strong support for language creation, a testament to its design philosophy that emphasizes flexibility and extensibility. This ability to create new languages and DSLs (Domain-Specific Languages) within Racket could be expanded to explore novel approaches to language design. Future research might focus on integrating advanced type systems or new paradigms into Racket's ecosystem, potentially influencing how languages are designed and implemented more broadly.

On the front of compiler design, Racket's implementation of its own compiler infrastructure is an interesting aspect for exploration. The language's approach to compiling and runtime systems could be used as a basis for investigating new compilation strategies, optimizing techniques, or even entirely new compiler architectures. For instance, improving Racket's Just-In-Time (JIT) compilation or exploring Ahead-Of-Time (AOT) compilation strategies could lead to significant performance improvements, making Racket more suitable for high-performance applications.

Additionally, with the increasing interest in compiler construction and optimization, Racket could leverage its existing infrastructure to experiment with and demonstrate new compilation techniques. This includes exploring alternative intermediate representations or optimizing existing representations to better support emerging hardware architectures or application domains.

In parallel with these advancements, integrating Racket with cutting-edge technologies remains a pivotal area for future exploration. As technologies like artificial intelligence, quantum computing, and blockchain continue to evolve, Racket's adaptability and extensibility provide a foundation for experimentation. For example, integrating Racket with AI frameworks could enable new forms of symbolic computation or facilitate the development of new tools for machine learning research. Similarly, exploring Racket's integration with quantum computing frameworks could provide a unique approach to quantum programming languages, leveraging Racket's language features to model and interact with quantum systems.

Racket's unique position in the landscape of programming languages also lends itself to further exploration in the context of functional programming advancements. Functional programming continues to be an area of active research, with ongoing developments in how functional paradigms can be applied to real-world problems. Racket's strong support for functional programming concepts could be further enhanced with new abstractions or optimizations that support more complex or novel use cases. For instance, the incorporation of new functional programming techniques such as monads or advanced type systems could enhance Racket's capabilities and usability.

Another intriguing area of development is the evolution of Racket's integration with existing development tools and environments. Enhancing interoperability with other languages and tools can expand Racket's applicability and make it more versatile for various development scenarios. This could involve improvements in integration with popular development environments or tools, as well as creating new interfaces or libraries to bridge gaps between Racket and other languages or technologies.

Furthermore, the exploration of advanced debugging and profiling tools tailored to Racket's features and paradigms could offer deeper insights into application performance and behavior. Developing sophisticated tools for analyzing Racket programs could aid in understanding complex interactions and optimizing performance, contributing to a more robust and efficient development environment.

Finally, considering the growth of the software development ecosystem, Racket could explore new paradigms for software development, such as new forms of code generation or software architecture patterns. Investigating how Racket can support or benefit from these emerging trends could provide valuable insights and position Racket at the forefront of new programming methodologies.

In summary, the future of Racket is ripe with opportunities for exploration and advancement. From refining its existing features and expanding its integration with emerging technologies to pioneering new approaches in language theory and compiler design, Racket's flexible and extensible nature positions it well for continued innovation. As these areas evolve, Racket's adaptability and foundational principles will play a crucial role in shaping its future and maintaining its relevance in the ever-changing landscape of programming languages and technologies.

www.ingramcontent.com/pod-product-compliance
Lightning Source LLC
Chambersburg PA
CBHW052140220526
45471CB00004B/1454